Reporting Global while being Local

International news has long been studied and understood as produced by outsiders – foreign correspondents working in exotic, international locales. This book challenges this established view by putting the spotlight on the insiders working in their own countries producing news for international audiences.

Western male foreign correspondents who report from areas affected by crises and conflicts for an 'audience back home' have long stood in as visible metaphors of international news production. But the understanding of who produces international news is starting to shift as scholars come to take into account the often-invisible role played by locally based, non-Western news-workers who have always been part and parcel of international news production. The roles and responsibilities of these professional, specialised locals within the global flow of news have only increased as falling news industry revenues have meant reductions in non-local staff in foreign news bureaus. Available research shows that the involvement of local journalists and fixers, as well as NGOs, as sources of news and information in international news production is marked by economic, socio-cultural and practice-related tensions. To shed light on these growing yet relatively less investigated changes happening in international news-making, this book brings together the latest of studies conducted on this form of journalistic labour around the world.

This book will contribute to both the breadth and depth of our future understanding of local news-work that benefits distant audiences, and also help cement the place of such journalistic work as a vital topic of analysis in its own right.

The chapters in this book were originally published as a special issue of *Journalism Studies.*

Saumava Mitra investigates the gendered and geopolitical inequities inherent in the reporting of – and the acts surrounding reporting of – violent and social conflicts around the world. Prior to joining DCU, Mitra worked in journalism, communications and academia in South Asia, East Africa, the North and Central Americas and in Western Europe.

Chris Paterson researches the production of international news and communication for development. He has led funded research on the representation of modern imperialism in Africa, the role of development funding for journalism and climate change communication in Africa. His books concern television news agencies and the safety of war correspondents.

Journalism Studies: Theory and Practice

Series editor: *Bob Franklin, Cardiff School of Journalism, Media and Cultural Studies, Cardiff University, UK*

The journal *Journalism Studies* was established at the turn of the new millennium by Bob Franklin. It was launched in the context of a burgeoning interest in the scholarly study of journalism and an expansive global community of journalism scholars and researchers. The ambition was to provide a forum for the critical discussion and study of journalism as a subject of intellectual inquiry but also an arena of professional practice. Previously, the study of journalism in the UK and much of Europe was a fairly marginal branch of the larger disciplines of media, communication and cultural studies; only a handful of Universities offered degree programmes in the subject. *Journalism Studies* has flourished and succeeded in providing the intended public space for discussion of research on key issues within the field, to the point where in 2007 a sister journal, *Journalism Practice*, was launched to enable an enhanced focus on practice-based issues, as well as foregrounding studies of journalism education, training and professional concerns. Both journals are among the leading ranked journals within the field and publish six issues annually, in electronic and print formats. More recently, 2013 witnessed the launch of a further companion journal *Digital Journalism* to provide a site for scholarly discussion, analysis and responses to the wide ranging implications of digital technologies for the practice and study of journalism. From the outset, the publication of themed issues has been a commitment for all journals. Their purpose is first, to focus on highly significant or neglected areas of the field; second, to facilitate discussion and analysis of important and topical policy issues; and third, to offer readers an especially high quality and closely focused set of essays, analyses and discussions.

The *Journalism Studies: Theory and Practice* book series draws on a wide range of these themed issues from all journals and thereby extends the critical and public forum provided by them. The Editor of the journals works closely with guest editors to ensure that the books achieve relevance for readers and the highest standards of research rigour and academic excellence. The series makes a significant contribution to the field of journalism studies by inviting distinguished scholars, academics and journalism practitioners to discuss and debate the central concerns within the field. It also reaches a wider readership of scholars, students and practitioners across the social sciences, humanities and communication arts, encouraging them to engage critically with, but also to interrogate, the specialist scholarly studies of journalism which this series provides.

For more information about this series, please visit: https://www.routledge.com/Journalism-Studies/book-series/JOURNALISM

Reporting Global while being Local

Local Producers of News for Distant Audiences

Edited by
Saumava Mitra and Chris Paterson

Routledge
Taylor & Francis Group
NEW YORK AND LONDON

First published 2021
by Routledge
605 Third Avenue, New York, NY 10017

and by Routledge
2 Park Square, Milton Park, Abingdon, Oxon, OX14 4RN

Routledge is an imprint of the Taylor & Francis Group, an informa business

Library of Congress Cataloging-in-Publication Data
A catalog record for this title has been requested

ISBN 13: 978-0-367-75873-8 (hbk)

Typeset in Myriad Pro
by codeMantra

Publisher's Note
The publisher accepts responsibility for any inconsistencies that may have arisen during the conversion of this book from journal articles to book chapters, namely the inclusion of journal terminology.

Disclaimer
Every effort has been made to contact copyright holders for their permission to reprint material in this book. The publishers would be grateful to hear from any copyright holder who is not here acknowledged and will undertake to rectify any errors or omissions in future editions of this book.

Contents

Citation Information

The chapters in this book were originally published in the *Journalism Studies*, volume 20, issue 12 (July 2019). When citing this material, please use the original page numbering for each article, as follows:

Introduction

Reporting Global While Being Local: Local Sources of News for Distant Audiences
Saumava Mitra and Chris Paterson
Journalism Studies, volume 20, issue 12 (July 2019) pp. 1671–1678

Chapter 1

Fixers as Entrepreneurs
Colleen Murrell
Journalism Studies, volume 20, issue 12 (July 2019) pp. 1679–1695

Chapter 2

"Fixing" the Journalist-Fixer Relationship: A Critical Look Towards Developing Best Practices in Global Reporting
Shayna Plaut and Peter Klein
Journalism Studies, volume 20, issue 12 (July 2019) pp. 1696–1713

Chapter 3

Beyond Puppet Journalism: The Bridging Work of Transnational Journalists in a Local Field
Ruth Moon
Journalism Studies, volume 20, issue 12 (July 2019) pp. 1714–1731

Chapter 4

The Development of Roles in Kosovo: From Fixers to Journalists
Abit Hoxha and Kenneth Andresen
Journalism Studies, volume 20, issue 12 (July 2019) pp. 1732–1746

Chapter 5

One Foot in Prison and One Foot Out: State-Appointed Local Journalistic Labor in North Korea
Soomin Seo
Journalism Studies, volume 20, issue 12 (July 2019) pp. 1747–1763

Chapter 6

Hierarchies of Editorial Power in International NGOs
Muganzi M. Isharaza
Journalism Studies, volume 20, issue 12 (July 2019) pp. 1764–1781

Chapter 7

"Translating" Russia: News Fixers and Foreign Correspondents in an Era of Political Uncertainty
Lindsay Palmer
Journalism Studies, volume 20, issue 12 (July 2019) pp. 1782–1797

Chapter 8

Reporting Global While Being Local—Commentary for Special Issue of Journalism Studies
Stephen Jukes
Journalism Studies, volume 20, issue 12 (July 2019) pp. 1798–1802

Chapter 9

Empowerment Journalism – Commentary for Special Issue of Journalism Studies
Maya Lefkowich, Britney Dennison and Peter Klein
Journalism Studies, volume 20, issue 12 (July 2019) pp. 1803–1809

Contributors

Kenneth Andresen Department of Nordic and Media Studies, University of Agder, Kristiansand, Norway.

Britney Dennison Global Reporting Centre, University of British Columbia, Vancouver, Canada.

Abit Hoxha Department of Nordic and Media Studies, University of Agder, Kristiansand, Norway.

Muganzi M. Isharaza School of Media and Communication, University of Leeds, UK.

Stephen Jukes Faculty of Media & Communication, Bournemouth University, UK.

Peter Klein University of British Columbia, Vancouver, Canada.

Maya Lefkowich Global Reporting Centre, University of British Columbia, Vancouver, Canada.

Saumava Mitra School of Communications, Dublin City University, Dublin, Ireland.

Ruth Moon Manship School of Mass Communication, Louisiana State University, Baton Rouge, USA.

Colleen Murrell School of Communications, Dublin City University, Dublin, Ireland.

Lindsay Palmer School of Journalism and Mass Communication, University of Wisconsin-Madison, USA.

Chris Paterson School of Media and Communication, University of Leeds, UK.

Shayna Plaut University of Winnipeg, Winnipeg, Canada.

Soomin Seo Department of Journalism, Klein College of Media and Communication, Temple University, Philadelphia, USA.

Introduction: Reporting Global While Being Local: Local SourcesofNewsforDistant Audiences

Saumava Mitra and Chris Paterson

ABSTRACT
This essay introduces the special issue entitled Reporting Global while being local: Local sources of news for distant audiences. It discusses the rationale behind this special issue's focus on local newsworkers who contribute their labour to international news-reporting and reviews research conducted on the work and working conditions of these newsworkers to date. The article then goes on to describe the articles that appear in the special issue.

There has been copious research over the decades concerning foreign correspondents who report on distant crises and conflicts for audiences back home, but news professionals working *in their own countries* but *for distant audiences* have only garnered passing attention of researchers. But such news-staff – termed "local-foreign" by Hamilton and Jenner (2004) – have long played essential roles within international news production, as the foreign correspondents and news reporting teams who depend on them tend to readily admit. This special issue is intended to shift the attention of those who study journalism to the largely neglected informal industry of local newsworkers who facilitate, and (perhaps) actively shape, global news reporting. Such people are typically known as fixers (logistical, cultural and linguistic aides), stringers, and translators, but can include a far wider variety of roles including reporters, photojournalists, videographers, technicians and more.

In scholarly debate about how cultural goods flow around the world (Schiller 1976, [1969] 1992; MacBride [1980] 2004; Tomlinson [1991] 2001; Park and Curran 2000; Thussu 2006; Hesmondhalgh 2013), international news has long been seen as dominated by large media institutions based in Western countries, resulting, many have argued, in an ideologically Western or even Anglo-American formulation of global news (e.g., Boyd-Barrett and Rantanen 1998, 2004; Thussu 2004; Wasserman and de Beer 2009; Paterson 2011).

This understanding has been challenged by a more recent suggestion that international news should now be seen as "hybrid" and not Western (Bromley and Clarke 2012, 1–16; Waisbord 2013, 222–233). This view sees international journalism for global audiences as "a transnational and collaborative process" (Palmer 2018a, 317). But while a more cosmopolitan "international space" (Murrell 2015, 7), helped by globalization may have come to create a "messier" reality in international news production (Palmer 2018b, 1333), patterns of Western dominance in global news cannot be said to have simply disappeared (Bromley and Clarke 2012, 12; Paterson 2011, 10–18).

Who Produces International News?

The tacit understanding that international news meant for global audiences is produced solely by Western journalists is no longer tenable, with the traditionally invisible labour of local newsworkers producing news for distant audiences becoming ever more visible. This is simultaneously giving rise to calls for addressing the issues of precarity and heightened insecurity which those local newsworkers face every day. Most recently this was seen in the case of the Reuters journalists from Myanmar, Wa Lone and Kyaw Soe Oo, who were imprisoned for reporting on state violence against Rohingyas. Lone and Oo were subsequently pardoned and released after an international outcry from the public, civil society, policymakers and governments (Lewis and Naing 2019). Academic understanding of the emerging problems and issues in contemporary international news production reflects this growing awareness of the role played by local newsworkers in producing news for global audiences.

In the case of the traditionally less-investigated form of journalism performed by local newsworkers, researchers are striving to understand the emotional, cultural and *journalistic* aspects of the labour they perform. Scholars are also paying attention to how long-criticized hegemonic practices within international news production which prioritize Western perspectives and norms are giving rise to frictions within international systems of news production as local news-staff come to terms with them. Challenges to the stereotypes and biases in news produced from Western perspectives are emerging (see e.g., Bunce, Franks, and Paterson 2017), but such challenges to traditional dynamics of Western dominated storytelling have also been shown to be dependent on change in the current configurations of the established hierarchies of editorial power. Relatedly, locally-based activists and NGO workers have come to be accepted within international news production as sources of news and information, creating another set of tensions and struggles between professional journalism and advocacy-based information sharing (Wright 2018).

Reliance on local fixers and journalists within international news production continues unabated today as does the reliance on locally-based non-journalistic sources. We hope for this special issue of the *Journalism Studies* to contribute to both the breadth and depth of our future understanding of who produces international news.

Focus on the Professional, Specialized *Locals*

The journalistic work and practices of foreign correspondents who report from areas affected by crises and conflicts for an "audience back home" have long been part of popular consciousnesses. From *Scoop* by Evelyn Waugh set in Imperial era Africa to *Somewhere I'll Find You* starring Clark Gable in 1942 to 2019s *The Hunt*, a 5-minute-video released online associated with the camera company Leica (BBC 2019), the profession has long been idealized and valorized (or satirized by Waugh) in such ways that Western males occupy centre stage. Unsurprisingly, the role of the Western male foreign correspondents – the "professional, specialized tourists" as Susan Sontag described them (2003, 17) – had been the most studied and discussed in different contexts and conflicts (Hallin 1984; Pedelty 1995; Thussu and Freedman 2003; Allan and Zelizer 2004; Hannerz 2004; Knightley 2004; Tumber and Webster 2006; Paterson 2019).

However, this entrenched understanding of who produces international news, especially of conflicts, is shifting within academia and beyond it. In addition to the role played by female journalists (e.g., Orgeret 2016; Palmer and Melki 2018), scholars have to started to recognize the role played by non-Western newsworkers who are (and one might say long have been, if for example we think of Cambodian journalist Dith Pran on whose life the 1984 film *Killing Fields* was based) part and parcel of international news production.

Pedelty (1995) was perhaps the first researcher to observe and describe the role played by local journalists who worked alongside Western foreign correspondents. He mentioned that there were "many indicators that Salvadorian and foreign journalists work within very different social and psychological contexts" (1995, 208). Nonetheless, apart from this brief observation, studies of local newsworkers engaged within international news production have been scarce.

The roles and responsibilities of these "professional, specialized locals" within international news production have increased as falling news industry revenues have meant reductions in non-local staff assigned to foreign news bureaus and the need to hire cheaper (and more ad hoc) journalistic labour has grown (Hamilton and Jenner 2004, 301–321; Hamilton 2012, 211–222; Otto and Meyer 2012; Murrell 2015, 1–22). There is also a growing "safety culture" in international news production as recent conflicts have tended to be more dangerous for foreign journalists (Palmer 2018c); that culture seeks to shield foreign correspondents while relying on news produced by journalists who call conflict-affected countries their primary or secondary home. For example, Paterson (2014, 166–168) found in his study of US-inflicted journalists' deaths in "the 9/11 wars" (Burke 2011), that over half (17 of 32) involved the killing of a local media worker assisting with international reporting. As Palmer (2018a, 316) has noted, "it is only in the age of the so-called 'war on terror', when conflict zones have become increasingly dangerous and the dependence on local news staff more pronounced," that the acknowledgement of agency of local sources in international news has been growing: both within journalistic circles and in academia.

Local Sources of News for Distant Audiences

While Hannerz (2004, 147–178) made a passing mention of the role of news fixers within his ethnographic study of foreign correspondents, Erickson and Hamilton (2006) discussed the role of fixers as vital support systems for foreign correspondents. Tumber and Webster (2006, 106–115) dedicated a chapter describing the work of fixers based on interviews with British journalists within their study on war reporting. In the following year, Palmer and Fontan (2007) specifically focused on the role of fixers in co-producing news about the Iraq war. Their study, like Tumber and Webster's, was also based largely on interviews with foreign journalists working in the country and concentrated largely on their role as linguistic aides to foreign correspondents. However, exploring the work and practice of fixers within international news production has since then incrementally shifted to start making sense of their work largely from their own perspectives and perceptions (Paterson, Andresen, and Hoxha 2012; Palmer 2018a, 2019).

While Hamilton and Jenner acknowledged the role of local-foreign correspondents back in 2004, Bunce's (2010) study of the cultural clash in the East Africa bureaus of international news organizations, where Kenyan journalists worked side by side with foreign journalists, was the first to seek to understand first-hand the work and practices of local journalists within international news production. A relatively lesser-known study by Khan (2011) was published in an edited volume (on forces of globalization at work in Afghanistan), and explored the work of local journalists in Pakistan who worked for and with international journalists to report on the Afghan war. Khan has since returned to the issue and provided more recent insight on fixing work undertaken by journalists in the frontier areas of Pakistan for international news media (2019). Seo (2016) has shed light on the role played by "local journalistic hires" in foreign bureaus run by the global news agency Associated Press over the last few decades by utilizing archival interviews kept by the news organization. A relatively neglected area for long, the work of local photojournalists who provide images for global audiences have also started to come into focus in recent scholarly investigations (Istek 2017; Mollerup and Mortensen 2018; Mitra 2019).

Another emerging and perhaps better-researched trend in this respect is the growing influence of locally-based activists, advocacy groups and non-governmental organizations, on international news production (Fenton 2010; Waisbord 2011; Chouliaraki 2015; Conrad 2015; Powers 2016). The growing inclusion of local non-journalistic agents who produce news, information and images for international audiences is also a consequence of budget-slashing by global news media. Particularly in their exploration of the agency of local NGO workers and activists' contributions to international news, this area of study shows that "local-foreign news production" can be understood as expanding today not only in magnitude but also in the kind of actors involved.

Available research shows that the involvement of local journalists and fixers as well as non-journalistic sources of news and information in international news production – a small part of what might be a larger shift towards transnational and collaborative international news-making – is far from being harmonious and is marked by economic, socio-cultural and practice-related tensions. Tensions have been noted to arise from non-recognition of the journalistic labour provided by the local news-staff by their news organizations (Murrell 2015; Seo 2016; Palmer 2018a; Khan 2019) as well as because of differing employment conditions of the local newsworkers as opposed to their international colleagues. In this context, research has shown that the work of local-foreign newsworkers is typified by more precarious, and often dangerous, conditions of employment (Tumber and Webster 2006, 106–115; Bunce 2011; Khan 2011; Paterson 2014; Mitra 2017; Palmer 2018c, 2019). Apart from these tensions within the context of the professional experience of local journalists and fixers, some researchers have also investigated differences in news values and role perceptions (Bunce 2011; Khan 2011; Mitra 2019) as well as similarities (Murrell 2015) compared to international journalists: another potential site of tension.

Finally, some researchers have pointed to how processes of news production within local-global journalism are affected by "'inside'/'outside' cultural dichotomy" (Bunce 2010, 527) because the identity-based affiliations and affinities, as well as the local knowledge and familiarity of the local journalists and fixers, are perceived as important factors in international news production by local newsworkers (Bunce 2015; Murrell 2015; Palmer 2019). While early research on the role of fixers, tended to view such differences as negative influences on news production (Tumber and Webster 2006; Palmer and Fontan 2007), increasingly researchers are also recognizing the potential positive influence that such local affiliations and affinities, knowledge and familiarity of the local journalists and fixers can have on international news (Paterson 2011; Bunce 2015; Mitra 2017; Palmer 2018b, 2019).

Reporting Global While Being Local

International news today needs to be understood as a chorus of voices – both foreign and local as well as professional and non-professional. Not all voices might yet have the same potential to be heard around the world however because research has shown that international news production can be shaped by both local story-telling objectives as well as efforts to conform news narratives to those perceived as preferred by foreign clients and audiences (Bunce 2015; Mitra 2019).

In this complex, messy reality of international news production of today where past patterns and present factors are shaping the future of foreign news, one thing is certain. International news production is morphing in ways and forms that are both geo-culturally specific to areas and regions, but also socio-economically comparable across the world. This special issue is inspired by the need for geographically broad, theoretically deep, methodologically sound, and culturally sensitive understandings of the processes and people shaping international news.

This issue grew out of dialogues the editors have had with peers and colleagues engaged in research on local newsworkers who produce news for distant audiences. We organized a panel bringing many of these researchers together for the 2018 ICA conference, and, in collaboration with UNESCO, this topic was also the focus of a panel we organized for the 2018 conference of the IAMCR. Several of these panelists have contributed to this special issue. We have also broadened the scope of the issue to attract relevant contributions from researchers interested in this topic.

The issue begins with research by news agency journalist turned educator Colleen Murrell examining the entrepreneurial nature of local newswork for foreign audiences, and then presents survey research by Shayna Plaut and Peter Klein which helps us grasp the extent and dimensions of such work. With their studies, Moon, Seo, Hoxha and Andresen, and another experienced author in this field, Palmer, examine internationally focused local newswork in Rwanda, North Korea, Kosovo, and Russia respectively. Isharaza guides our focus to the neglected site of local news story production within the communications apparatus of international NGOs. This issue also includes two short essays which the editors invited to offer additional insight into "local-foreign" journalism from the perspective of journalists' safety (from news agency veteran turned educator Stephen Jukes) and new practices being adopted to make local-foreign collaboration more inclusive (from researcher-journalists of the media organization Global Reporting Centre).

It is our hope to bring together the very latest of studies being conducted which will shape our future understandings of local newswork meant for distant audiences, and help to cement the place of that journalistic work as a vital topic of analysis in its own right.

Disclosure statement

No potential conflict of interest was reported by the authors.

ORCID

Saumava Mitra http://orcid.org/0000-0002-8622-7091

References

Allan, S., and B. Zelizer, eds. 2004. *Reporting War: Journalism in Wartime*. New York: Routledge.

BBC. 2019. "Leica China Video Sparks Backlash Over Tiananmen Square Image." BBC.com, April 19. Accessed July 7, 2019. https://www.bbc.com/news/world-asia-china-47987817.

Boyd-Barrett, O., and T. Rantanen, eds. 1998. *The Globalization of News*. London: Sage.

Boyd-Barrett, O., and T. Rantanen. 2004. "News Agencies as News Sources: A Reevaluation." In *International News in the 21st Century*, edited by C. Paterson and A. Sreberny, 31–46. Eastleigh: Luton University Press.

Bromley, M., and J. Clarke, eds. 2012. *International News in the Digital Age: East West Perceptions of a New World Order*. New York: Routledge.

Bunce, M. 2010. "'This Place Used to be a White British Boys' Club': Reporting Dynamics and Cultural Clash at an International News Bureau in Nairobi." *The Round Table: The Commonwealth Journal of International Affairs* 99 (410): 515–528.

Bunce, M. 2011. *The New Foreign Correspondent at Work: Local-national 'Stringers' and the Global News Coverage of Darfur*. Oxford: Reuters Institute for the Study of Journalism, 1–36.

Bunce, M. 2015. "International News and the Image of Africa: New Storytellers, New Narratives?" In *Images of Africa: Creation, Negotiation and Subversion*, edited by J. Gallagher, 42–62. Oxford: Oxford University Press.

Bunce, M., S. Franks, and C. Paterson, eds. 2017. *Africa's Media Image in the 21st Century: From the "Heart of Darkness" to "Africa Rising"*. New York: Routledge.

Burke, J. 2011. *The 9/11 Wars*. London: Penguin UK.

Chouliaraki, L. 2015. "Digital Witnessing in Conflict Zones: The Politics of Remediation." *Information Communication & Society* 18 (11): 1362–1377.

Conrad, D. 2015. "The Freelancer–NGO Alliance: What a Story of Kenyan Waste Reveals About Contemporary Foreign News Production." *Journalism Studies* 16 (2): 275–288.

Erickson, E., and J. M. Hamilton. 2006. "Foreign Reporting Enhanced by Parachute Journalism." *Newspaper Research Journal* 27 (1): 33–47.

Fenton, N. 2010. *New Media, Old News: Journalism and Democracy in the Digital Age*. London: Sage Publications.

Hallin, D. 1984. "The Media, the War in Vietnam, and Political Support: A Critique of the Thesis of an Oppositional Media." *The Journal of Politics* 46 (01): 2–24.

Hamilton, J. M. 2012. "Foreign Correspondence: One Age Ends, Another Begins." In *International News in the Digital Age: East West Perceptions of a New World Order*, edited by M. Bromley and J. Clarke, 311–322. New York: Routledge.

Hamilton, J. M., and E. Jenner. 2004. "Redefining Foreign Correspondence." *Journalism: Theory, Practice & Criticism* 5 (3): 301–321.

Hannerz, U. 2004. *Foreign News: Exploring the World of Foreign Correspondents*. Chicago: Chicago University Press.

Hesmondhalgh, D. 2013. *The Cultural Industries*. 3rd ed. London: Sage.

Istek, P. 2017. "On Their Own: Freelance Photojournalists in Conflict Zones." *Visual Communication Quarterly* 24 (1): 32–39.

Khan, A. 2011. "The "Afghan Beat": Pukhtoon Journalism and the Afghan War." In *Globalizing Afghanistan: Terrorism, War and the Rhetoric of Nation Building*, edited by Z. Jalalzai and D. Jefferess, 79–94. Durham: Duke University Press.

Khan, A. 2019. "Fixers in Corporate Media: Pashtun Journalists Under Threat in North Western Pakistan." *Conflict and Communication Online* 18 (1): 1–9.

Knightley, P. 2004. *The First Casualty: The War Correspondent as Hero and Myth-maker from the Crimea to Iraq*. Baltimore: Johns Hopkins University Press.

Lewis, S., and S. Naing. 2019. "Two Reuters Reporters Freed in Myanmar After More Than 500 Days in Jail." Reuters.com, May 6. Accessed July 7, 2019. https://www.reuters.com/article/us-myanmar-journalists/two-reuters-reporters-freed-in-myanmar-after-more-than-500-days-in-jail-idUSKCN1SD056.

MacBride, S. [1980] 2004. *Many Voices, One World: Towards a New, More Just, and More Efficient World Information and Communication Order*. New York: Rowman & Littlefield.

Mitra, S. 2017. "Adoptability and Acceptability of Peace Journalism Among Afghan Photojournalists: Lessons for Peace Journalism Training in Conflict-affected Countries." *Journal of the Association for Journalism Education UK* 6 (2): 17–27.

Mitra, S. 2019. "'Picturing Afghan Women' for Western Audiences: The Afghan Perspective. *Journalism*. doi:10.1177/1464884919849359.

Mollerup, N. G., and M. Mortensen. 2018. "Proximity and Distance in the Mediation of Suffering: Local Photographers in War-torn Aleppo and the International Media Circuit." *Journalism*. doi:10.1177/1464884918793054.

Murrell, C. 2015. *Foreign Correspondents and International Newsgathering: The Role of Fixers*. New York: Routledge.

Orgeret, K. S. 2016. "Women Making News. Conflict and Post-conflict in the Field." In *Journalism in Conflict and Post-conflict Conditions. Worldwide Perspectives*, edited by K. S. Orgeret and W. Tayeebwa, 99–114. Göteborg: Nordicom.

Otto, F., and C. O. Meyer. 2012. "Missing the Story? Changes in Foreign News Reporting and Their Implications for Conflict Prevention." *Media, War & Conflict* 5 (3): 205–221.

Palmer, L. 2018a. "Being the Bridge': News Fixers' Perspectives on Cultural Difference in Reporting the 'War on Terror." *Journalism* 19 (3): 314–332.

Palmer, L. 2018b. "Lost in Translation: Journalistic Discourse on News "Fixers"." *Journalism Studies* 19 (9): 1331–1348.

Palmer, L. 2018c. *Becoming the Story: War Correspondents Since 9/11*. Urbana, IL: University of Illinois Press.

Palmer, L. 2019. *The Fixers: Local News Workers and the Underground Labor of International Reporting*. New York: Oxford University Press.

Palmer, J., and V. Fontan. 2007. "'Our Ears and Our Eyes' Journalists and Fixers in Iraq." *Journalism* 8 (1): 5–24.

Palmer, L., and J. Melki. 2018. "Shape Shifting in the Conflict Zone: The Strategic Performance of Gender in War Reporting." *Journalism Studies* 19 (1): 126–142.

Park, M. J., and J. Curran, eds. 2000. *De-westernizing Media Studies*. London: Routledge.

Paterson, C. 2011. *The International Television News Agencies: The World from London*. New York: Peter Lang.

Paterson, C. 2014. *War Reporters Under Threat: The United States and Media Freedom*. London: Pluto Press.

Paterson, C. 2019. *Foreign Correspondents. Oxford Research Encyclopedia of Communication*. Oxford: Oxford University Press.

Paterson, C., K. Andresen, and A. Hoxha. 2012. "The Manufacture of an International News Event: The Day Kosovo Was Born." *Journalism: Theory, Practice & Criticism* 13 (1): 103–120.

Pedelty, M. 1995. *War Stories: The Culture of Foreign Correspondents*. New York: Routledge.

Powers, M. 2016. "NGO Publicity and Reinforcing Path Dependencies: Explaining the Persistence of Media-centered Publicity Strategies." *The International Journal of Press/Politics* 21 (4): 490–507.

Schiller, H. I. [1969] 1992. *Mass Communications and American Empire*. New York: Avalon.

Schiller, H. I. 1976. *Communication and Cultural Domination*. White Plains, NY: International Arts and Sciences Press.

Seo, S. 2016. "Marginal Majority at the Postcolonial News Agency: Foreign Journalistic Hires at the Associated Press." *Journalism Studies* 17 (1): 39–56.

Sontag, S. 2003. *Regarding the Pain of Others*. New York: Picador.

Thussu, D. K. 2004. "Media Plenty and the Poverty of News." In *International News in the 21st Century*, edited by C. A. Paterson and A. Sreberny, 47–61. Eastleigh: Luton University Press.

Thussu, D. K., ed. 2006. *Media on the Move: Global Flow and Contra-flow*. New York: Routledge.

Thussu, D. K., and D. Freedman, eds. 2003. *War and the Media: Reporting Conflict 24/7*. London: Sage.

Tomlinson, J. [1991] 2001. *Cultural Imperialism: A Critical Introduction*. New York: Continuum.

Tumber, H., and F. Webster. 2006. *Journalists Under Fire: Information War and Journalistic Practices*. London: Sage

Waisbord, S. 2011. "Can NGOs Change the News?" *International Journal of Communication* 5: 142–165.

Waisbord, S. 2013. *Reinventing Professionalism. Journalism and News in Global Perspective*. Cambridge: Polity Press.

Wasserman, H., and A. S. de Beer. 2009. "Towards De-westernizing Journalism Studies." In *The Handbook of Journalism Studies*, 448–458. London: Routledge.

Wright, K. 2018. *Who's Reporting Africa Now? Non-governmental Organizations, Journalists and Multimedia*. New York: Peter Lang.

Fixers as Entrepreneurs

Colleen Murrell

ABSTRACT
This article examines how fixers and local journalists are increasingly organising among themselves to manage working contracts with foreign correspondents venturing into their countries. This study first reflects on the traditional modus operandi of foreign correspondents and fixers, as covered in the work of authors such as Hannerz, Maxwell-Hamilton, Murrell and Paterson et al. It then moves on to update the narrative of one group of fixers, from being ad hoc hires to becoming media entrepreneurs. This study also explores the growing number of online organisations that are turning this long-standing newsgathering role into a trading profession, that is opening up beyond the news media into other areas of practice such as film-making and business. It explores a range of new media organisations from large transnational ones to boutique operations, and gathers data from some of the key people behind these changes. As local fixers, producers and journalists remain uniquely exposed to violence and danger in the course of their jobs, this study also explores if any changes are being implemented to try and ensure better safety standards.

Introduction

Local journalists, producers or fixers have played a part in Western foreign correspondence for as long as there have been despatches sent from abroad to the readers back home. However, being largely "back room" people, assisting the out-front reporters, their work remains largely hidden from view and is thereby little understood. The majority of fixers remain to this day temporary workers who can be picked up and dropped by foreign correspondents at a moment's notice. They often lack power and agency in their media work and are forced to accept sub-standard employment conditions. Nonetheless, a growing number are adopting a more entrepreneurial stance, and are advertising their skills on websites and are forming their own companies. This research project is interested in finding out the reasons for moving in this direction and the consequences of this change to fixers' lives.

The term "fixer" has become a handy catch-all name for the person hired overseas to assist in the job of news gathering being carried out by a visiting reporter. For several years now, there have been ongoing debates in reporting, fixing and academic circles as to whether or not this term is pejorative, and is thereby under-selling the importance of the role. The suggestions that perhaps the terms "local producer" (Murrell 2009), "local journalist" or "journalist-fixer" (Klein and Plaut 2017) would be better substitutes have been canvassed, but not adopted. Given that the term "fixer" is still in widespread use, and is employed by so many fixers themselves for the purposes of advertising their skills, experience and availability, this article will use the term on the understanding that fixers are crucial players in the pursuit of international news gathering, as illustrated by the growing number of research projects discussed below. In scholarly work the role of a fixer has been defined as a locally-employed media worker, who facilitates the coverage of news stories by a visiting reporter in both a logistical sense (for example related to travel, permits, filming, and location access), and in an editorial sense, through teamwork in the generation of story ideas, contacts, translation, analysis and interviewing (Murrell 2009).

Literature on Fixers

Fixers have only been researched as a separate group of media workers in the past decade. If you examine the copious literature on foreign correspondents (books, articles and journalists' autobiographies), you mostly find only passing references to the work of fixers. In the official history about international newsgathering, their voices are not readily heard and correspondingly they appear to have little power. In Mark Pedelty's ethnographic work (1995, 211) about foreign correspondents in San Salvador, he referred to fixers as mere "logistical aides" who helped the elite staff reporters with their newsgathering. For Hannerz (2004, 154), fixers were a "polymorphous" group, who tended to use the role as "a stepping stone to a journalistic career." Erickson and Hamilton (2006, 40) understood them to be the "support systems" for travelling reporters. This same "assisting" frame was employed by Tumber and Webster (2006) in a book chapter devoted to fixers, which did not assign to them a significant role in generating ideas or original news stories. For Palmer and Fontan (2007, 12) fixers were mostly translators and interpreters with good local contacts. They concluded that their hiring was a "necessary evil" during the 2003 invasion of Iraq, due to the danger for Westerners and their lack of Arabic language skills. They decided that employing fixers weakened "the traditional model of the foreign correspondent" (2007, 22). However, Iraq was not unusual as a dateline for hiring fixers, as the traditional foreign correspondent has been employing fixers as a default production process for decades. What was unusual about Iraq, in the years following 2003, was that the situation became so dangerous that the role of fixers expanded, and they started conducting the interviews and news gathering themselves, sometimes even in place of the foreign correspondents (Murrell 2010).

In a doctoral thesis and associated articles that examined the working relationships and news production teamwork between fixers and foreign correspondents (Murrell 2009; 2010; 2011) it was found that fixers had considerable editorial sway in story generation and analysis that was often being poorly reflected in either journalists' or scholars' accounts. This qualitative research project examined the power differentials and the teamwork of both parties to this newsgathering game. Drawing on field theory and the acquisition of cultural capital by Pierre Bourdieu (1986, 243–244 and 248; Benson and Neveu 2004) this research found that the short and long-term agency and power resided with the correspondents, and that fixers could gain only limited and short-term profit from the working exchange. Whereas ground-breaking or exclusive stories could lead to significant cultural capital for reporters (promotions, book deals, entry to the well-paid lecture circuit, etc.) fixers were only as good as their last job and their names were rarely attached to the stories published or broadcast (Murrell 2009).

This project posed mirrored questions to both fixers and correspondents about their production practices, in order to compare and contrast the different ways that they worked and understood their roles. Through applying a grounded theory approach, what emerged from the data were findings about their respective levels of cultural capital, power and agency. Data from interviews carried out between 2007 and 2008, revealed that contacts for fixers were still held securely in reporters' own notebooks or in company databases (in the case of UK organisations). These databases - particularly those from the BBC and ITN - recorded details about the fixers' locations, languages, political and religious beliefs, and personal circumstances (Murrell 2011, 165–177). Reporters and producers who worked with fixers were tasked with updating the databases, following their latest experiences "on the road." The correspondents could give free rein to their thoughts about these people, including musings about their abilities, skills, personalities and whether or not they were "difficult" about certain stories or in particular situations. These internal accounts would then affect fixers' chances of securing further employment when a reporter from the organisation next went abroad. These databases were open for perusal by any employee on the newsgathering side of the media companies concerned, however, there was no way for fixers to access or correct such accounts. If a fixer had been employed many times over the years, especially in conflict zones, then they might have a quiet word with a foreign editor to try and pass on any problematic issues they experienced while working with staff members. However, this could easily land them in the "too tricky to work with" category for future jobs.

The fixers who were interviewed about how they found work (Murrell 2011, 177–180) said that they mostly got jobs through contacts made during previous fixing work, via the apparent serendipity of being in the right place at the right time, or by proactively going to hotels favoured by foreign correspondents and asking around for jobs. Once they had built up a solid reputation, then they could get further jobs through "word of mouth" or recommendations passed on from one reporter to another. When a particular story or location was running hot, or was in an enclosed place where fixers were thin on the ground, then pay and conditions were good, and skilful fixers were fought over by keen reporters (Murrell 2011, 175). Several correspondents admitted that they would not pass on the contacts of really good fixers, except to their own organisations or very close friends. Ironically therefore, fixers' work prospects could be diminished if they were very good, but they might never know the reason for this paucity of opportunity. Even today, most fixers continue to be ad hoc hires, taken on for particular stories, and engaged on a daily basis. A lucky few have retainers for a set number of days per year to work with particular companies. Others get hired longer term, such as by the BBC or CNN in Baghdad in the years following the 2003 war, as it can be safer for all parties to have longer term and trusted employees in ongoing dangerous situations (Murrell 2010).

The favourite type of fixer cited by western journalists, is a local reporter (Murrell 2011, 164–177 and 205–211). Correspondents believe this type of person understands the nature of the job and the local scene, tends to be proactive and well connected and is highly adaptable. Fixers generally agreed with this interpretation. A fixer from Bali, Dr. Darma Putra, explained this succinctly:

> Because my background is journalist I have a similar kind of mission, vision, or let's say it with the big word, ideology. So, I'm a citizen of journalism, of the world called journalism. I'm not a Balinese or not an Indonesian in that case. So, whatever's new, whatever is news then we always share it. [...] There's only one journalism. (Murrell 2015, 137)

Another major finding (Murrell 2011, 2013) was that successful fixers, the ones who were chosen most regularly by reporters, tended to be globalised citizens and "people like us." They spoke English, bartered for jobs, were persistent and were increasingly knowledgeable about the international media market and their part in it. These are all personality traits that are inherently entrepreneurial.

Research undertaken in the past few years has further emphasised the fixers' perspectives on their role in newsgathering. Paterson, Andresen, and Hoxha (2012, 117) examined the role of fixers in "constructed news coverage," related to the declaration of independence by Kosovo in 2008, finding that the participation of young fixers, "allowed the story to move beyond the confines set by those orchestrating it." Palmer (2018) interviewed 21 fixers in a project that concentrated on the cultural differences between fixers and correspondents, and explored their expectations and experiences during the newsgathering process. In a large global study, Klein and Plaut (2017) surveyed 435 news gatherers and asked if they considered themselves to be journalists, fixers or "journalist-fixers." Data from the respondents, showed that 167 identified as fixers or journalist-fixers and 19 in the latter category participated in follow-up interviews. Their findings showed that "underlying tensions" simmered and were related to the unequal power dynamic that often remained hidden during their work together. One of their foremost findings was that, "While safety was foremost for correspondents, a larger concern for fixers was money." Another major preoccupation was by-line credit, as most correspondents claimed to rarely give fixers credit, with most fixers saying they would like to have credit. The importance of the editorial aspect of the fixing job is underlined by correspondents in their stated preference for working with fixers who are local journalists (Murrell 2011). This is borne out in a series of interviews with fixers called "Unbylined," from the website "Roads & Kingdoms." According to "local colleague" on the site, Borpujari (2016), the name "fixer" does not do justice to the role of someone who works as a local journalist, and has to hand over their hard-earned resources to the parachuting correspondent:

> My contact list that I have accrued over the years. My convincing for interviews for your story. My translation of tragedies and emotions into words you may best understand. My experience that protects, or encourages you to walk the street with your camera at night, and yet, the by-line belongs only to you. The awards are won only by you. The one to be addressed as journalist is only you.

Democratising Platforms

In the same way that fixers are beginning to emphasise their separate category as "journalist-fixers," so are some beginning to assert their rights to better negotiate hiring contracts. These people are now forming their own companies or collectives to secure better deals for themselves. This latest move has been part of a continuum, that began a few years back with the setting up of websites devoted to freelance news gathering. An early social media news gathering site along these lines was a "closed" and later "secret"

Facebook site called "The Vulture Club," which was set up by NGO workers and freelance journalists. One of the findings of research into this site (Murrell 2014) was that it was mostly about locating fixers, and that the most active members were freelance journalists, seeking help with newsgathering overseas. However, already there were signs that fixers were beginning to advertise themselves for hire in posts that they themselves initiated on the site. Later still, fixers started to branch out and set up their own Facebook pages, specific to particular places or to organisations or individuals. In addition, larger advocacy groups stepped into the space to help, advise or provide a platform for fixers to communicate with other fixers, reporters and NGO workers. These platforms are gradually leading to a merging of the separate categories of fixers and reporters. The "Frontline Freelance Register" (FFR) which began in 2013, advocates for better hiring and safety conditions for freelancers, including many journalists who also work as fixers. In a similar way "The Rory Peck Trust," offers resources, prizes and safety and editorial training for freelance media workers. "Hostwriter" is a free, open network which connects 3800 journalists from 136 countries with the aim of breaking down the barriers between Western journalists and journalists from other countries, by giving them an online space to link up to conduct joint reporting projects. In a similar fashion "Round Earth Media" pairs up American reporters with reporters in particular locations where "hard to report" stories are happening.

A similarly large platform is "WorldFixer," which proclaims itself to be, "Home of the best local producers, fixers and journalists" (WorldFixer). According to its founder, Mike Garrod, WorldFixer has on its books, "8,000 fixers, producers, service companies and some journalists" (emailed interview, 2018). This platform brokers jobs between fixers and a wide variety of news, filming, business, and NGO clients. This free platform allows people to put up their profiles, listing their languages, skills, testimonials and previous work in the role. They also get vetted and their references are contacted. The site lists the different categories of media workers and fixers available to hire:

> General Fixer; Camera Operator/Photographer; Charity Worker/NGO; Driver; Guide; Law Enforcement/Security; Local Journalist; Local Producer/Coordinator; Location Manager/Scout; Medical Professional; Other; Researcher; Runner/General Assistant; Translator; Travel Ind. Fixers; Visas and Permits Fixers. (WorldFixer, 2018)

According to the site's owner, Mike Garrod, the online space makes it easier and more transparent for fixers and hirers to conduct fair negotiations.

> In the event of pay disputes arising from connections through the site I do step in to mediate regularly. [...] We also remove clients and fixers from the site who engage in bad practice but that depends on people telling me about it - I have a "three strike rule" on this for fixers (to account for personality clashes) and a zero tolerance on clients for no pay or encouraging fixers to engage in hostile environments without proper cover. (Garrod email interview, 2018)

The organisation "HackPack" also operates as a cross-category broker for 8434 media professionals from 163 countries (HackPack, 2018). Justin Varilek (email interview, 2018) who runs the site, says that the advantages of a large platform to fixer members are numerous:

> It is easier to source a variety of different jobs and attain a more or less consistent revenue stream. When a rather large client is running late on payments, then it is easier to force them to pay by declaring that the entire group won't work on further projects until payments are made.

Entrepreneurialism, Media and the Film Industry

Alongside these initiatives from the newsgathering side, connections are also being made from the film industry side. Because the fixer role is so "polymorphous" (Hannerz 2004, 154), it is ideal for project-based work that outsources distinct tasks. Here is how a film and television production company "NeedaFixer" (2018) explains this new merging of categories on its website, while emphasising the logistical rather than editorial aspects of the role:

> The term "fixer" came from journalism. Foreign correspondents in an unfamiliar place would hire a helper to arrange parts of their story or interview. Fixers would take care of all the details: translation, transportation, accommodation, and so on. Their local knowledge often proved vital to the journalist's piece. "Fixing" eventually made its way to the film and television industry. These days, a fixer is anyone who provides support and helps to coordinate film projects. And at NeedaFixer, we're all fixers because we FIX amazing projects and bring stories to life.

Temporary and outsourced jobs are, increasingly, the way of the future, and companies working loosely within the creative arts field are as much a part of this development as any others in the business and service industries. According to creative entrepreneur Alex Vero (2017):

> Like it or not, the general macro trend is towards a freelance global workforce. Fewer and fewer agencies and production companies are working on retainers and are increasingly operating on a project-by-project basis. Gartner predicts that 50% of the US workforce will be freelance by 2020.

Deuze and Witschge (2018, 167) have examined entrepreneurialism in media work, declaring it to be "part of a profession that can best be seen as a self-organising social system through which shifting coalitions of participants are linked, and that is interdependent on a variety of other systems." Media workers may be entrepreneurial in setting up their portfolio of jobs, but they still need to fit into a complicated arrangement of part-time agreements. This "patchwork-career" (Michel 2000) of impermanence is likely to become the new normal.

In 2019 while these Western-based larger fixer sites are growing in size and number, they represent only a fraction of the ways in which fixers find work. Klein and Plaut's study (2017) confirmed that "word of mouth" remains the main way that fixers are recruited by foreign correspondents. Their survey and interviews found that 92% of hires were still being done via word of mouth (usually journalist via journalist). They also discovered that fixers accessed online recruitment 48% of the time, whereas journalists did so only 25.5% of the time. According to Plaut (emailed interview 2018), while

> Fixers would sometimes have Facebook pages, [it was] more to let journalists know they existed or were available, but this was new, one to two years' old and not as common, and even then, it was expected that the journalists talked to one another before reaching out to a fixer.

This research project will examine an evolving strategy of entrepreneurial fixers, who have taken a further step towards independence in their working practices. The questions posed to fixers were designed to discover the reasons why they felt a need to set up their own companies, and what challenges and benefits accrued from this move, in terms of finances and safety precautions. Where previous studies have emphasised the "sole-trader" aspects of fixers' production practices, this article examines the motives of fixers who have embraced entrepreneurialism through team-building, thereby banding together with colleagues to draw on strength of numbers in negotiations.

Methodology

Following on from research that examined fixers' working lives as ad hoc hires by reporters (Murrell 2011, 2015; Klein and Plaut 2017), and a project that charted fixers beginning to advertise for jobs via online websites (Murrell 2014), the findings concerning power and agency from those earlier projects were embedded in the concepts that influenced the design of this particular project. The questionnaire contained sensitising, theoretical, structural and guiding questions, as recommended by grounded theory scholars Strauss and Corbin (1998, 77–78). The catalyst for reassessing changes in Bourdieu's "journalistic field" (Benson and Neveu 2004), was the recent proliferation of online sites that appeared to show that fixers were gathering together to form their own companies and – with strength in numbers – negotiate the terms of their jobs. The questionnaire was designed to collect qualitative data that explored themes related to the possible redressing of the power imbalance between journalists and fixers. The questions were therefore written to tease out if forming companies (as opposed to being a single freelancer) improved the financial circumstances and safety of fixers. The questions were also designed to further explore Klein and Plaut's finding (2017) that fixers' overriding interest was financial rather than being related to safety concerns.

Purposive sampling was conducted via prominent journalists and fixers, in order to locate relevant fixers who had set up their own companies. Likely candidates were also located via online sites which marketed themselves as catering for fixers. On finding a promising candidate, an exploratory email was sent out to see if the person had in fact set up their own company and to find out if they would agree to fill out a questionnaire. Along the way, many fixers were contacted whom international journalists had recommended as being "likely to have set up their own company." However, often they were simply entrepreneurial individuals who were active in securing work but had not formed companies or collectives of their own. While in this stage of discovery, it was also found that many online fixers' sites now offered, "film services" for feature filming and advertising as well as traditional services for news gathering. Some companies were very large, for example, "Skoti Collins's Global Producers/Fixers" website on Facebook (FB), which had 2436 members (2018). Others, such as "Steppe Fixers Mongolia" just had Facebook and online pages which stated simply what they did, and offered contact numbers and email addresses.

In the end, through online investigations, purposive sampling and asking other researchers, 30 questionnaires were sent out to specific entities to see if they fitted the bill of being organisations run *by* fixers *for* fixers. Of these 30, 20 were completed and returned, of which 18[1] fitted the aforementioned criteria. Included in the 18 were two apparent "lone traders" because, on closer inspection, they worked and shared jobs in an organised collective with a defined community of other fixers. For example, *Zeghy* from Brazil, operated as a company in conjunction with others and had always wanted to start up his own legal company but was stymied by local bureaucracy from making this official (see below). Hassan Ashwor, a multi-award-winning fixer, was included as he helps to run the website *The Fixer* which sources and advertises fixing work for others. Separately, and not included in the findings, emailed interview exchanges were conducted with three people[2] for the purpose of background knowledge. Two were in charge of major fixer websites (quoted in the literature review section), and a third was a scholar who had conducted a large survey of fixers, about which I had further questions.

Findings: Name, Size and Location

The questions were grouped into loosely themed areas (drawing on findings of previous research) which sought information linked to concepts of power, agency and improvements to financial and safety conditions. Overall, the questions canvassed answers relating to the size and location of the companies, the jobs being carried out, the reasons for setting up the companies in the first place and the consequences of these decisions. Four questions elicited short answers about their names, whether or not they wanted anonymity, how big were their operations and in which countries they operated. All respondents agreed to have the names of their organisations published, but three wanted their personal names anonymised, and therefore only the names of the organisations are given in these findings. Nine operated in single country locations: those in Jordan, Gaza, Bangladesh, Pakistan, Rajasthan, Brazil, Tunisia (x 2) and Iraq. Others operated across regions that were connected geographically or ethnically. For example, *The Fixer*, a Yazidi organisation advertising on Facebook, operated "within the areas of Sinjar, Rabiah, Dohuk, Erbil and Syria" providing fixers who spoke Arabic, Kurdish and English. This organisation operated around the boundaries of zones controlled by the so-called Islamic State. *Fixers.Press* stated that it had people in "Estonia, Latvia and Lithuania," separating and concentrating on the Baltic states. *Fixer in India* was located in the neighbouring states of Thailand, Nepal, India and Bangladesh, while *Mali Tama Expedition SARL* operated across the expanse of West Africa. *Film Fixers Balkans* brought together another large geographic area, spread across nine separate countries: Bulgaria, Romania, Slovakia, Croatia, Cyprus, Turkey, Macedonia, Serbia, and Bosnia and Herzegovina. The size of these operations varied, but most employed a handful of people with the largest one (*Highlight Films, Israel*) reporting that it had 14 fixers on its books, with eight on the payroll and six operating as "freelance" workers. In Gaza, 12 fixers were employed by *Tantesh Media Services*.

Findings: Power, Agency and Overcoming Hardship

The open-ended question, "Why did you decide to start up this organisation?" led to some interesting insights. Some answers were specifically about seizing an opportunity for growth and drawing on their own experience to harness more power and agency in their working lives. For some of these people, local conditions of hardship prompted them to branch out. A few examples were:

- *I decided to work as a fixer and production service provider because it's a unique profession in the context of Bangladesh and the opportunity to work with foreigners staying in my home country was a bonus. The country is still struggling economically with a substantial, educated unemployment rate. So, I wanted to do something out of the box to have a better living.* (BangladeshFixer)

- *Tourism dried up after 9/11, plus my background. Looking at our strength of knowledge, travel experience, contacts and ability to execute made us come this way.* (Vista, Pakistan)
- *I established "Highlight Films" in 1998 in order to produce my own documentary films and series. I soon realised that many colleagues and friends-of-friends asked me for assistance in productions taking place in Israel, and I realised that there are no professional solutions to providing these services. So, I re-arranged the company to specialise in providing production services.* (Highlight Films, Israel)
- *After 25 years of journalism and producing news for international papers and TV channels, I decided to do it by myself.* (Dangerous Works, Turkey)
- *After the Revolution, there have been many events and many foreign journalists who started to come to Tunisia to cover the country's current affairs. [...] I worked really hard with journalists and fulfilled the work assigned to me, so I developed a kind of good reputation. Then I started to get more journalists contacting me thanks to the "word of mouth," so I was thinking that it was the time to establish my own small business.* (Ahmed Ellali, Tunisia)
- *To work on bigger projects.* (Mesopotamia Agency, Iraq)

Findings: Pragmatism

Other answers revealed a theme of choosing to start up a company for purely pragmatic reasons. For these people, the decision was based on the perception that a company would be seen as more serious than a single individual looking for work. Here are some examples:

- *I started as a freelance business, but we were forced by local authorities to start our company after limiting the fixing and translation services to authorized companies.* (Tantesh Media Services, Gaza)
- *To have more stability and also because it's better seen by the client to have a company, it's always better than as a freelancer.* (Gladiators Agency, Tunisia)
- *I have done this because when I used to work with some of the NGOs or UN Agencies as an individual, most of the time I didn't get my payment, so I decided to have my own organisation.* (Kanga Africa Media Production, South Sudan)
- *Because I was getting clients who wanted to hire companies.* (CoverStoryNews, Uganda)

Findings: Helping People and Advocacy

A final group of answers to the above open question gave reasons related to "helping people" or advocacy. Here there is a suggestion of a higher calling to help either make their community better known or advance the cause of journalism or film-making. The final response is about more than advocacy, it is about activism:

- *To help the international crews in working at the places and with the people within our reach, for better coverage and access to the required location or group of people. We aim towards making the world a better place not only for us but also for the coming generations, through our efforts.* (Fixer in India)

- *We really wanted to help people making TV.* (Film Fixers, Balkans)
- *As a journalist I have always wanted to have my own company. As my expertise lies in journalism and communications, I decided to focus on that. I also saw how little coverage Estonia, Latvia and Lithuania got in international news. I thought it would be great to help international media organisations report more and better stories from my region – i.e., put my country on the map.* (Fixers.press, Baltics)
- *To be able to help my customers and refer them to people I trust if I am not available to work with them.* (Honeybee Tours, Jordan)
- *I started because I escaped from ISIS and I left my area. I want to work against ISIS. I find working as a fixer is against them.* (The Fixer)

Findings: Chosen Platforms and News Versus Film-making

In terms of how they advertised their organisations, all of the people surveyed said they used a mixture of their "own websites" and "social media." Some went on to mention specific sites or methods: word of mouth/reputation (8); Facebook sites (12); Linkedin (5); Instagram (1); Twitter (1); Lightstalkers (1), and WorldFixers (2). Respondents were asked to classify the percentage of work they undertook that could be defined as *news fixing,* as opposed to fixing for film-making or other businesses. Most of the organisations said they undertook a combination of news fixing *plus* other roles. For a few, news comprised only a small amount of work, versus work carried out for film companies – for example, *Highlight Films* in Israel reported only 10% of its work was in the news field. Whereas, for *Tantesh Media Services* in Gaza, 85% of the work was in the area of news. Similarly, *The Fixer* did 90% of its work in news and Coverstorynews in Uganda did 100% of its work in news. Most were positioned in the mid-range (40–60%), with four companies reporting a straight 50–50% split between news and film production.

In answer to the open question, what else does your organisation do? The data showed that the majority of the companies, in addition to editorial news fixing, offered a range of camera work, driving, translation, hotel booking and security. In Gaza they even proffered "high speed internet upload." The *Mesopotamia Agency* in Iraq reported:

> We are a team consisting of two journalists who are doing most of the journalism-related work while the others are taking care of the logistics. This mainly includes just five people but this would go as high as 9 or 11 or perhaps more, depending on the size and the budget of the project. The additional number would include a camera operator, photographer, drivers, guards, sound engineers and translators.

In companies that also worked for film production, they could supply various extra services, from location scouting and crew sourcing, to filming permits, post-production and viewing. The most comprehensive list came from *BangladeshFixer*:

> Most of the times I have to team up my team with professional film and media crews like local directors, DOPS, camera operators, a production manager and AP, gaffer, sound recordist, drone operator, spark, grip, hair and makeup artist, art director, script supervisor, production coordinator, location manager, competent AD, runner, driver, local medics and catering team, rigger, AC/focus puller, security, Steadicam operator, electrician, translators and data

wranglers and just about any other crew position that my clients might require at the most competitive rates. [...] I, along with my production team, provide logistical support, facilitate permits, arrange entry through customs and immigration, location management, talent acquisition, crew sourcing, offshore filming, equipment supply, line producing, accommodation and transport arrangements.

In response to the question asking if fixers inside their organisations had *other* jobs, four answered no. The rest indicated a variety of roles, but with most being media-related. These answers again spoke to needing to maintain a portfolio career or "patchwork-career" (Michel 2000), when working on the boundaries of the precariat. Here are some typical responses:

- *Journalists, drivers, guards, translators, actors.* (Film Fixers, Balkans)
- *Yes. Related to the media.* (Dangerous Works, Turkey)
- *Yes, they have a local job. Most of them work in local media houses and they have the experience of "if anything happens" then they know how to deal with it.* (Kanga Africa Media Production, South Sudan)
- *Yes. Running their own business. Covering parties, wedding parties and selling news to local TV and radio.* (Coverstorynews, Uganda)
- *Yes. One has a camera shop, one is a journalist and one is a retired English teacher.* (Honeybee Tours, Jordan)
- *They work as teachers, taxi drivers, general workers.* (Tantesh Media Services, Gaza)
- *We do employ local fixers and they are mostly working in the media or journalism related organisations. (Vista, Pakistan)*
- *Usually they are working as stringers for another media organisation.* (Mesopotamia Agency, Iraq)
- *Most of the crew I work with, work as freelancers on a regular basis.* (Zeghy, Brazil)
- *Generally, yes. They work in journalism, research and media fields.* (Fixers.Press, Baltics)
- *Most of them work in the TV/cinema production field.* (Gladiators Agency, Tunisia)
- *They are either students or translators or English teachers who always wait for an opportunity to work for foreign journalists.* (Ahmed Ellali, Tunisia)

Findings: Improvements in Finances and Safety?

The final questions were related to whether or not creating and running their own organisations led to better conditions in terms of money and safety. These were posed as separate questions, but were often returned in a single, merged fashion, and so all are reported in this way in the findings below. This may have been a fault of the grouping of questions in the questionnaire, as this was done consistently by respondents. This was frustrating as both questions were important in their own right. Seven respondents were clear that financial and safety conditions had both improved:

- *Much better on both fronts.* (The Crew, Rajasthan)
- *We increased the daily rate and always provide 100% safety conditions.* (Film Fixers Balkans)
- *The money has improved in a good way and safety conditions are not affected.* (Dangerous Works, Turkey)

- *Yes, in terms of money, but only in terms of seniority and experience. Yes, we have strict security protocols and are often using professional security agents who are part of the crew.* (Highlight Films, Israel)
- *Money: We are getting more referrals for work. Safety: One translator is female and she feels very safe working with my customers because she trusts me that I will not put her in harm's way.* (Honeybee Tours, Jordan)
- *Fixers are usually offered several times (up to 5 times) the average local wages offered by private businesses in the territory. In terms of safety, we provide fixers and drivers with press jackets with clear markers to make them clearly visible, especially in time of wars and clashes. Flak jackets and helmets are not allowed into Gaza, so we cannot provide them unfortunately* (Tantesh Media Services, Gaza).
- *Money has changed quite significantly in recent years.* […] *I would always prefer to play the game safely rather than be in trouble working on any risky assignments although the payment can be irresistible. So, in my work ethics, safety is the most important priority.* (BangladeshFixer, Bangladesh)

Other respondents gave more nuanced answers, reflecting that setting up businesses was a work in progress and that financially, times were still difficult. They stressed that they were concentrating on making sure things were done correctly, rather than being able, necessarily, to improve wages for all within a short time-span. Some answers only explained how things were done now, rather than making a comparison with how they were done before.

- *The money varies with who is employing us. International media groups and news organisations pay better than [film] production houses. Safety has not improved as there are no credible safety trainers in Pakistan.* (Vista, Pakistan)
- *In terms of money, I don't see much improvement after the World Cup and Olympic Games boom in Brazil. The competition is tough. In terms of safety, we are working always under a strict attention to safety, sometimes against the clients' will. As you know, Brazil's film subjects are often the Indian tribes, favelas and crime.* (Zeghy, Brazil)
- *We are working case by case, and it depends on the size of the project.* […] *The fees are usually decided on the nature of the mission, the number of the work days and the experience and the relationship of the fixer. Experience is very essential in some places and it is more important than anything else in the war zones and this of course will be essential when it comes to money. It hasn't changed in terms of safety conditions.* (Mesopotamia Agency, Iraq)
- *We lost around 90% of our incomes because Tunisia is not in the focus of the newsrooms and because of security after the terrorist attacks. Documentary, entertainment, and movie producers were afraid to come and film in Tunisia. After seven years of revolution the conditions are better [regarding safety] because the security forces are used to working with foreign crews and they understand better what they are looking for.* (Gladiators Agency, Tunisia)
- *I just link between them and the client, later they will be paid directly from the client. I don't make a profit margin. Since we are all freelancers, the client pledges to take all security measures.* (Ahmed Ellali, Tunisia)
- *We work on fixed-fees and don't take up assignments that are underpaid. As fixers, we still want to take similar risks as we took ten years ago.* (Fixer in India)

- *We work together based on a contract. We manage that as a team. As our work is based on a contract so regarding safety there is not much [difficult] conditions. We manage that as a team.* (*Mali Tama Expedition SARL*)
- *For many of our fixers it is the first time offering fixing services (we are a young company), so it is not possible to compare just yet. However, we can make sure that our fixers get paid fairly. Likewise, with safety. It is not possible to say just yet (we started our company in the summer of 2017), but part of our company's role is to take care of our fixers and make sure they have fair and safe working conditions.* (Fixers.press, Baltics)

Discussion and Conclusion

The role of fixers, local producers and fixer-journalists is in transition. Where Western reporters were once in total control of the hiring practices of fixers and held all the power and agency (Murrell 2011), Bourdieu's journalistic field (here related to foreign correspondence) has refracted to encompass challenges to the power dynamic from local journalists and media workers. A decade ago, contacts for fixers were held in isolation by foreign correspondents, media companies or NGOs. There were no common places where one could find or advertise for a fixer, and nowhere for fixers to advertise themselves as being available for work. Although staff journalists might add fixers' names to shared company databases (Murrell 2009), and pass on to colleagues some information about individual fixers, there was no way that fixers could tell if this information affected hiring practices. To cap it all, the contacts of highly skilled fixers were often a closely-held secret as competitive correspondents did not always want to share a valuable editorial and logistical resource. Fixers in this employment situation had next to no agency or autonomy. This began to change around six years ago when NGO workers set up a couple of closed (and later secret) groups on Facebook to help reporters and fixers to find each other (Murrell 2014). From then on, freelance reporters had access to contacts and networks that previously were only available to staff correspondents, and fixers were able to both respond to reporter requests and also to initiate their own employment by soliciting work via the sites. Later still, fixers began setting up their own Facebook sites, which were largely, but not always geo-specific. In this latest iteration of fixers asserting their own power and agency, some have been turning their personal cultural capital into organisations, companies and loose collectives, with a view to improving their bargaining positions. This is still not the main way that most fixers find work, but it is growing steadily. According to Klein and Plaut (2017), "word of mouth" (journalist-to-journalist) is still the way that most fixers access news work. However, this new research shows that these local entrepreneurs are putting their faith in the power of the internet – websites and platforms – to initiate hiring decisions.

The first finding from this research is that social media and digital communications have enabled some companies to cover several countries and large swathes of land, leading to economies of scale. However, localised conflicts also mean that other companies have to operate in single countries only (e.g., Israel, Gaza and Iraq). Another finding is that these companies usually employ just a handful of people, although this number can expand as necessary to suit the job (particularly in film). This elasticity in employment terms gives the companies a competitive edge. In answer to the open-ended question about why did these fixers start up their own organisations, the reasons most often cited were related to opportunity, money, agency and pragmatism. With regards to money, the answers pointed to fixers wanting to take control of the financial negotiations with clients on behalf of a group. A number of participants replied that news and film organisations preferred to work with and bill *organisations* rather than individuals. Many cited their accumulated years of experience in the job and said it therefore made sense to set up on their own. These responses related to agency, and leveraging one's skills to become self-governing. In taking back some power in negotiations, fixers are seeking a little more stability in their working lives than negotiating on an ad hoc basis allows. For some who work in conflict zones or countries in crisis, working with international organisations affords an opportunity to transcend local economic and/or political difficulties. These relate to constrained circumstances (Gaza), terrorism putting off tourists (Tunisia and Bangladesh) and economic downturns (in Brazil, Pakistan and Bangladesh).

The finding that these companies are branching out into working for the film industry, shows that fixers are increasing their opportunities to keep up a steadier flow of work. The data reveal that most fixers juggle work in other media-related fields, or as teachers or drivers. In keeping up a portfolio of jobs, they improve their options for financial gain. This patchwork career mixes part-time entrepreneurial roles with steady income jobs. In answer to questions concerning whether or not these new organisations had improved people's finances or made the work safer, fixers tended to be more expansive about the former than the latter, which is in line with the findings from Klein and Plaut regarding the overriding importance of financial gain in the fixing role (2017). On the financial side, seven thought things had clearly improved. The rest gave more nuanced answers which nonetheless revealed that they were working together as teams to continue to improve negotiations. Often the financial rewards depended on the hirer and the task involved, and several respondents said they always agreed on daily rates. A few noted that it also depended on the sector, and that news paid better than film production. Several were concerned with settling matters correctly with their employees, and paying experienced people more money, particularly if they had conflict experience. The theme of "agency in the field," a concept Bourdieu relates to power, emerged from the answers about why they set up the companies and whether or not things had improved financially. Overall, the answers gave a sense that company owners were consolidating their skills and experience and gradually taking more control over their working lives, but business was still hard going.

With regards to safety, it was acknowledged that this was often a common goal of the collective, based on a keen, localised understanding of the security situation. Some of these organisations work in very dangerous locations – Iraq, Northern Syria, South Sudan, Gaza and Mali, or, the job requires them to stray into some particularly dangerous localities like the favelas in Brazil. The Israeli company *Highlight Films* has its own security operatives, whereas in Pakistan, tellingly, "safety has not improved as there are no credible safety trainers in Pakistan." Gaza was another place where fixers were working to improve safety but ultimately this continued to be problematic as the authorities would not allow residents to own flak jackets or helmets. The majority said the safety conditions were the same or better than before. While some fixers earned more money for dangerous jobs, others chose to avoid these kinds of situations altogether, despite the increased financial incentives. Safety therefore, while looming less large as a preoccupation, was more under the companies' control.

These are early days for most fixer-entrepreneurs setting out to run their own businesses and these companies remain small in number. Sometimes these organisations may be little more than loose collectives of people who gather under the umbrella of a company for specific project work, when it is available. As scholarly work has recently demonstrated how vital and wide-ranging is the fixer's role, it is not surprising that it is now being co-opted by film and television production companies which have no news gathering mission. There is wider knowledge and more transparency about this role than there was a decade ago, and this is for the good. The neo-colonial approach of elite journalists hiring fixers in an ad hoc fashion as helpers, and not acknowledging the importance of their work, or doing little to keep them safe, is out of fashion with the times. Bad or abusive behaviour on both sides of this relationship can become public knowledge on social media, as can any lack of payment. Organisations such as *Hostwriter* or *Round Earth Media* envisage the local-international relationship as co-dependent and emphasise the benefits that can be accrued when both sides work together to tackle newsgathering situations. Social media have enabled disadvantaged voices to be heard, and unfair work situations to be aired in a way that never would have been possible earlier. The job of international newsgathering is also in the process of devolving more to the people on the ground. Today, rather than having the power remain the preserve of Western correspondents, power has to be more carefully and transparently negotiated. The power balance has shifted between the two players in the field of journalism, in keeping with these financially challenging times for Western media and also with changing views on equality and diversity. But media entrepreneurialism does not necessarily guarantee instant profits at this lower level of structural change. As Deuze and Witschge (2018, 177) point out, the journalistic field is "ambient" (Hermida 2010) and "liquid" (Deuze 2008). It is a "moving object and … a dynamic set of practices and expectations – a profession in a permanent process of becoming." This "permanent instability inside the news industry" is something with which fixers – like the rest of us – will have to grapple.

The companies surveyed:

Film Fixers, Balkans
The Crew, Rajasthan
Fixers.press, Baltics
Mesopotamia Agency, Iraq
Tantesh Media Services, Gaza
Honeybee Tours, Jordan
Ahmed Ellali, Tunisia
Gladiators Media Agency, Tunisia
Vista, Pakistan
Dangerous Works, Turkey
BangladeshFixer, Bangladesh
Highlight Films, Israel
The Fixer, Syria/Iraq
Zeghy, Brazil

Kanga Africa Media Production, South Sudan
Coverstorynews, Uganda
Mali Tama Expedition, SARL. Mali.
Fixer In India, India

Emailed Interviews for Context

Mike Garrod, Owner, *WorldFixer*. Emailed interview (27 April 2018).
Shayna Plaut, UBC scholar. Emailed interview (28 March 2018).
Justin Varilek, Owner, *HackPack*. Emailed interview (8 April 2018).

Notes

1. See list of companies at the end of the paper.
2. See list of interviewees at the end of the paper.

Acknowledgements

I would like to thank the two anonymous reviewers for their helpful comments.

Disclosure statement

No potential conflict of interest was reported by the author.

References

Benson, Rodney, and Erik Neveu. 2004. *Bourdieu and the Journalistic Field*. Cambridge: Polity Press.

Borpujari, Priyanka. 2016. "IFJ Blog: Who Fixes, Who Reports?" *International Federation of Journalists*. https://www.ifj.org/media-centre/news/detail/category/asia-pacific/article/ifj-blog-who-fixes-who-reports-2.html.

Bourdieu, Pierre. 1986. "The Forms of Capital." Chap. 9 In *Handbook of Theory and Research for the Sociology of Education*, edited by J. Richardson, 241–258. New York & London: Greenwood Press.

Deuze, Mark. 2008. "The Changing Context of News Work: Liquid Journalism for a Monitorial Citizenry." *International Journal of Communication* 2. https://ijoc.org/index.php/ijoc/article/view/290.

Deuze, Mark, and Tamara Witschge. 2018. "Beyond Journalism: Theorizing the Transformation of Journalism." *Journalism: Theory, Practice & Criticism* 19 (2): 165–181. doi:10.1177/1464884916688550.

Erickson, Emily, and John Maxwell Hamilton. 2006. "Foreign Reporting Enhanced by Parachute Journalism." *Newspaper Research Journal* 27 (1): 33–47. doi:10.1177/073953290602700104.

Frontline Freelance Register website: https://www.facebook.com/frontlinefreelanceregister/.

Hackpack website. https://hackpack.press/.

Hannerz, Ulf. 2004. *Foreign News: Exploring the World of Foreign Correspondents*. Chicago and London: The University of Chicago Press.

Hermida, Alfred. 2010. "Twittering the News: The Emergence of Ambient Journalism." *Journalism Practice* 4 (3): 421–436.

Hostwriter website. https://hostwriter.org/.

Klein, Peter, and Shayna Plaut. 2017. "Fixing the Journalist-Fixer Relationship." *Nieman Reports*. http://niemanreports.org/articles/fixing-the-journalist-fixer-relationship/.

Michel, Lutz. 2000. *Qualifikationsanforderungen in der Professionellen Multimedia–Produktion*. Cologne: AIM.
Murrell, Colleen. 2009. "Fixers and Foreign Correspondents: News Production and Autonomy." *Australian Journalism Review* 31 (1): 5–17. ISSN: 08102686
Murrell, Colleen. 2010. "Baghdad Bureaux: An Exploration of the Inter-Connected World of Fixers and Correspondents at the BBC and CNN." *Media, War and Conflict* 3 (2): 125–137.
Murrell, Colleen. 2011. "Correspondents and Fixers: An Investigation of Teamwork in International Television News Gathering." PhD thesis, University of Melbourne.
Murrell, Colleen. 2013. "International Fixers: Cultural Interpreters or 'People Like us?'." *Ethical Space: The International Journal of Communication Ethics* 10 (2/3): 72–79.
Murrell, Colleen. 2014. "The Vulture Club: International Newsgathering via Facebook." *Australian Journalism Review* 36 (1): 15–27.
Murrell, Colleen. 2015. *Foreign Correspondents and International Newsgathering: The Role of Fixers*. New York: Routledge Research in Journalism series.
NeedaFixer website. https://www.needafixer.com/.
Palmer, Lindsay. 2018. "'Being the Bridge': News Fixers' Perspectives on Cultural Difference in Reporting the 'War on Terror'." *Journalism* 19 (3): 314–332. doi:10.1177/1464884916657515.
Palmer, Jerry, and Victoria Fontan. 2007. "Our Ears and Our Eyes': Journalists and Fixers in Iraq." *Journalism: Theory, Practice & Criticism* 8 (1): 5–24. doi:10.1177/1464884907072419.
Paterson, Chris, Kenneth Andresen, and Abit Hoxha. 2012. "The Manufacture of an International News Event: The Day Kosovo Was Born." *Journalism: Theory, Practice & Criticism* 13 (1): 103–120. doi:10.1177/1464884911400846.
Pedelty, Mark. 1995. *War Stories: The Culture of Foreign Correspondents*. New York: Routledge.
Skoti Collins Global Producers/Fixers closed website on Facebook. https://www.facebook.com/groups/1490677660985149/.
Strauss, Anselm and Juliet Corbin. 1998. *Basics of Qualitative Research: Techniques and Procedures for Developing Grounded Theory*. Thousand Oaks: Sage.
Tumber, Howard, and Frank Webster. 2006. *Journalists Under Fire: Information War and Journalistic Practices*. London: Sage.
Vero, Alex. 2017. "What Next for Brands, Agencies and Production Companies." *The Drum Network*. Accessed April 25 2018. http://www.thedrum.com/opinion/2017/01/30/what-next-brands-agencies-and-production-companies.
World Fixer website: https://worldfixer.com/.

"Fixing" the Journalist-Fixer Relationship: A Critical Look Towards Developing Best Practices in Global Reporting

Shayna Plaut and Peter Klein

ABSTRACT

Sociologists and media scholars have offered a robust body of literature regarding the daily workings of global journalism – both in newsrooms and with freelancers. Within this literature, which is both critical and reflexive, the role of *fixers* is acknowledged, but rarely questioned. Such work often fails to critically examine power dynamics inherent in the actual institutional and global arrangement. This project aims to fill this gap, focusing on the realities and constraints of editorial agency by fixers. Through a large-scale survey (450 responses from more than 70 countries) followed by 35 semi-structured interviews with journalists, fixers and people who identify as both, we map current trends and highlight nuanced dynamics and tensions within the practice. Specifically, we sought to understand what effect, if any, the fixer has in shaping the content of a story, highlighting the disjuncture between journalists and fixers in recognizing the potential editorial impacts. Lastly, the work examines the inequality between international journalists and their local *fixers* worldwide, and seeks to examine how the relationship is understood culturally within the rapidly changing field of global journalism. This article not only identifies problems within current practices, but also explores potential remedies.

While driving along a highway in Hyderabad, India, with Sanjay Jha, a longtime "fixer," Peter Klein, one of the authors of this piece, made reference to the term *fixer*. Jha, who has worked for CBS News, CNN and Now Public, took issue with his title, asking: "What exactly am I fixing? Your toilet? Am I a plumber?" Jha pointed out that for nearly two decades he has written and produced for the top news organizations in India. He prefers a more accurate description of his role: *journalist*. But he rarely receives the recognition and benefits that come with that title. Why?

The inherent power dynamic between the *correspondent* and the *fixer* is a topic of concern for many individual journalists and fixers, and yet the practice itself is rarely questioned (Klein and Plaut 2017). Although precise definitions differ – and unearthing the various definitions of "fixing" is a goal behind this research – fixers typically engage in activities such as: booking hotels and transportation, serving as translators, finding

Supplemental data for this article can be accessed at https://doi.org/10.1080/1461670X.2019.1638292.

interview subjects, securing access to government officials and scouting out dangerous locations (Erickson and Hamilton 2006; Murrell 2010; Mojica 2015; Vandevoordt 2015). Although Western news organizations rarely credit them, fixers are typically paid well, especially compared to local income standards (Murrell 2010; Paterson, Andersen, and Hoxha 2012). The financial benefits, as well as access to global audiences, are often the primary (although by no means only) motivations for people to work as fixers. Note that, following Ward (2010), we have chosen to use the term "global journalism" rather than "international reporting" as "international" will assume a stable center and periphery.

There is a consistent body of work that looks at the *ethics* of journalism as a field and the ethical dilemmas faced by journalists themselves. Such work offers a more critical understanding of positionality and a journalist's role in creating and (re)presenting a story (Bell 1997; Zelizer 2004; Alzner 2012; Carr 2013; Ward 2010, 2013) – but little research has specifically addressed the role of the *fixer* from a critical position of power. The use of fixers is considered standard practice, with the fixer often invisible and unidentified. When studies are done on fixers, typically it focuses on issues of safety of the fixers or how credit is allotted or denied in the final piece; rarely is there a focus on how the fixer-journalist dynamic may affect the production and *content* of the piece. One notable exception is the 2011 piece on the international coverage of the war in Kosovo, where Paterson, Andersen and Hoxha speak about the socio-economic realities of fixing, recalling how the local journalists at the Kosovo Institute of Journalism and Communication were recruited by international journalists.

The questions guiding our research are threefold and interrelated: What are the power dynamics between fixers and foreign correspondents? How does this manifest in terms of finances and safety for both parties, as well as in the content of the stories themselves? And, lastly, are these dynamics and issues being addressed and remedied? In order to provide a "map" of the current situation between fixers and foreign correspondents, as well as a more in-depth understanding of the dynamics, we utilized a mixed-methods approach. We got a sense of the big picture by employing a large-scale survey and then turned to self-selected in-depth interviews for nuance. We do not claim that either the survey or interviews are generalizable but rather, in keeping with a critical and constructivist approach, this mixed-methods approach provides a means of "gaining assurance" for a pattern that appears to be emerging (Stake 2006, 36).

Our project builds on Colleen Murrell's pivotal work on the role of fixers in global journalism, which was the "first to examine the ways in which the employment of local people can inject indigenous viewpoints into the story ... " (2015, 154). Her work detailed how "local fixers can change or subvert the ingredients of the newsgathering that become the finished story, as seen on our screens." However, she continues, "Correspondents mostly believe this happens rarely" (154).[1] Her project relied solely on interviews with journalists and executives and included only five fixers. In addition, her work was primarily focused on the news-making process and does not discuss the role of productive power (Barnett and Duvall 2005): the larger political implications of what this news *says* – and what this news *does* – in terms of domestic and international agenda setting. Our research expands on Murrell's work and seeks to address the gaps: we focused on *fixing* as a process, and we gathered information from both fixers and journalists (and those who identify as both). Our goal is not only understanding current problems, but also identifying what should change.

We chose to explore this topic partly because of our own experiences in the field. Both authors are from the global North, and have worked both as journalists and as fixers abroad. Both hold positions at academic institutions. Shayna Plaut is a critical and constructivist scholar, specializing in the intersections of human rights and journalism – especially media created by underrepresented communities. Peter Klein is a seasoned journalist who teaches global journalism and founded the Global Reporting Centre. Collectively they have worked in more than two dozen countries and in as many languages, and bring these experiences to this research.

Between Journalist and Fixer – Shifting Contexts; Shifting Roles

Although they are mostly invisible, fixing and fixers are essential to the creation of global journalism as we know it. Without fixers, the current practice of global journalism – where a journalist from one country, usually in the global North, can fly somewhere without literacy, let alone fluency, in the linguistic, cultural or social context(s) and report on a story for audiences worldwide who also lack the linguistic, cultural and social context(s) – could not function. But although journalists have always worked with local people in order to secure a story, because of changes in news business models as well as an increased concern regarding security, the fixer has taken on many of the duties and responsibilities of a journalist. The roles have become blurred and, as we demonstrate in our research, sometimes the same person will be a journalist one day and a fixer the next.

Much of the current literature highlights the US-led invasion of Iraq in 2003 and the subsequent ongoing civil war as a turning point regarding the increasingly pivotal role of fixers in identifying and constructing a global news, arguing that the turmoil brought severe risks to journalists, both international and domestic (Murrell 2010, 2015). CNN reporter Nic Robertson said the situation in Iraq was "unique" because he and his colleagues felt they'd become "the target." (Murrell 2015, 116) Although ITN's Alex Thomson disagrees: "I bet if you spoke to journalists in Russia, Mexico or Algeria [they would not be surprised at this level of targeting and violence, rather] I think we've just joined the world where journalists are under threat." That said, according to the Committee for the Protection of Journalists (CPJ), as of June 2019 at least 292 journalists and "media support workers" were murdered since the start of the Syrian war specifically because of their journalistic work. As CPJ notes, "Far more journalists, for example, were murdered in targeted killings in Iraq than died in combat-related circumstances." This caused a rethinking of how much risk news organizations and individual journalists were willing to take.

It is within this context that international journalists began relying on fixers not only to help facilitate the story, but also to actually unearth and report the story (Murrell 2010, 132–133; Paterson, Andersen, and Hoxha 2012, 111–113). According to former CNN executive Eason Jordan, starting in the mid-2000s in Iraq, "the distinction between journalist and media worker [was] blurred because Iraqi media workers [became]de-facto reporters, serving as the eyes and ears of foreign correspondents" (Murrell 2015, 116). Because of security concerns, many of the British, Australian and American media companies closed their already-shrinking bureaus in Iraq, and thus the use of freelancers and local journalists (often working as fixers) increased. According to CPJ, the 127 journalists who have died to date during the Syrian civil war, and the increasing death toll in Mexico of journalists covering narco-trafficking, has increased attention on the real, physical dangers of conducting journalism which challenges traditional reporting practices. We argue the change in reporting practices will inevitably shape what is reported as "the story."

It is easy to cast the fixer as either a victim of neo-colonial relations, stripped of agency by the foreign journalist, or as a manipulative, sneaky local who is trying to dupe the journalist into telling his or her story. Both versions play on colonial stereotypes where the foreign journalist (the West) still plays the primary role (Said, 1978, 1982). We argue, rather, that fixers – who are often journalists themselves – are intimately aware of what is needed to create, and sustain, global journalism (Skrubbeltrang 2015). Our findings show that the creation of a news story is a process shaped by the interactions of various actors. These actors include: the news bureau, the audiences back home, the journalist and the local sources. All of these actors have different motivations, as well as varying, but often uneven, levels of power. As Maggie O'Kane notes, "The traditional model of the foreign correspondent is a pretty colonial approach" (Murrell 2015, 144), but by no means are fixers simply victims, nor exploiters, in this process.

Both fixers and journalists are engaged in a process of *framing* the story, making myriad decisions and judgements that will determine what facts are presented and how the truth is defined. This can have severe political, policy and military implications (Strömbäck, Shehata, and Dimitrova 2005, 2008). According to media scholars such as Fairclough (1992, 1995) as well as scholars of international relations (Barnett and Duvall 2005; Carpenter 2007; Brysk 2013), the way an issue is framed both shapes, and is shaped by, existing power dynamics and interests that have tangible consequences. How an issue is framed determines how resources, such as time, money and attention, are allocated and, perhaps more importantly, what issues are *not* deemed worthy of said time, money and attention (Carpenter 2007).

Applying a Post-Colonial Lens

Our research is grounded in an understanding that power relations between people nations and institutions are neither inevitable nor static. As it currently stands, a foreign journalist often cannot work without a fixer, and the local fixer, by definition, cannot work as a fixer without being hired by a journalist.[2] The fixer and journalist are dependent on one another, but it is a relationship created, and generated, through the process of colonialism. We draw on Doty (1996) and Mamdani (2004, 2007) who, grounded in Edward Said's pivotal work (1978, 1981), remind us that the "Global North" and "Global South" (previously referred to as "the West" and "the East") were, and continue to be, *created* through media and policy discourse. There is an interdependent, but unequal (Memmi 1965), relationship between Western media outlets and local journalists/fixers. If we start with this premise, then how do these power dynamics manifest in terms of finances, content and safety, and how is this being addressed and/or remedied?

Our research indicates that although the journalist relies on the local knowledge and linguistic skills of the fixer, the journalist often fails to recognize the impact of this dependence when reporting. In the mind of the journalist, the *fixer* often ceases to be an individual and is seen simply as a tool for getting the *journalist's* story. In reality, by suggesting interview subjects or locations or providing local context, the fixer *is* framing the story for the journalist, though the journalist still maintains the illusion of individualism and power. The fixer recognizes and operates within uneven power dynamics, but is not without agency. Fixers are constantly engaged in framing the journalist's reality, and thus shaping the story, but they often do so in ways that are unseen by the journalist. The practice of fixing is a constant negotiation of power and trust.

The work of feminist and critical race scholars such as Mohanty (2003), Razack (1999), and Hill Collins (1986) can offer much to this conversation, recognizing not only the pivotal role that those who are marginalized play, but also the unique perspective and insight they often bring in understanding how larger systems of power and agency work within colonial and racialized dynamics. In discussing both black female domestic workers, as well as black female sociologists, Patricia Hill Collins (1986) coined the term "outsiders within" as people who, because of their unique perspective – being both inside and outside the centers of power (the home and academia) – can often have a clearer view of the machinations of power, particularly in terms of understanding the production of knowledge. As "outsiders within" the world of global journalism, fixers, and particularly those who identify as both journalists and fixers, have a particularly clear understanding of the *making* of traditional global journalism.

Methods of Inquiry

The limited research on fixers has been based on semi-structured interviews with some prior content analysis of the journalist's work; this may not work as well when evaluating an entire field. Using this approach, one can get a more complete and multifaceted understanding of the institutional practice of fixers within the changing field of journalism.

Although there have been changes over the past decade, journalism as a profession is still very grounded in a positivist ("God's eye") notion of objectivity (Hackett and Zhao 1998; Zelizer 2004; Plaut 2014, 2015). Post (anti) colonial approaches offer tools to better understand the *ongoing* process of maintaining global hierarchies within the practice, and production, of global journalism. In addition, feminist and post (anti) colonial methodological approaches emphasize the interweaving of theory, method and content. Thus, to best explore these questions, we chose to allow for inductive and deductive definitions of what it is to be a fixer, and the practice of fixing more broadly. Recognizing that categories are rarely stable, we encouraged people to self-identify as a fixer, journalist or both (which we refer to in this article as "journalist-fixer").

Our methodological approach enabled us to triangulate (Yin 2009; 2011) our data between what is evidenced statistically through our survey and nuances that came to light through interviewing. We recognize that triangulating does not provide "proof," but rather is a means of "gaining assurance" for an emerging pattern (Stake 2006, 36). Recognizing that the definitions and practices of journalism are in a period of rapid flux, we were happy to receive many responses from free-lancers, stringers and producers. That said, we maintained that financial compensation was a key part of the definition for both journalists and fixers, thus focusing on "fixing" as a recognized journalistic practice.

With few exceptions (mostly coming from Brazil or Scandinavia), nearly all of the existing research conducted on fixers and fixing is based on English language interviews. After conducting an extensive review of academic literature, trade publications, websites and journalistic forums available online in English and Spanish to survey the field and identify major trends, we developed a 20-question survey for fixers and journalists, respectively.[3] We allowed people to self-identify as *fixers* those who have been hired by journalists, as *journalists* as those who have hired fixers, or both fixer and journalist. This category (fixer-journalist) is a methodological contribution to the field. By providing people with the opportunity to self-identify without rigid, binary categories, we discovered a more nuanced picture of the dynamic journalist/fixer relationship. Nearly 20% of respondents self-identified as fixer-journalists. As can be seen later in the analysis, they hold a unique role in global journalism.

Our means of outreach was based on our strengths: a vast network of connections within the worlds (note plural) of journalism. We circulated our survey through existing journalistic, fixer and media forums including, but not limited to: Frontline Club, "I need a Fixer!" Vulture Club, Global Investigative Journalism Network, Committee to Protect Journalists and Open Society Foundation's Journalism Program. We shared the link through our personal and professional connections, utilized the Global Reporting Centre's social media contacts, as well as our personal online presence, and reached out to well-connected media professionals worldwide and in multiple languages. In this way, we utilized a broad approach to "snowball sampling" that enabled anyone with an email or social media presence, and connection to journalism, to participate in the research. We make no claims to generalizability and recognize that people who self-select to participate in the research may not represent the vast majority of those who could, potentially, participate. As critical theory reminds us, it is always important to see who is *not* present in the conversation. That said, a large-scale survey does provide us with the basis to start asking, exploring and perhaps answering some questions.

The anonymous survey included basic demographic information (age, gender, languages, journalistic medium, years of experience, salary), as well as questions specifically geared toward defining the roles of a fixer (logistics, interpretation, editorial).[4] We also had a series of questions focused on issues of security and trust. We engaged in what could be termed "cyber snowball sampling," distributing the survey for the month through English and Spanish language social media (Twitter and Facebook), journalistic forums and our own extensive professional and personal networks.[5] The survey was available for one month.

Those responding were a mix of ages from the mid-20s to later 60s working in a variety of journalistic mediums with many working in mixed media (television, print and online video). The vast majority of those who responded the survey (fixers, journalists and those who identify as both) had over 10 years of experience; many quite seasoned with over 25 years in the field.

Slightly more than 10% (48 people) of those who completed the survey registered on a separate page to be interviewed by either phone or Skype in English, Spanish or French. (As noted previously, the quantitative survey data remained anonymous). By the time we closed the survey, 450 people from 70 countries completed the survey, and 35 people from 20 countries were interviewed. All interviewees were asked at the end of the interview if they wanted to remain anonymous. The overwhelming majority (85%) wanted to be referenced by their real names (Figure 1).

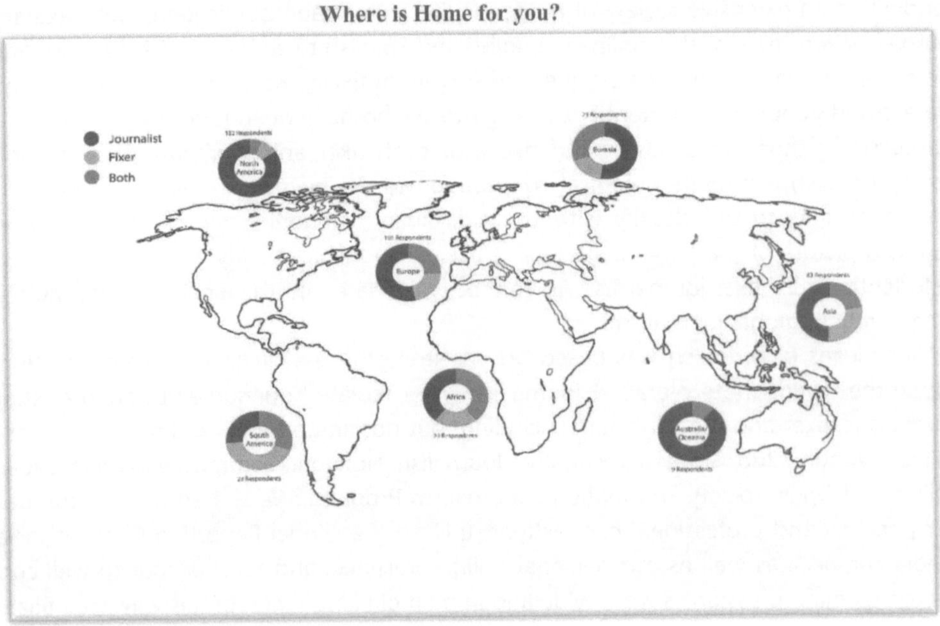

Figure 1. Geographic location of respondents, authors' data.

Limitations

While we publicized the survey worldwide, we had very few responses from Latin America and East Asia. Given that few people from these regions completed the survey, it also meant a few people from those regions were interviewed. The vast majority of the journalists were employed by US and Canadian media. Although we interviewed two fixers working in Latin America (both who had journalistic training), we did not interview any self-identified journalists from Latin America or East Asia. In addition, although we interviewed journalists and producers who had lived and worked in the Arab world, no fixers from there responded to our survey.

In addition, the findings and analysis of the journalists are primarily based on those working for English-language media – both public and private media outlets, as well as people who free-lance – in places as diverse as India, Kenya and Romania. Lastly, although there was a near-even split in terms of the gender of journalists (52% of respondents in the survey and interviewees were female), most of the fixers interviewed identified as male.

Findings and Analysis

Within the academic literature on global journalism, people are categorized as strictly journalists or fixers, but the reality is more fluid and nuanced. We took this into account when designing the survey, allowing people to self-identify as journalist, fixer or both – journalists who have hired fixers and have also been hired as fixers by other journalists. We refer to these people as "journalist-fixers." More than 20% of the people who answered the survey, and 30% of those interviewed, identified as journalist-fixers. This indicates the fixer-journalist dynamic is fuzzier than previously thought and is changing (as indicated by more shared bylines). The vocabulary used in newsrooms and project budgets has yet to catch up.

The Existence of the Journalist-Fixer

Returning to Hill Collins's (1986) concept of "outsiders within" one can understand that journalist-fixers have a clear perspective on the system and structures that make up the practice of global journalism, including the roles of fixers and journalists, and the dynamics between the two. Journalist-fixers make a clear distinction between the two roles. In fact, we found that journalist-fixers often adhered more strictly to traditional distinctions between "journalist" and "fixer" than those who identified solely as fixers. When they were working as a fixer, journalist-fixers repeatedly described their role as one that ensures that the *journalist* is able to craft the best story, noting in interviews that, "It is the journalist's story, it is not my story." They defined their work as a fixer as: suggesting and locating sources, securing interviews, taking care of travel and documents and arranging other logistics. "Roadie Ric," one of the rare fixers who works in the US (for a German media outlet), described his role as being the "guardrails to keep [journalists] on the road to where they want to go," but added, "It's up to them to decide which lane they want to go in."

Although all fixers and journalist-fixers recalled correcting a journalist for factual errors, they also clearly differentiated such corrections from attempting to shape a story. Journalist-fixers are often highly sought after by foreign journalists for their dual expertise in both the norms of journalism and the contexts and languages of their countries. "Good fixers are really producers, no? At least the best ones are," said Francis Hardin, a reporter with more than 30 years of experience, most recently with CNN.

Alexenia, a journalist-fixer from Bulgaria with more than 30 years of experience as a journalist and 10 years as a fixer, was adamant: "This is their [the foreign journalists'] project so I don't feel very comfortable to argue with them. If this was my project I would follow my agenda, but because it is not mine, I will completely agree with them." She also said that she would never tolerate a fixer correcting or outwardly influencing her stories when she is working as a journalist. In other words, journalist-fixers were more protective of the distinction between journalism and fixing in terms of editorial content, or what they often referred to as "control" of the story. Ana, a well-established fixer in Brazil who previously worked as a journalist in the US and the UK, explained her fixer role in clear terms: "I understand they have to do a story, they have a topic, an idea. And it is my role to get them what they need. It's not my story."

An unanticipated finding is that a significant portion (20%) of the journalist-fixers interviewed world-wide have in-country production companies and can thus offer multiple services (videography, editing, translation) in addition to fixing. The economics of this model help maintain an interdependent, although still unequal, relationship between local and foreign news production; media companies can get quality production done in-country at a much cheaper cost, and the fixers – who also work at or own the production companies – can get paid international rates for their work.

Security/Safety

As discussed above, journalists and media-workers are increasingly targeted in war zones, heavily criminalized areas and autocratic societies. This has led to an industry of "security training." Security training focuses on preparing people for recognizing and surviving in hostile-environments training and often includes life insurance and provisions for medivac and repatriation of remains if needed. Although available to journalists working for a major news bureau, such training and insurance is often an out-of-pocket expense for a free-lancer or fixer (Dart, Center 2015). Although traditionally, war-journalist are protected in principle, if not in law, by international norms, it is not the same with media workers (Kuwayame 2011; Myers 2011; Dart Centre 2015; OSCE 2016). But, as our research shows, the reality of who is a journalist and who is a media worker (including a fixer) is an increasingly "blurred distinction" (Murrell 2015, 116).

Security and safety of fixers have dominated the discussions in much of the literature and journalistic blogs. Interestingly, our findings indicate that security was *not* a major concern for fixers nor journalists in either our survey or interviews. In fact, in both the survey and interviews, journalists seemed most deferential to fixers' expertise when it involved issues of safety and security. All of the journalists and some of the fixers interviewed offered stories of either avoiding, or exiting, precarious situations thanks to fixer guidance. Many of the journalists credited fixers with knowing how to "read" situations noting that when a fixer said it was time to go – it was time to go. Journalists described fixers who were able to negotiate the physical safety for the team. Laurie Few, a seasoned investigative journalist and executive producer, reflected on a situation in Mexico a few years ago:

> I sent a crew down to Puerto Peñasco, and we were, loosely to state, chasing a bad guy. Because it would be a high-risk situation, I needed to know that the person that they were with not only would know the area, [but] would know when [something was off, and] would be alert. And sure enough, there was a situation where someone started tailing my team through that part of the town.
>
> They were taken into the cop shop. Now all of a sudden, my fixer is becoming my new negotiator ... So, in that case, I need somebody who can speak the language. I need somebody who can understand the situation. I need somebody who can, once my team is released from the police station, pardon my language, get them the hell out of there.

Journalists rely on fixers to recognize danger before it happens and to serve as navigators and interpreters if one does find themselves in a precarious situation. While much focus has been on the risks of journalists putting fixers in danger, it is often the fixer who keep journalists OUT of danger or, if they are in danger, they can mitigate the gravity of a risky situation.

According to the survey, 70.6% of journalists believe they "never" placed a fixer in immediate danger, whereas 56% of the fixers believed they were "never" placed in danger. For the vast majority of fixers (and fixer-journalists) security concerns (rather than content/editorial) were the only reason they chose to not take a story – and for this they were unapologetic.

Given this information, it is interesting to note that security and safety are still dominating the headlines within the industry in the limited, but growing, discussion of fixers. Perhaps this is due to the economics behind the "security training industry," or perhaps because a story of a kidnaped, injured or murdered media worker makes for good headlines. Either way, the issue of physical security is *not* the area that is of most concern to fixers themselves – and overwhelmingly the journalists defer to the fixer's judgment about issues of safety and security.

Credit

Most of the articles written about fixers have focused on the *journalist's* thoughts and opinions regarding the treatment of fixers. In both academic articles and more reflective trade pieces, According to survey respondents, 60% of journalist state that fixers "never" or "rarely" get credit. This is increasingly recognized by global reporters as problematic and there have been steps taken by certain journalists to try and change this. Perhaps most famously, *New York Times* journalist Sydney Schanberg, profiled in the movie *The Killing Fields,* repeatedly stated in interviews that, "My reporting could not have been done without [his reporting partner and fixer] Dith Pran." Lameck Baraza, a documentary photographer and journalist from Kenya who covers stories for European outlets and also works as a fixer for foreign journalists stated,

> Fixers are very important in the line of work that journalists do in general. I feel that fixers generally need to get some recognition, whether it's just a byline or just a form of recognition in journalists' work, because at the end of the day the journalist, even me personally, I could have not gotten a story if it wasn't [for] the fixer. Eventually, journalists do win big awards, but fixers they don't get too much recognition. I believe they should get recognition more than just being paid by journalists and then being forgotten.

Lameck's sentiment was not unusual, and it clearly points to the interdependent, but unequal, relationship between the fixer and the journalist. But our findings indicate that the issue of "credit" is more nuanced. There are times when fixers *do* want credit and times where they prefer to stay in the background. When the fixers were asked if they wanted to get credit for stories they worked on, 48% stated they would always like public credit, and 38% stated the wanted public credit "sometimes"; journalist-fixers had similar responses. As many of the fixers explained, after the journalist goes home, the fixer remains on the ground. Even when, credit is deserved, it might not be safe for a fixer to publicly accept credit. In other words, there is no uniform preference.

Money

Although the definitions of what a fixer does changes based on context and on the relationship with the journalist, "fixing" is a job, and those hired are paid for their work. That said, very few people rely on fixing as their primary occupation or source of income. According to the survey, 75% of fixers said they have another profession, stating that fixing is only a minor or moderate source of income. This not only shows that the fixer has multiple professional identities, and thus access to multiple worlds, but also that they are quite aware of the fluid, perhaps even fickle, financial nature of working within the foreign correspondent model of global journalism. In fact, when asked about times that their "trust has been violated," nearly all the examples in the survey and in the interviews focused on financial transactions. When we examined websites that bring together fixers and journalists; the most common discussion subjects initiated by fixers were the honesty, ease and reliability of getting paid by the journalist or bureau.

Once again, trust becomes the key ingredient in the "fixing" relationship, as fixers and journalist-fixers (73% and 90%, respectively) negotiate their rate directly with a journalist (or with a producer). Although we did not ask directly about payment in the follow-up interviews, without prompting, fixers would often reflect on times when they were shorted, and the lessons they learned in terms of business practices to avoid future shortfalls.

Word of Mouth

Although fixers sometimes advertise their services via Facebook, and many journalists are familiar with online groups such as "Vulture Club" and "World Fixer," most recruitment is done by word of mouth. In fact, 92% of survey respondents, and all but one of those interviewed, cited "word-of-mouth" as the primary means of hiring. As a producer and cameraman for CBC with more than 25 years of experience explained,

> Being in the business for a while, I have personal connections with lots of people at BBC or ITV/ITN and Al Jazeera. And usually I start with personal contacts and usually … it's such a small world that they have people who know people.

For those in the world of global journalism, word of mouth is simply the way the system works. More than 70% of journalists and fixers surveyed maintained contact with one another, keeping each other abreast of travel plans and availability. In addition, many fixers worked with the same journalists multiple times over a series of years and rely on these journalists to recommend other potential clients.

Being aware that one's livelihood, reputation and physical safety are intertwined has interesting implications. Given that journalists tend to check in with other journalists when searching for potential fixers, a question arises: who is left out or never considered? As one Canadian producer from Al Jazeera, based in the Middle East, explained, "because they [fixers] are recommended by people we trust, you kind of take it for granted that they're legit. You know?" But what are the consequences of this blanket trust? And what do fixers have to do – or not do – to remain "legit" in the eyes of a journalist? As previously illustrated, fixers often see their role as helping to find and create the story the reporter already has in mind.

Political/Personal Affiliation

In the survey, we asked fixers if they disclosed their political affiliation with the journalists with whom they were working. We also asked journalists if they inquired about such affiliation from fixers or potential fixers. More than one-third of the fixers stated they had no political affiliations and one-third of journalists reported they never ask. About 50% of the journalist's report asking sometimes or always, but only 6.6% of fixers disclose their political affiliation "often" or "always."

This is a startling difference and became a bit more nuanced in the interviews, where the question seemed to take many journalists by surprise – some stating they had never thought to ask, but that it was probably a good idea to do so. We also broadened the discussion to include "political leaning," since "political affiliation" might only be interpreted as party membership by some. About one-fourth actively recognized that the political or ethnic affiliation of a fixer could affect a story, so they said they took some precautions. In one case, Anca, a journalist from Romania, was interviewing ethnic Hungarians in a mixed city. Her fixer and translator was a local ethnic Romanian who spoke Hungarian. It quickly became obvious to Anca that her fixer's ethnic and political affiliation was influencing his translation and interpretation:

> I could tell from his way of reporting ... of telling me things, that he was translating everything through this thick glass, [like he was] still feeling, like, under siege ... He had the mentality of a person who'd been under siege from the ethnic Hungarians ... Because of what happened in [this particular town] in the past, like, 50 years before, his account was, let's say, tainted ... From my perspective, his view was skewed. Nevertheless, because I was aware of his position, I was able to not let that seep into my reporting, and in my final edit ... I just used the data and made sure that whatever he provided me was balanced with information that I could get telling the other point of view.

Only two fixers directly addressed how their ethnic or tribal identity may influence access to a story. Khalid Waseem discussed how his father being Pashto enabled him to understand the language and to gain access to tribal areas in Pakistan that might otherwise be off limits. Lameck Baraza, a journalist-fixer from Kenya who is Christian, discussed how he could not access certain areas (such as a mosque) when working as a journalist. But when he worked as a fixer for foreign journalists he was more willing to push for entry.

Aside from Nejc, a fixer in Slovenia who had previously been involved in municipal politics, none of the fixers acknowledged working for the government. Some said they were open about their own thoughts on the politics of their country ("I let my opinions be known" or "I have my opinions and I have no filter"), but they often distinguished their personal opinions of the politics of the country from their work as fixers. Josh, a veteran TV producer based in New York, gave a typical response when asked if he ever inquiries about a fixer's personal or political affiliations: "I don't see how that's relevant." Very rarely were there any accusations of overt manipulation or malice; rather, the fixer was a tool – not a person – for the journalists' story.

Michael Armstrong, a Montreal-based reporter for Global TV's news program Global National, explained it well. When asked if his reporting was impacted by a fixer's political or ethnic identity, he responded, "I don't think so. I don't believe I would let that [kind of influence] happen." Then he paused and reflected a bit more:

> I think I'm perhaps sensitive to that. No, that's not correct. Not sensitive to their political leanings or affiliations affecting me. What I'm sensitive to is *anything* from them affecting me. So, I do my job. They have their job to do. So, I *have* to trust them.

It is important to understand that fixers also often held this view of their professional role. As can be seen with the example of Lameck, who gained access to a mosque for a journalist, fixers often prioritize a journalist's needs or story, but they remain keenly aware that their tribal, caste, ethnic or gender identities *could* influence the story. Even

Mandy Clark, a reporter based in the UK who was otherwise adamant that one should "never trust a reporter who takes editorial guidance from a fixer," shared a telling example of a time when she was reporting in Afghanistan. She noticed that people, mostly women, were not answering her questions directly. Her fixer, who was also her translator, explained that his gender – as a man – might be affecting the reporting, and thus shaping the story.

Editorial Agency

One of the key findings is the difference in how much influence journalists think fixers have on framing the story versus how much influence fixers believe they have in shaping the story. In both the survey and interviews we referred to this as "editorial guidance," and it was clear that fixers, including journalist-fixers, believe they have much more influence over the editorial content of a journalistic piece than is recognized by journalists.

The survey identified a significant disconnect: Whereas 78%of fixers reported questioning/challenging the editorial focus of a piece, only 44% of journalists reported being questioned/challenged by fixers. Half the journalists said they were corrected by a fixer, whereas 80% of fixers reported having corrected a fixer. In the survey, 38% of journalists said they *never* rely on fixers for editorial guidance, whereas 15% of fixers say journalists *always* rely on them for editorial guidance. Journalists and fixers are literally experiencing the realities of "fixing" differently.

Within the interviews, many journalists bristled at these questions. Mandy Clark, who has worked as a journalist in Britain for over 17 years, stating flatly, "Certainly I would never take editorial guidance from a fixer! That would compromise my journalism." Others were more nuanced, distinguishing between fixers who provided local context and perspective, which was welcomed, from those who provide editorial guidance. Many found the idea of editorial guidance or being "corrected" by a fixer in terms of content as crossing over into the professional role of a journalist, and thus inappropriate for a fixer.

This begs the question as to whether fixers really "never" directly shape the telling of a story, as asserted by Clark, or whether journalists fail, or choose to overlook, a fixer's impact on the editorial content of a piece. As Armstrong explains, to acknowledge a fixer's influence could compromise the self-identity of the journalist. Interestingly, most people who identified *only* as fixers (rather than journalist-fixers) acknowledged that they *do* influence the editorial content, particularly in terms of who they recommended for interviews/sources. This can be seen in the examples offered by Khalid and Nejc in the previous sections, as well as the example provided by Haroon (a fixer from Afghanistan) below. These fixers take pride in their depth and breadth of contacts, noting that pairing up such connections to the needs of the story is what makes them "a good fixer." Thus, the fact that they can sift through their contacts and offer a selection of sources inherently influences editorial content. According to the fixers, this is not manipulative, but rather a part of their work. This is a very different interpretation from that of the journalist who often fails to recognize, or at least acknowledge, the fixer's editorial agency. In other words, although both journalists and fixers acknowledged unequal power differentiation, journalists identified it in terms of safety and bylines, whereas fixers identified it significantly in terms of lack of professional respect and recognition of their expertise.

Fixers saw their duties and responsibilities as fairly consistent: interpretation, suggesting and locating sources, logistics and sometimes tasks that are specific to a region, such as security, currency exchange or access. According to the fixers, the space for editorial agency could not be generalized; rather, it was relationship-dependent. As fixers became more familiar with individual journalists, they felt more comfortable directly offering opinions and suggesting content, as well as recommending story ideas. For example, Haroon, a fixer from Afghanistan (now living in Washington, DC) discussed how he was able to help shape a journalist's book on "the new generation" in post-Taliban Afghanistan. He was concerned that this was too broad of a topic: "It's really hard to define each individual, because the new generation covers a big number of the people." Instead, he suggested a way to focus the subject,

> Let's pick a couple of them that I know who works for the international organizations, who are educated recently, they are the new generation ... and invite them together to my house ... in order to get a better sense of the general feeling.

When asked if he felt like this influenced the outcome of the story (in this case a book), Haroon did not hesitate, "Yes. In terms of logistics and content. And it was a more interesting and accurate story because they could also talk to each other." But he was quick to add that he could only suggest this diversion from the standard protocol because of the level of trust he had with this particular journalist.

Fixing, and the level of agency that a fixer possesses, is not static. It is highly context-specific, depending on the familiarity of the journalist with the language, background, contacts and political volatility of a given region. In addition, and just as importantly, the fixers and journalists develop their own dynamic and level of trust, which shapes the parameters of what is acceptable, and possible, within each working relationship.

It became clear through the interviews that fixers are quite attuned to how the stories they are helping to create are going to be consumed by an international public. There is a concern for accuracy and a fear of generalization, over-simplicity and sensationalism. At the same time, they are aware that their editorial influence must not be seen as a threat to the journalist's role, but rather an asset to make the journalist's story better. To achieve that outcome, fixers pay careful attention to establishing credibility and trust with journalists.

By contrast, journalists seem to feel that a determination of trust is inevitable and can be established quickly. According to the journalists, the most important thing was that the fixer can help the journalist do a good job – and the level of the fixer's engagement (or editorial agency) was based on the *journalist's* familiarity with the language and/or region. In other words, journalists believe they set the parameters of trust and the degree of fixers' agency.

Fixers are keenly aware that journalist clients need to believe they have editorial control, or it compromises their professional identity as journalists. Asked if he had ever corrected a journalist who he believed was misrepresenting a story, Khalid, a fixer from Pakistan who previously ran a tourism company, was cautious:

> [M]y job is not to, you can say, give them a sense of direction on their agenda, but [rather] my job is to facilitate them and if they are putting stuff wrong I will warn them that they are deviating from the story, from the on-the-ground reality ... But it is their film, their project, their story. My job is to make them aware of the situation and then it is purely his call.

Ana, the fixer from Brazil who had previously worked as a journalist in the UK and the US, concurred: "I wouldn't say I have influenced the story, but I have given the journalist all the elements that he needs to put a good story, or at least, a fair story." Many fixers reflected on instances when journalists explained what they wanted for a story – and then the fixers offered a variety of sources *knowing* which option would be most attractive. Khalid illustrated his point, giving the example of a journalist from Channel NewsAsia – Singapore who wanted to run a story on human rights. Khalid provided a number of options for interviews, including the chairman of the Pakistan Human Rights Society and a female human rights activist who is also a constitutional lawyer. Although he wrote up background information on them all, he had a sense that the female activist who was also a constitutional lawyer would be the most attractive to the journalist. "I've got a fair idea about it, but I will not push my decision down their throat, I will give them an option," he said. And he was right – the story ran and was reportedly quite popular.

Although numerous fixers, as noted above, discussed how their role in suggesting and identifying sources shaped the ultimate story, *none* of the journalists brought this up as an example of editorial influence. Rather, Laurie Few, the veteran journalist whose crew had trouble in Mexico, summed it up: "As a journalist you should always be the one vetting … I make all decisions." Such was the consistent storyline by *all* journalists interviewed.

Implications and Conclusion

In sum, throughout the interviews it became clear that journalists often rely on fixers in multiple ways, but have a hard time letting go of the idea that it is *their* story. However, at the same time she was quick to point out that at the end of the day, she signs off on the story because it is still *her* story. This is the tension – the possession of "the story," and, by extension, "the truth," as if the truth is owned by a single person rather than a process that involves many people with different avenues and angles.

The use of fixers has been an unquestioned component of international reporting – but our research shows that both fixers and journalists find the current dynamic problematic. One of our primary contributions is to expose a dynamic that had previously been so normalized, it has been beyond question. Fixing – as a process within global journalism – is both a result and a continuation of unequal power between a journalist and fixer, and within the global media landscape as a whole. In other words, how a story is made frames the story itself, influencing political and policy decisions, which in turn influence the dominant narratives of truth. "The story" holds up existing structures, and dynamics, of power (Fairclough 1995).

And this is where the Indian "fixer" Sanjay Jha, who wants to be identified as a journalist not a repairman, throws up his hands in frustration. When asked if he is consulted or engaged for editorial guidance, he replied,

> No, that is the sad part. Some of them maybe they do because they ask me, 'Sanjay what do you think of the story? How else should we play it out?' But most of the time they have a preconceived idea about the story before coming to do the story and they just want me to facilitate them in terms of access, the contacts, that is all … Sometimes I have discussions, but I obviously don't challenge them as such because it's their perspective. I try and change that, but no. Sometimes I feel their perception of the subject is different than what is the

reality so I try and tell them. Obviously, I do not have a control of the content on editorial side, so they do what they feel good about it.

We hope this research opens up conversations around the newsroom – including with editors, payroll and audiences, as well as journalists and fixers – about that which had previously only been questioned on an individual level. In addition, we suggest putting together a handbook of best practices for fixers. The handbook could both codify practices and identify common concerns. This would enable fixers to gain more protection and offer more industry-specific guidance to journalists, thus providing leverage for editors and others in the newsroom.

Notes

1. Murrell concludes that "fixers provide a useful and exploitable division of labour that can be squeezed and then set aside," but she is hopeful that this is changing, at least for English-language bureaus.
2. It should be noted that although the majority of the time the journalist is from the global North and the fixer from the global South, there are some circumstances where local journalists hire fixers in countries with diverse languages and cultures, such as Nigeria, Kenya, India and Romania.
3. The surveys and interview guides are included in the appendices; in addition, the demographic breakdown of respondents can be found at https://globalreportingcentre.org/fixers/
4. Given that answers were being compiled, we had people choose from pre-formulated responses, but also provided spaces for people to offer long-form answers and examples.
5. We are grateful to Dr Rafeal Weiner for helping come up with this term.

Acknowledgements

This project would not have been possible without the research assistance of Peter Mothe and Olivier Musafiri and the technological and outreach skills of Ashley Nicholson and Britney Dennison. Graphic representation of data was created by Sharon Nadeem and can be found at https://globalreportingcentre.org/fixers/

Disclosure statement

No potential conflict of interest was reported by the authors.

Funding

Funding for this work was provided by the Canadian Media Research Consortium.

References

Alzner, B. 2012. We're Only Human: The Case for Altruism and Advocacy Journalism. [online]. The Canadian Journalism Project. Retrieved April 1, 2014 Accessed April 1, 2014. http://j-source.ca/article/we%E2%80%99re-only-human-case-altruism-and-advocacy-journalism.

Barnett, M., and R. Duvall. 2005. "Power in Global Governance." In *Power in Global Governance*, edited by M. Barnett and R. Duvall, 1–32. Cambridge: Cambridge University Press.

Bell, M. 1997. "TV News: How Far Should We Go?" *British Journalism Review* 8: 7–16.

Brysk, A. 2013. *Speaking Rights to Power: Constructing Political Will*. New York, NY: Oxford University Press.

Carpenter, R. C. 2007. "Setting the Advocacy Agenda: Issue Emergence and Non-Emergence in Transnational Advocacy Network." *International Studies Quarterly* 51 (1): 99–120.

Carr, D. 2013. Journalism, Even When It's Tilted. *The New York Times*. Accessed Apr. 1, 2014. http://www.nytimes.com/2013/07/01/business/media/journalism-is-still-at-work-even-when-its-practitioner-has-a-slant.html.

Dart Center. 2015. "University Based Organization Devoted to Educating and Advocating for Ethical and Thorough Trauma Reporting" [online]. Dart Center for Journalism and Trauma. Accessed Nov. 17, 2017. http://dartcenter.org/content/global-safety-principles-and-practices#.VfBU1WSrQy5.

Doty, R. L. 1996. *Imperial Encounters*. Minneapolis: University of Minnesota Press.

Erickson and Hamilton. 2006. "Foreign Reporting Enhanced By Parachute Journalism." *Newspaper Research Journal* 27 (1): 33–47.

Fairclough, N. 1992. *Discourse and Social Change*. Cambridge: Polity Press.

Fairclough, N. 1995. *Media Discourse*. London: Edward Arnold.

Hackett, R. A., and Y. Zhao. 1998. *Sustaining Democracy: Journalism and the Politics of Objectivity*. Toronto: Garamond Press.

Hill Collins, P. 1986/2008. "Learning From the Outsider Within: The Sociological Significance of Black Feminist Thought." In *Just Methods: An Interdisciplinary Feminist Reader*, edited by A. Jaggar, 308–320. Boulder, CO: Paradigm.

Klein, P., and S. Plaut. 2017. "Fixing" the Journalist-Fixer Relationship, *Neiman Reports*. http://niemanreports.org/articles/fixing-the-journalist-fixer-relationship/.

Kuwayame, T. 2011. "Which of Us Dies First?" [online] Gizmodo. http://gizmodo.com/5795745/which-of-us-dies-first.

Mamdani, M. 2004. *Good Muslim, Bad Muslim*. New York, NY: Three Leaves Press.

Mamdani, M. 2007. "On Blasphemy, Bigotry and the Politics of Culture Talk." Public Lecture: Istanbul, Turkey. http://lb.boell.org/sites/default/files/uploads/2007/05/mamdani-blasphemy_bigotry_culture_talk.pdf.

Memmi, A. 1965. *The Colonizer and the Colonized*. Boston, MA: Beacon Press.

Mohanty, C. T. 2003. *Feminism Without Borders: Decolonizing Theory, Practicing Solidarity*. Durham, NC: Duke University Press.

Mojica, J. 2015. Why News as You Know It Wouldn't Exist Without Fixers. *Vice News*, [online]. https://news.vice.com/article/why-local-freelancers-are-the-real-heroes-of-international-news.

Murrell, C. 2010. "Baghdad Bureau: An Exploration of the Interconnected World of Fixers and Correspondents at the BBC and CNN." *Media, War & Conflict* 3 (2): 125–137.

Murrell, C. 2015. *Foreign Correspondents and International Newsgathering*. New York, NY: Routledge.

Myers, S. 2011. What News Organizations Owe the Fixers They Rely On, Leave Behind in Foreign Countries. *Poynter*, [online]. http://www.poynter.org/2011/what-news-organizations-owe-the-fixers-they-rely-on-leave-behind-in-foreign-countries/132724/.

OSCE. 2016. Conflict sensitive journalism: best practices and recommendations. [online]. http://www.osce.org/ukraine/254526?download=true.

Paterson, C., K. Andersen, and A. Hoxha. 2012. "The Manufacture of an International News Event: The day Kosovo was Born." *Journalism* 13 (1): 103–120.

Plaut, S. 2014. "Fact Based Storytelling" or Fact Based Activism? Tensions, Strategies and Next Steps of Human Rights and Journalism." In *SAGE Handbook of Human Rights*, edited by A. Mihr and M. Gibney. Thousand Oaks, CA: Sage.

Plaut, S. 2015. "Reshaping the Borders of Journalism: Lessons Learned From Transnational Peoples' Journalism." *Journalism Practice*, 1–32. DOI:10.1080/17512786.2015.1092391.

Razack, S. 1999. *Looking White People in the Eye: Gender, Race and Culture in Courtrooms and Classrooms*. Toronto, ON: University of Toronto Press.

Said, E. 1978/1994. *Orientalism*. New York, NY: Vintage Press.

Said, E. 1981. *Covering Islam: How the Media and Experts Determine How We See The Rest of the World*. London: Vintage Books.

Skrubbeltrang, J. 2015. "Research: The Role of the Fixer in Foreign News," *European Journalism Observatory*. http://en.ejo.ch/research/research-role-fixer-foreign-news?utm_source=DMM%2002%2F27%2F2015&utm_campaign=DMM%209-5&utm_medium=email.

Stake, R. 2006. *Multiple Case Study Analysis*. New York, NY: Guilford Press.

Strömbäck, J. 2005. "In Search of a Standard: Four Models of Democracy and Their Normative Implications for Journalism." *Journalism Studies* 6 (3): 331–345.

Strömbäck, J., A. Shehata, and D. V. Dimitrova. 2008. "Framing the Mohammad Cartoons Issue: A Cross-Cultural Comparison of Swedish and U.S. Press." *Global Media and Communication* 4 (2): 117–138.

Vandevoordt, R. 2015. "Why Journalists Covered Syria the Way They Did: On the Role of Economic, Social and Cultural Capital." *Journalism* 18 (5): 609–625.

Ward, S. J. A. 2010. *Global Journalism Ethics*. Montreal: McGill-Queens.

Ward, S. J. A. 2013. *Global Journalism Ethics: Problems and Perspectives*. West Sussex: Blackwell.

Yin, R. K. 2009. *Case Study Research: Design and Methodology*. Thousand Oaks, CA: Sage.

Yin, R. K. 2011. *Qualitative Research Methods from Start to Finish*. Thousand Oaks, CA: Sage.

Zelizer, B. 2004. "When Facts, Truth and Reality Are God-Terms: On Journalism's Uneasy Place in Cultural Studies." *Communication and Critical/Cultural Studies* 1 (1): 100–119.

Beyond Puppet Journalism: The Bridging Work of Transnational Journalists in a Local Field

Ruth Moon

ABSTRACT

This article examines the position and relative power of local journalists who produce foreign correspondence in contemporary authoritarian states. The study uses field theory to examine the forms of capital and the field positions these journalists hold in a context where the local field imposes strong, unwritten boundaries around acceptable methods and forms of storytelling—leaving local journalists to practice what one correspondent called "puppet journalism." This study draws on data collected during seven months of fieldwork, including participant observation in several newsrooms and interviews conducted in and around Kigali, Rwanda. I find that local-foreign correspondents in Rwanda occupy a bridging position, drawing from local and transnational journalism fields to construct their understanding of the journalism game (in Bourdieu's terms, their habitus). These journalists incorporate values into their work routines and news coverage that align with the transnational field, while adapting these values to better coexist with the expectations of the local field. This analysis offers insight into the routines and capital of local-foreign correspondents in a development-oriented authoritarian country and, more broadly, unpacks the ways that a journalist might draw from multiple fields to construct a bridging habitus.

The role played by local-foreign journalists in global news production is the subject of increasing interest. Recent research examines the tenuous position occupied by local fixers, stringers, and journalists for Western news outlets, pointing out that reporters living in and reporting on their native countries for Western news outlets put their security, their homes, and their livelihoods on the line for the work they do (Palmer 2018). And yet, such employees constitute a growing percentage of foreign correspondents (Wu and Hamilton 2004). I draw on participant observation and interview data collected over seven months in Rwandan newsrooms to examine the relationship of local-foreign correspondents with the local journalism field, asking the following research question: What are the advantages and disadvantages facing local-foreign correspondents in an authoritarian context, and how do they intersect with the local field?

This study clarifies the way particular players in the field of journalism construct their *habitus*—their understanding of the journalistic game—and the forms of power, or capital, they acquire in the process. In a strong state like Rwanda, where local journalists are encouraged to produce news that supports official narratives and promotes government policy, foreign correspondence allows these actors to enter a transnational journalism field. Local-foreign correspondents occupy a bridging position, drawing from local and transnational fields to construct their unique understanding of the game they play. The habitus of these journalists includes rules about journalism practice and newsworthiness, drawn from the transnational field, combined with an understanding of what journalism is and how journalists should behave, drawn from the local field. In bridging these two fields, local-foreign correspondents acquire cultural capital from the transnational field while sacrificing social capital in the local field.

Capital, Doxa, Habitus, and the Journalism Field

Field theory posits that social agents, including journalists, can accrue different kinds of resources based on their positions in an occupational field (Bourdieu 2011). Economic, cultural, and social capital are particularly important to the journalism field. Economic capital refers to monetary income as well as other financial resources and assets, or the ability to translate one's abilities into income. Cultural capital includes the capacity to define and legitimize moral and artistic values, standards, and styles in a particular field, or to produce things meeting these standards. This can include the ability to define socialized habits, valued cultural objects such as paintings, and formal educational qualifications and training. It also includes an element of symbolic power—the ability to determine whether something is "real" journalism or not (Bourdieu 1989). Social capital refers to the resources that can be mobilized through one's social network (Anheier, Gerhards, and Romo 1995). In the journalism field, economic capital is measured by circulation, advertising revenues, or audience ratings (Benson and Neveu 2005). The level and kinds of capital an organization or person possesses relative to others in the field determine that agent's placement in the field and thus the kinds of forces that act upon that agent and the behaviors the agent can undertake (Benson and Neveu 2005). Individuals and organizations can be mapped relative to other organizations in the journalism field based on the levels of capital they possess (English 2016).

Journalists can gain and lose different kinds of capital through their affiliations with particular news organizations, as in the case of journalists who were constrained and empowered to cover Syrian political conflict in particular ways by their organizations' budgets and editorial identities (Vandevoordt 2017). Journalists can also build capital through their interactions with each other, for instance using Twitter discussions to increase social followings, drive web traffic, and build awareness of social media best practices (Barnard 2016). They analyze the capital of others, particularly sources, calling on various levels of cultural and social capital in choosing sources to interview and in written portrayals of those sources (Munnik 2017). They can also trade capital across fields, for instance using skills acquired through journalism careers to find higher levels of economic capital (that is, salaries) in other occupations (Davidson and Meyers 2016).

Journalists acquire and sacrifice capital within the context of a *doxa*: "a set of professional beliefs which tend to appear as evident, natural, and self-explaining norms of journalism practice" (Schultz 2007, 194). The journalistic doxa contains the set of professional beliefs shared within the field, defining what is and is not contained within its boundaries. The doxa is one factor shaping an individual journalist's *habitus*: the "feel for the game," which for a journalist includes a sense of what is or is not newsworthy (Bourdieu 1989; Willig 2013). The habitus is constructed from a variety of individual experiences and interaction with social structures, including his or her position within the journalistic field and interaction with particular levels of capital (Compton and Benedetti 2010). A journalist relies on his or her habitus to determine appropriate behavior within a given field, whose boundaries and unspoken rules are defined by its doxa.

Fields are typically considered and assessed within national boundaries, as occupational fields are shaped in part by political and economic context and other factors determined at a national level. A journalist's ability to acquire capital depends on the position of the journalism field relative to other fields of power, such that journalists within a field dependent on market forces have different capacities than those in fields more strongly shaped by other forces (Powers and Vera Zambrano 2016). With this in mind, local historical and sociopolitical dynamics inform the doxa of a field and the position of various actors within it (Benson and Neveu 2005). To understand the position of local-foreign correspondents in Rwanda, one must understand both the unusual field position of foreign correspondents with respect to local journalism practice and the Rwandan journalism field.

The Field-Bridging Work of Foreign Correspondents

Local journalists producing foreign correspondence perform a type of transnational journalism work. Transnational journalists bridge multiple sets of journalistic norms and gatekeeping processes; they are required to cooperate with the local field's standards for and expectations of journalists, while producing news content that satisfies the publication standards of a news organization in a different country (Hellmueller 2017). While transnational journalism work is done in many contexts by diverse individuals and organizations, the work of foreign correspondence has historically been conducted primarily by Western employees of Western organizations stationed in non-Western countries to provide news briefs and updates to their readers back home (Silberstein-Loeb 2014). To do this, wire services have historically relied on news produced in bureaus staffed with international correspondents foreign to the country they report on (Silberstein-Loeb 2014). However, foreign correspondence is conducted by an increasingly diverse range of actors, including locals writing for a variety of foreign audiences (Hamilton and Jenner 2004). By 2001, the balance of reporters working as foreign correspondents for U.S. outlets had shifted so that 69% were foreign nationals, though most still identified as white or European (Wu and Hamilton 2004). From the news organization's perspective, employing foreign nationals is a good business decision; Wu and Hamilton found that their average salaries were around half that of U.S. national foreign correspondents at the time. Foreign national employees also lower the cost of sense-making by cultivating networks of local sources, knowing local customs and politics, and explaining background to particular stories (Hamilton 2010).

While foreign correspondents are increasingly diverse, they share some common characteristics that set them apart from the local journalism field. A survey of foreign correspondents working for U.S. organizations found that all respondents, including foreign nationals and U.S. nationals, prioritized news values similarly (Wu and Hamilton 2004). A study of foreign correspondents in China found that they tend to perceive their roles in line with the roles journalists hold in the home countries of their employers, but the entire press corps prioritized "pursuing detached, independent journalism with an emphasis on objectivity and the audience" (Zeng 2017, 8). By contrast, local Chinese journalists tend to practice frequent self-censorship and produce media in line with state messaging (Stockmann and Gallagher 2011). These findings suggest that journalists working as foreign correspondents, whatever their nationality, are playing by different rules than their local counterparts and are heavily influenced by the norms of their employing organizations' countries. They can be thought of as belonging to two fields of journalism: they physically inhabit a journalism field in geographic space, while at the same time producing content that meets the expectations of a field located elsewhere.

Compared to news produced for local audiences, news produced for multinational audiences often relies on different frames and news values to make the content accessible and meaningful for audiences from different histories, cultures, and societies (Atad 2017). Western wire services, such as Reuters, Agence France-Presse, and the Associated Press, require their employees to produce content adhering to standards of news reporting and writing acceptable across a range of audiences in different Western countries. This means avoiding partiality, relying on demonstrably correct factual information, and producing a report that will be satisfactory to editors with a variety of political views, editorial values, and publication schedules (Fenby 1986). These news values can thus be considered part of the doxa of the transnational journalism field.

These requirements imply that journalists producing news for transnational organizations navigate multiple fields of practice in doing their jobs. Not only must they behave appropriately as defined by the local field of journalism, but they must also produce news with a focus and style appropriate to the country or countries of the media organization's home and audience, which are generally situated in the West.

Method

This study is informed by a desire to both observe journalists' actions and understand their motivations (Gans 1999). Data come from a seven-month ethnographic study of Rwandan newsrooms conducted in 2017. Field sites were selected using a network ethnography (Howard 2002). This methodological approach is especially suited to the study of African newsrooms, where virtual networks influence news decisions and journalism culture but physical locations are also important (Mabweazara and Mare 2017). The social network analysis was conducted using network data scraped from news organizations active on Twitter, a social media platform that is increasingly popular across sub-Saharan Africa as a way of sharing information (Portland 2016). Journalists use the tool to share breaking news and other information, live-blog, and cultivate sources (Hermida 2013). Key organizations identified from the Twitter analysis became the starting points for participant observation and interviews in Rwanda. The study also pairs participant observation with interviews to observe and understand journalists' behavior, drawing on the strength of ethnographic methods to highlight the dynamic and embedded nature of cultural production (Cottle 2007).

The field sites for this study included two local news organizations: the *New Times*, an influential English-language newspaper founded shortly after the end of the 1994 genocide and a central node in the social network of Rwandan journalism organizations, and

KT Press, a newer, influential web publication. This study also draws from firsthand observations and interviews conducted at several transnational media organizations with employees in Rwanda. In 2017, these organizations included Deutsche Welle, Agence France-Presse, Associated Press, Reuters, Bloomberg, Voice of America, and a regional news organization, the *East African*. The *East African*, a news organization based in Nairobi, Kenya, with an audience across Tanzania, Kenya, Uganda, and Rwanda, had a Kigali bureau employing multiple local staff; most of the other agencies in Kigali employed one local stringer, and some stringers worked for multiple outlets. This study refers to these journalists as local-foreign correspondents. To maintain confidentiality, organizations are identified only where relevant to an observation.

Interviews for this study were conducted in English,[1] recorded, and transcribed. In the field, I adopted the role of an observer and editor, spending an average of 15–20 hours per week in newsrooms (Lindlof and Taylor 2010). I observed editorial meetings and edited articles for English-language fluency and organization, accompanied reporters on field assignments to press conferences, and spent time with journalists in lunchrooms and on breaks. I jotted field notes in real time and supplemented them later each day with memos and observations; I then organized field notes and interview transcripts through an open coding process to better identify and understand relevant observations (Emerson, Fretz, and Shaw 2011).

Rwandan Journalism Context

Local Journalism Field and Doxa

The Rwandan journalism field rewards members who adhere to norms of non-critical news coverage, with specific values outlined in a national code of ethics available to journalists in the country (Rwandan Media Fraternity 2011). Journalists build social capital by following these expectations and, at elite media organizations, they accrue economic capital through a process dominated by advertising revenue.

The pressure to produce non-critical news coverage stems in part from the history of journalism in Rwanda. As in many African states, Rwanda's journalism field grew within a context of historical tension between democratic liberation movements and Marxist and Africanist one-party statism (Rønning and Kupe 2000). Through the 1970s, Rwanda, along with a dozen other countries in sub-Saharan Africa, had a legally enforced one-party political system that shaped the role and freedom of the local press (Jose 1975).

At the same time, the Rwandan journalism field became embroiled in the political and social forces spurring ethnic conflict. Tensions between Rwanda's two major ethnic groups —Hutu and Tutsi—dates back to the early twentieth century, when Belgian colonists assigned identity cards and corresponding roles of power to Rwandans based on physical features, cattle ownership, and linkages to the country's Tutsi monarchy, thereby unsettling the area's social equilibrium and political status quo (Barnett 2002). These divisions were further entrenched in 1959, when Hutu uprisings led thousands of Tutsi to flee to neighboring countries. Cycles of ethnic tension recurred in the decades after independence in 1962, with almost 500,000 Rwandans, the vast majority of them identifying as Tutsi, living as refugees in neighboring countries by the early 1990s (United Nations, n.d.). Ethnic violence climaxed in 1994, when president Juvénal Habyarimana's plane was shot down over Kigali on April 6, marking the beginning of the genocide. Over the following 100 days, an estimated 800,000 people, primarily of Tutsi ethnicity, were killed (Prunier 1997). The genocide ended in early July when the Rwandan Patriotic Front—comprised mainly of Tutsi refugees from neighboring Uganda—took command of the country. RPF leader Paul Kagame was elected president in 2000 and was reelected to a third term in 2017.

Media outlets reflected and enhanced ethnic division throughout the genocide and the period leading up to it. Political alignment and ethnic alignment were synonymous in the late twentieth century (Thompson 2007). Throughout the early 1990s, journalists—particularly those in radio—worked with the government to proliferate messages of division and violence between Hutu and Tutsi (Cruikshank 2016). Leading up to the genocide, government censors reviewed news content prior to publication, ensuring that it aligned with the official messaging of the anti-Tutsi governing regime (Barton 2001). Along with this broad messaging, popular media outlets, including *Radio-Television Libre des Milles Collines* and the newspaper *Kangura*, were instrumental in stirring up violence and paving the way for the genocide (Kellow and Steeves 1998). The domestic media's involvement in the genocide is memorialized locally: A portion of the Kigali Genocide Memorial depicts the role played by local media outlets and journalists in the genocide (author visit). According to this exhibit, more than 20 newspapers and journals spread hate messages against Tutsi in the run-up to the genocide. The exhibit depicts examples of racist cartoons and other forms of media coverage that deepened the perceived divide between Hutu and Tutsi.

Following the genocide, government and journalism leaders reshaped Rwanda's journalism field. Within the field, professional education, documents, and incentives encouraged journalists to produce independent and watchdog-oriented work. The main school of journalism in Rwanda, the School of Journalism and Communication at the National University of Rwanda, faced a shortage of local journalism instructors when it was formed after the genocide in 1996 (Skjerdal and Ngugi 2007). To address the shortage, the university partnered with Carleton University in Canada, which sent journalism faculty to instruct Rwandan students and facilitated an internship exchange program from 2006 to 2011 (CBC News 2011). Several reporters said these instructors emphasized the value of independent press to democratic governance. "One teacher taught us, 'be the voice of the voiceless,'" a journalist said, explaining that Carleton instructors had taught students that journalism's role is to "afflict the comfortable," investigating and speaking truth to power (personal communication, May 26, 2017).

In 2011, Rwandan journalists with support from USAID and the Rwanda Media Strengthening Project of the International Research and Exchanges Board (IREX) produced a nonbinding code of ethics to be "voluntarily embraced by Rwandan journalists and … widely used in newsrooms and classrooms as a guide for ethical behavior" (Rwandan Media Fraternity 2011, 2). That code of ethics, available to local journalists, is similar to the code of ethics published by the U.S. Society of Professional Journalists (Society of Professional Journalists 2014). It emphasizes the obligation of Rwandan journalists to "defend the universal human values of peace, tolerance, democracy, human rights, social progress, and national cohesion" (Rwandan Media Fraternity 2011, 3). It entreats journalists to pursue honesty and to present facts to the public, noting that journalists should not suppress "essential information," should only present information that is true and accurate, and should not stir up racial, tribal, ethnic, or religious hatred. The code of ethics also notes that journalists should be independent and "withstand ... external or internal pressure aiming at having them modify or distort information" (p. 9). In 2017, professional organizations within the field—notably Pax Press and the *Association Rwandaise des Journalistes* (ARJ)—had recently offered cash rewards to journalists producing investigative reporting for local news organizations.

However, external forces encourage a different style of journalism. While some provisions protect media—guaranteeing press freedom and freedom of speech, and mandating the availability of some information (Gonza 2012)—the current political system is designed to curtail the flow of information through legal sanctions and harassment. While it is beyond the scope of this article to define the current form of government in Rwanda, many scholars have compellingly argued that it is a development-oriented authoritarian state, and media policies align with this model (see e.g., Friedman 2012; Matfess 2015). Limits on media freedom have been adopted to sustain the power of the ruling elites and to prevent the return of hate media (Cruikshank 2017; Sobel and McIntyre 2018). Legal restrictions forbid divisionism—broadly defined as inciting conflict among Rwandans—and any messages perpetuating genocide ideology. There are strong penalties for breaking either law, and the ARJ had campaigned unsuccessfully before 2017 to have defamation decriminalized. In 2003, the government instituted licensing requirements for media organizations, updating requirements in 2009 (Rwandan Parliament 2009) and 2013 (Rwandan Parliament 2013). The constitution created an external regulatory body, today called the Media High Council, to oversee media freedom, responsibility, and professionalism. Since 2009, news organizations operating in Rwanda must register with the government (Puri 2014). Journalists register for press passes with the ARJ, which means the names and information of the country's practicing journalists are readily accessible. Taken together, these laws ensure that Rwandan government officials are familiar with local news organizations and journalists and that they have legal capacity to censure journalists producing unwanted messages. The independence of the judicial system, at least in its transitional form, is contested (Loyle 2018), and courts tend to side with government officials against journalists, according to many sources interviewed for this research. Journalists who committed minor infractions could be fined or have their licenses suspended, the ARJ director said in an interview.

Media organizations are also restricted and encouraged to self-censor by the economic context (Holliday 2017). Rwanda's journalism field, like many, is market-oriented, meaning news organizations depend on advertisements for funding. In Rwanda, this dependency is further complicated by the fact that the largest businesses and thus the most lucrative advertisers in the country are government organizations, or are private corporations substantially owned by the government. The private Rwandan holding company Tri-Star Investments/Crystal Ventures Ltd.—fully owned by the RPF—holds a majority share in 11 Rwandan companies, most of which lead their sectors with only international competition (Booth and Golooba-Mutebi 2012). Thus, when advertisers request or demand that news organizations cut critical stories or run positive coverage, the government often has a stake in the requests. "The advertisers are our biggest problem," an editor at *KT Press* said. "We always have to think very hard about how we will balance letting the journalists do their work and maintaining an income so they can be paid" (personal communication, March 20, 2017). Editors faced with demands from advertisers often cut articles or changed programing to accommodate advertisers' demands, according to a director of the ARJ. These editors fear that losing major chunks of advertising revenue will damage their ability to stay afloat as a business. Most attempts to control Rwandan journalism come from the financial sector. "It will not be somebody threatening to jail you or beat you or do whatever, but to cut the ads," this person said. "We understand. If you are running a business, you have to work; at the end of the month, you have to pay taxes, you have to pay dues" (personal communication, May 31, 2017). Senior editors across local media outlets named advertiser pressure as a major factor influencing news content. While editors would, occasionally, strategically resist, they learned to avoid particularly controversial forms of news that would invite conflict with advertisers.

As a result, the journalism field in Rwanda cultivates a doxa that promotes standardized coverage of positive or non-critical news and avoids rigorous debate (Gonza 2012). According to a chairman of the ARJ, critical content declined dramatically around the time of the 2010 presidential election, when many news outlets critical of the government were banned and news outlets forced into exile. Since then, he said, critical content had decreased so that, by 2017, most of the many news outlets in Rwanda "don't scrutinize real power" (personal communication, May 31, 2017). Citizens likewise avoid controversy: Public comment functions are increasingly available on news sites, but commentators avoid debating politics or pointing out problems that would incriminate superiors or government officials, even when journalists seek them out as sources (Nduhura and Prieler 2017).

Transnational Journalism Field and Doxa

Transnational news organizations in Rwanda, show evidence of similar news values and priorities as transnational organizations elsewhere (Atad 2017; Hellmueller 2017). They encourage detachment, objectivity, and independence, aligned with the news values and expectations of Western European and U.S. home countries. One way the organizations encourage this behavior is by offering encouragement and protection to reporters who follow these guidelines. One local-foreign correspondent had been harassed online after researching a story for a local radio station, where he had worked briefly while also freelancing for a wire service. He had been researching the members of a commission created to investigate allegedly genocide-denying broadcasts by the BBC Rwanda (for which the Rwandan government banned BBC broadcasts in Kinyarwanda). He wanted to find out what connections each commissioner had to verify government claims that the board was neutral and independent of the government. He produced and aired a broadcast story about the independence of the commission, and within days became the subject of a smear campaign by unnamed social media accounts that he attributes to the government. In detailed and lengthy statements, phantom Facebook and Twitter accounts called him a "genocide denier," an accusation that, if proven, carries a strong penalty in Rwanda. He told his employers about the campaign and his editor offered to step in and defend him, saying that the news organization had the power to ask the government to find out who was behind the harassment. Another employee of a transnational news organization had been arrested the previous year for a critical story but was detained for only a few hours because the organization immediately threatened to run a story about the arrest. These examples illustrate an aspect of the transnational field's doxa: Promoting independent journalism by supporting employees who produce it. By contrast, the first reporter had been suspended from a local news organization for producing a show that criticized government programs, and reporters in the local field shared stories of past arrests of journalists over news coverage with the narrative that such arrests had been deserved.

Analysis: The Habitus of Rwandan Local-Foreign Correspondents

The habitus of the local-foreign correspondent in Rwanda is constructed within the context of these two fields. As a result, it incorporates elements of each field, resulting in points of tension and limitation while also including behavior that is discouraged by the Rwandan doxa. This local-foreign correspondence habitus thus combines two perspectives: The transnational field encourages transnational journalists to practice independent, critical journalism. In contrast, the local field encourages Rwandan journalists to remain loyal to the state and to follow the local field's rules of engagement. The local-foreign correspondence habitus incorporates lessons and expectations from both fields, resulting in a set of rules that allows the reporter to bridge the two fields and accrue or lose capital in each while not belonging fully to either.

Transnational Field: Encouraging Independent, Critical Journalism

The transnational doxa encourages journalists to practice independent, critical journalism through widely shared news values of creativity and difference, contradicting the local field's values of standardization and uniformity in content creation. Local-foreign correspondents are motivated to incorporate these values through editorial encouragement and the high levels of cultural capital associated with those stories.

In contrast to the way journalists in the local field are encouraged to produce positive coverage without applying an editorial news filter, journalists at wire agencies and other transnational media organizations in Rwanda are rewarded for and trained in producing news reports that assess a variety of angles of a story and are independent from preferred government narratives, embodying a news value of *creativity*. These reporters were encouraged to pursue angles that were creative, investigative, and often critical of powerful government leaders. "You have [independence] to discover stories, to investigate stories," a local-foreign correspondent explained. "As long as you have your facts backed up on a computer somewhere or a recorder somewhere, the editor will run the story. There is no censorship" (personal communication, June 8, 2017). Even when covering events, wire reporters were encouraged to push beyond descriptions of what happened and to look for deeper newsworthy elements that could be emphasized in their writing. Another wire reporter explained that a journalist working for international organizations would be encouraged by his or her editors to "try to probe" beyond an official narrative for his or her reporting:

> If people are being evicted, the *New Times* is going to say, "people are being evicted for the good of all." ... They are not going to tell you that 20 people were evicted, but not given alternative housing. We are going to say that government is not compensating those guys. (personal communication, May 16, 2017)

This practice was encouraged in editorial meetings at the *East African*'s Kigali bureau. At one late June meeting, reporters gathered around a large conference table pitched stories to the bureau editor, who rebuffed and critiqued ideas, calling for more development so that stories would not make "organizations feel good," approving an ambitious story about a fire code development promoted by the Rwandan government that the editorial staff deemed unrealistic, and concluding the meeting with praise for one idea: "Good, something about this is a story the *New Times* won't publish." The reporter who pitched the final story suggested that he get additional quotes from public officials "to soften it," but the editor responded, "No, we don't need to soften it. A story is a story."

Transnational journalists are also motivated by the news value of *difference*, taking a different angle or sharing new information from stories that have already been published. This news value is evident in editorial communication and in the discourse of local-foreign journalists. A local-foreign correspondent described attending a press conference with other local reporters and checking the *New Times* website the next day to be sure that his story idea had not been scooped by the daily paper. "You look for the story the following day to see if they beat you to something, and there is nothing," he said. "They have given us this void, this vacuum in which we can operate. As long as a story is critical—or something they call negative here—we know we are going to break it" (personal communication, June 8, 2017). Thus, reporters at transnational organizations were encouraged to produce critical and investigative content, both by their editors and by the lack of local competition seeking to pursue those stories.

The foreign correspondence habitus encouraged these news values of difference by imbuing them with economic and cultural value. Some local-foreign correspondents were paid on retainer, meaning they received monthly salaries fairly equivalent to those of journalists at elite local organizations, but they are paid regardless of the number of stories written in a month. Unusually high production in a particular month (more than 20 stories, in one case) merits a bonus. Other transnational news organizations compensate their stringers on a per-story basis, with compensation rate tied to the length of the published article. Thus, while salaries are equivalent to those at elite, local organizations, the compensation practice differs. Journalists in the local field are paid a monthly salary only if they meet a story quota, often requiring 30 or more stories per month. By contrast, the foreign correspondent is rewarded for taking his or her time on stories, exploring creative possibilities, writing longer articles, and focusing only on news coverage that clearly merits international attention.

Local-foreign correspondents gained cultural capital by producing content with these news values of difference and creativity. One way this happened was when local organizations would report on the stories produced by transnational organizations. One local-foreign correspondent wrote a story on a human rights report issued by a European organization for his news agency. A Rwandan minister quoted in the story asked him not to run the story, but the article ran anyway. The next day, the journalist found an article in the *New Times* commenting on his story. Through this and similar occurrences, local-foreign correspondents felt that, even though they wrote to an international audience, their work had an effect on local discussions by introducing dynamics of independence with which local media could contend and interact. The news produced by local journalists for wire services would thus introduce new discussion topics to the local press, who could report on the news by reporting what their colleagues had published for transnational outlets. On another occasion, a local-foreign correspondent described how a colleague at the *New Times* had learned of a news story involving Twitter censorship during the election campaign. Unable to report the story for that outlet, the reporter had sent a news tip to a colleague working for a transnational organization, who then reported and broke the story in a form of news rescue (Vergobbi 1992).

The cultural status afforded this sort of news content is also evident in the reactions of powerful political actors to news produced by local-foreign correspondents. In the Twitter censorship example outlined above, government officials reversed the official policy within days of the story breaking in international news outlets. More generally, reporters often heard from local officials who were unhappy with how they had been represented to international audiences, or saw policies change as a result of their work. One local-foreign correspondent said:

> Rwanda … wants to be seen well internationally, so they will change if you write a story that is true. It may be fake change, like provisional change, maybe to show the international community, which is huge in this country, that something has changed—but it will be there. (personal communication, May 26, 2017)

This person and other reporters had been critiqued by local and national authorities for taking independent and sometimes critical angles on news stories. This criticism signaled the relative power the journalists were perceived to hold in the journalism field—power to impact public opinion with an important, transnational audience.

Local-foreign correspondents also measured their cultural capital in terms of the number of readers their online stories attracted. As one explained, "When you start getting out these critical stories, you go on Twitter and check the reach—it's in the thousands, and tens of thousands, if it's a critical story" (personal communication, June 8, 2017). Other journalists echoed this feeling of satisfaction from knowing they were producing news that would be read by a wide audience including Rwandans and international readers or listeners. They felt they gained name recognition and respect in their roles as journalists from audiences interested in reading an alternate perspective free from local economic pressure. The same person noted that he had heard from many readers who appreciated the perspective the paper offered. "I've listened to quite a number of people and they appreciate our role in Rwanda," he said. "Most people find us an alternative for information, to find their way to the right information" (personal communication, June 8, 2017). Local-foreign correspondents valued the ability to produce news that aligned with values they learned in journalism school and that would be widely read and respected with the potential to create change—in other words, accruing cultural capital.

Local Field: Encouraging Loyalty and Rule-Following

Rwandan local-foreign correspondents are also embedded in the local journalism doxa, which encourages behavior aligned with the values of *loyalty* and *rule-following*. The habitus of the local-foreign journalist incorporates these values, and this is evident especially in the ways journalists justify their practices and talk about their routines. Local-foreign journalists discuss their work for transnational organizations in terms of loyalty to Rwanda and Rwandan organizations. Journalists often faced criticism for being disloyal, but rather than dismissing loyalty as an invalid or unimportant value, they defended their decisions to work for transnational organizations as embodying loyalty, just in a different form from that of their local peers.

One local-foreign correspondent noted that reporters working for wire services were occasionally told by government officials that, by working for international employers, they were "betraying the country." Many reporters in Rwanda attend a multiweek education program, run by the RPF, where attendees learn about the history and culture of Rwanda. This reporter said officials at these events spread messages about how working for international outlets was unpatriotic because those outlets look for negative news. He countered that, in other countries, including France and the U.S., local and national outlets published critical news without being perceived as disloyal.

> They will be telling them, "No, don't work for those international media. Those are people who want negative things from us, nothing positive." That is total bullshit ... I cover some positive stories—economic growth, investment, investors coming around. (personal communication, May 26, 2017)

This journalist defended his position by arguing that he produced news about positive developments in Rwanda alongside news about events perceived as negative. Another foreign correspondent, who had previously worked for the *New Times*, also couched his decision to pursue foreign correspondence—and particularly creative, critical news angles—in terms of loyalty to the country. He traced his family history to the genocide, noting that he was grateful that the RPF had helped his family obtain food, shelter, and other necessities in the aftermath. However, even very good governments are not perfect, he said:

> There is nothing wrong in holding whoever is doing nothing accountable. I am very grateful for what this current government did for my family, for me, but I don't think I should be restrained to tell them look, this is not good. (personal communication, June 27, 2017)

These examples illustrate how the Rwandan local-foreign correspondent's habitus incorporates the local field's value of loyalty in explaining and justifying work in the transnational field.

The local journalism habitus also imposes negative sanctions on journalists who do not follow the local field's rules. To accommodate this constraint, local-foreign correspondents incorporate a habit of careful adherence to rules of journalistic ethics and news production into their newsgathering and production routines. They also self-censor, declaring some topics off-limits even for reporters who inhabit a transnational habitus.

Journalists who produce news content at odds with the local field's doxa encounter criticism from local authorities in the form of critical observation, sometimes followed by attempts to censor the journalist or disqualify his or her professionalism by scrutinizing reporting practices. One local-foreign correspondent explained, "If you are really a good journalist—not just a puppet journalist ... you will always be scared that you are being watched. You will face criticism any time" (personal communication, May 26, 2017). Another local-foreign correspondent, who had previously worked at the *East African* and the *New Times*, explained the process of this critical observation, telling how his reporting history had been scrutinized in light of one critical story he wrote for the *East African*. He had written an article about a press conference, and a minister said she had been misquoted in the article. The reporter later learned that the minister took the opportunity to call his entire work history into question, taking the confrontation directly to the Aga Khan family, which owns the publication. "Later I found out that they had lined up all my stories I worked on before," he said. "They were saying, 'You see, there is this history which means this person is doing it intentionally'" (personal communication, May 16, 2017). Because this reporter was working for an independent publication and had a reputation for producing news that broke the norms embedded in the local doxa, he found that political officials were quick to criticize his journalistic practices as unprofessional and call for him to be fired.

Because this sort of scrutiny is common, reporters working for wire agencies are cautious, not just in reporting but also in their daily lives. They were concerned that they would be harassed for a reporting mistake or, in extreme cases, that they would be followed and harassed in their personal lives. One wire reporter said he felt sure that government officials and others constantly scrutinized his work looking for errors, which he called "small problems."

> When you get a small problem, they can use that—they will not be punishing you for that small problem, but they will be punishing you because of what you do. You have to be very smart, in the sense that you try to do your work properly, not to give them the chance to get you. (personal communication, May 16, 2017)

Foreign correspondents know that their work flies in the face of local field expectations around news norms, and in many cases they have been criticized for "small problems" with their work. As a result, they are cautious in their reporting—"very smart" to be sure that it will not provide an opportunity for critics to complain. News reporters for local organizations, by contrast, did not tend to warrant strong criticism for such "small problems" as misspellings and factual errors. Several such errors came to light in editorial meetings at the *New Times* and *KT Press*. Occasionally, a reporter would be chastised by his or her editor, but the corrections were typically friendly and collegial in tone.

Local-foreign correspondents in Rwanda are scrutinized because their work is contrary to local norms, and because in working for international organizations, they are sometimes considered disloyal to Rwanda. The latter critique is also leveled against foreign correspondents who are not nationals of the countries they report in, suggesting that nationality does not protect foreign correspondents from official critique. In facing extra measures of criticism for their work and affiliations, Rwandan local-foreign correspondents lose the benefit of being "on the same side" as their local peers within or outside the journalism field. They instead face scrutiny for small decisions and for their employers—thus losing social capital compared to their peers in the local field.

Foreign correspondents also self-censored, noting some topics they would not cover, even with the protection afforded by the economics and status of the transnational field. Topics that local-foreign correspondents said they would not cover included the personal lives of President Paul Kagame, his wife Jeannette, or their four children; the Rwandan conglomerate Crystal Ventures Ltd., which is held by the RPF and holds investments in nearly every business venture in the country; and stories involving the Rwanda Defense Force. "Those are the kinds of stories that will get you whupped," a local-foreign correspondent said. "Even if a source came and told me that the president may be misusing this and this amount of money, I wouldn't write that story. I would be crazy to write it

... those are the kind of stories that I run away from" (personal communication, date withheld). The consequences for writing these stories would be beyond an organization's ability to control; foreign correspondents said that they could lose their jobs and would likely face strong public censure for writing on such topics. Thus, local-foreign correspondents incorporate the local doxa's values of rule-following and loyalty into their habitus by following careful protocol when producing critical news coverage and by avoiding coverage entirely on particularly high-profile, controversial topics.

Transnational employers accommodate their local employees' judgment about the level of danger associated with particular articles. One local-foreign correspondent said his regional editors were aware of the sensitive and sometimes risky nature of newsgathering in Rwanda and would check in before publishing stories to ask whether a particular story was too sensitive and would bring trouble. "They make sure that the stories are well-researched, especially in countries like this," one wire reporter said. "They understand the context here, the fragility ... Sometimes they even ask, 'this story, don't you think it will cause you problems?'" (personal communication, May 16, 2017). These examples illustrate how the local-foreign correspondent's habitus is removed from but shaped by the local field's values of loyalty and rule-following.

Conclusion

This article unpacks how doxa and rules from different fields of journalism intersect to form the habitus—the accumulation of experiences that construct the boundaries of appropriate social action—for the local-foreign correspondent. In Rwanda, this habitus is influenced by both the journalist's local journalism field, inhabited through training and geographic presence, and a transnational field, inhabited through organizational affiliation. This suggests that local-foreign journalists hold an unusual, field-bridging position. One consequence of this position is that they accumulate relatively high levels of cultural capital from the transnational field while sacrificing social capital in the local field.

There are, of course, limitations to this study. It analyzes the role of local-foreign correspondents in one country with a small journalism field. Rwanda's journalism field has unique characteristics, including the impact of the relatively recent genocide on field dynamics. However, Rwanda can also be seen as an important example that is not idiosyncratic but rather illustrative of governance and journalism practices in similarly authoritarian contexts around the world, including Turkey, Hong Kong, Singapore, Ethiopia, and Indonesia. Not only is Rwanda exemplary of many countries governed by a contemporary authoritarian regime, but it is a bellwether for governance across sub-Saharan Africa. Rwanda is a model of efficient development policy, exhibiting rapid growth over the past two decades in gross national income and per-capita income, declining poverty rates, and improved scores on a variety of development indices, including the United Nations' Human Development Index, World Banks Doing Business rankings, and Millennium Challenge Corporation's country scorecards (Molt 2017). The strength and durability of Rwanda's governance model shows that it is possible to cultivate economic development through foreign investment while also suppressing political dissent and preventing the development of strong civil society spaces (Matfess 2015).

This study shows how transnational news organizations may intersect with local news fields in contemporary authoritarian countries. Rwandan journalists are encouraged through primarily economic incentives to self-censor and promote positive coverage (Freedom House 2017; Rwandan Governance Board 2016). Nongovernmental organizations like Pax Press promote independent media and critical reporting, but these organizations are dependent on government funding (personal communications, June 5 and May 31, 2017). Thus, journalists in the local field have little encouragement or protection to pursue independent journalism. This form of media control has parallels in many authoritarian countries. The present study shows why journalists in these places might choose to work for transnational organizations and what they gain and lose in so doing.

In this context, the position of local-foreign correspondents—bridging two journalism fields and navigating expectations and pressure from each—comes into focus as one that is both precarious and powerful. Local-foreign correspondents face greater scrutiny for their work than do local journalists producing field-aligned and government-aligned news content, and their labor and safety are likely undervalued by the foreign press (Palmer 2018). However, they also have the power to pursue news values discouraged by the local doxa. In addition, they introduce stories exhibiting these values into the local news ecosystem, providing a greater spectrum of information to local audiences and allowing local journalists to engage critically with news stories that would otherwise fall outside the field's boundaries. This study highlights how the position of local-foreign correspondents can bridge two fields, incorporating values from both into a habitus where power is both gained and lost.

Note

1. The primary language in Rwanda is Kinyarwanda, but almost all journalists spoke English at the elite news organizations where this study's interviews and observations were conducted, and editorial meetings took place primarily in English.

Acknowledgments

I would like to thank Philip Howard and Matthew Powers for valuable insight on research related to this study, and David Peyton and the anonymous *Journalism Studies* reviewers for thoughtful comments on the manuscript.

Disclosure Statement

No potential conflict of interest was reported by the author.

Funding

This article is based on material from a PhD dissertation funded by a Boren Fellowship, the University of Washington's Harry Bridges Center for Labor Studies, and the Chester Fritz International Fellowship.

ORCID

Ruth Moon http://orcid.org/0000-0002-2170-7385

References

Anheier, Helmut K., Jurgen Gerhards, and Frank P. Romo. 1995. "Forms of Capital and Social Structure in Cultural Fields: Examining Bourdieu's Social Topography." *American Journal of Sociology* 100 (4): 859–903. doi:10.1086/230603.

Atad, Erga. 2017. "Global Newsworthiness and Reversed Domestication." *Journalism Practice* 11 (6): 760–776. doi:10.1080/17512786.2016.1194223.

Barnard, Stephen R. 2016. "'Tweet or Be Sacked': Twitter and the New Elements of Journalistic Practice." *Journalism* 17 (2): 190–207. doi:10.1177/1464884914553079.

Barnett, Michael. 2002. *Eyewitness to a Genocide: The United Nations and Rwanda*. Ithaca, NY: Cornell University Press.

Barton, Gina. 2001. "New Beginnings in Rwanda." *Quill* (October). eprint: https://quill.spjnetwork.org/2001/10/04/new-beginnings-in-rwanda/.

Benson, Rodney, and Erik Neveu. 2005. *Bourdieu and the Journalistic Field*. Malden: Polity Press.

Booth, David, and Frederick Golooba-Mutebi. 2012. "Developmental Patrimonialism? The Case of Rwanda." *African Affairs* 111 (444): 379–403. doi:10.1093/afraf/ads026.

Bourdieu, Pierre. 1989. "Social Space and Symbolic Power." *Sociological Theory* 7 (1): 14–25. doi:10.2307/202060.

Bourdieu, Pierre. 2011. "The Forms of Capital (1986)." In *Cultural Theory: An Anthology*, Vol. 1, 81–93. Malden, MA: John Wiley & Sons.

CBC News. 2011. "Rwanda-Carleton Journalism Exchange Suspended." *CBC News*, September. eprint: https://www.cbc.ca/news/canada/ottawa/rwanda-carleton-journalism-exchange-suspended-1.1000304.

Compton, J. R., and P. Benedetti. 2010. "Labour, New Media and the Institutional Restructuring of Journalism." *Journalism Studies* 11 (4): 487–499. doi:10.1080/14616701003638350.

Cottle, Simon. 2007. "Ethnography and News Production: New(s) Developments in the Field." *Sociology Compass* 1 (1): 1–16. doi:10.1111/j.1751-9020.2007.00002.x.

Cruikshank, Sally Ann. 2016. "The Urban–Rural Divide: Building the News Media Agenda in Post-Genocide Rwanda." *African Journalism Studies* 37 (2): 77–94. doi:10.1080/23743670.2016.1173573.

Cruikshank, Sally Ann. 2017. "A Developing Chasm: Oppressive Structures, Media, and Journalism in Post-Genocide Rwanda." *International Communication Research Journal* 52 (1): 31–56.

Davidson, Roei, and Oren Meyers. 2016. "'Should I Stay or Should I Go?' Exit, Voice and Loyalty among Journalists." *Journalism Studies* 17 (5): 590–607. doi:10.1080/1461670X.2014.988996.

Emerson, Robert M., Rachel I. Fretz, and Linda L. Shaw. 2011. *Writing Ethnographic Fieldnotes*. 2nd ed. Chicago, IL: University of Chicago Press.

English, Peter. 2016. "Mapping the Sports Journalism Field: Bourdieu and Broadsheet Newsrooms." *Journalism* 17 (8): 1001–1017. doi:10.1177/1464884915576728.

Fenby, Jonathan. 1986. *The International News Services*. New York: Schocken Books.

Freedom House. 2017. *Press Freedom's Dark Horizon: Freedom of the Press 2017*. Technical report. Washington, DC: Freedom House, April.

Friedman, A. 2012. "Kagame's Rwanda: Can an Authoritarian Development Model Be Squared with Democracy and Human Rights?." *Oregon Review of International Law* 14: 253.

Gans, Herbert. 1999. "Participant Observation in the Era of 'Ethnography.'" *Journal of Contemporary Ethnography* 28 (5): 540–548. doi:10.1177/089124199129023532.

Gonza, Munganwa. 2012. *Media Sustainability Index 2012: Rwanda*. Research Report. Washington, DC: IREX.

Hamilton, James T. 2010. "The (Many) Markets for International News: How News from Abroad Sells at Home." *Journalism Studies* 11 (5): 650–666. doi:10.1080/1461670X.2010.502789.

Hamilton, John Maxwell, and Eric Jenner. 2004. "Redefining Foreign Correspondence." *Journalism* 5 (3): 301–321. doi:10.1177/1464884904044938.

Hellmueller, Lea. 2017. "Gatekeeping Beyond Geographical Borders: Developing an Analytical Model of Transnational Journalism Cultures." *International Communication Gazette* 79 (1): 3–25. doi:10.1177/1748048516656304.

Hermida, Alfred. 2013. "#Journalism: Reconfiguring Journalism Research about Twitter, One Tweet at a Time." *Digital Journalism* 1 (3): 295–313. doi:10.1080/21670811.2013.808456.

Holliday, Graham. 2017. "Sound and Fury: Two Decades Ago Rwandan Radio Was Monopolised by Voices Promoting Genocide, but Radio Is Still Not Free from Controversy." *Index on Censorship* 46 (3): 51–53. doi:10.1177/0306422017730957.

Howard, Philip N. 2002. "Network Ethnography and the Hypermedia Organization: New Media, New Organizations, New Methods." *New Media & Society* 4 (4): 550–574. doi:10.1177/146144402321466813.

Jose, Alhaji Babatunde. 1975. "Press Freedom in Africa." *African Affairs* 74 (296): 255–262. eprint: http://www.jstor.org/stable/721933.

Kellow, Christine L., and H. Leslie Steeves. 1998. "The Role of Radio in the Rwandan Genocide." *Journal of Communication* 48 (3): 107–128. doi:10.1111/j.1460-2466.1998.tb02762.x.

Lindlof, Thomas R., and Bryan C. Taylor. 2010. *Qualitative Communication Research Methods*. 3rd ed. Thousand Oaks, CA: SAGE Publications.

Loyle, C. E. 2018. "Transitional Justice and Political Order in Rwanda." *Ethnic and Racial Studies* 41 (4): 663–680. doi:10.1080/01419870.2017.1366537.

Mabweazara, Hayes Mawindi, and Admire Mare. 2017. "Researching the Fluid and Multisited Appropriations of Digital Technologies in African Newsrooms." In *Digital Technology and Journalism*, edited by J. Tong and S. H. Lo, 317–345. London: Palgrave Macmillan.

Matfess, Hilary. 2015. "Rwanda and Ethiopia: Developmental Authoritarianism and the New Politics of African Strong Men." *African Studies Review* 58 (2): 181–204. doi:10.1017/asr.2015.43.

Molt, Peter. 2017. *Rwanda as a Model*. Report. Bonn, Germany: Konrad-Adenauer-Stiftung, October. eprint: http://www.kas.de/wf/en/33.50364/.

Munnik, Michael B. 2017. "A Field Theory Perspective on Journalist–Source Relations: A Study of 'New Entrants' and 'Authorised Knowers' among Scottish Muslims." *Sociology*. doi:10.1177/0038038517696220.

Nduhura, Dominique, and Michael Prieler. 2017. "Citizen Journalism and Democratisation of Mainstream Media in Rwanda." *African Journalism Studies* 38 (2): 178–197. doi:10.1080/23743670.2017.1332659.

Palmer, Lindsay. 2018. *Becoming the Story: War Correspondents since 9/11*. Urbana, IL: University of Illinois Press.

Portland. 2016. "How Africa Tweets 2016". Accessed eprint: https://portland-communications.com/publications/how-africa-tweets-2016/.

Powers, Matthew, and Sandra Vera Zambrano. 2016. "Explaining the Formation of Online News Startups in France and the United States: A Field Analysis." *Journal of Communication* 66 (5): 857–877. doi:10.1111/jcom.12253.

Prunier, Gérard. 1997. *The Rwanda Crisis: History of a Genocide*. New York: Columbia University Press.

Puri, Shamlal. 2014. "For Rwanda's Media, the State Plays a Dominant Role." International Press Institute. eprint: https://ipi.media/for-rwandas-media-the-state-plays-a-dominant-role/.

Rønning, Helge, and Tawana Kupe. 2000. "The Dual Legacy of Democracy and Authoritarianism." In *De-Westernizing Media Studies*, edited by James Curran and Myung-Jin Park, 157–177. New York: Routledge.

Rwandan Governance Board. 2016. *The Status of Media Houses in Rwanda*. Report. Kigali, Rwanda: Rwandan Governance Board.

Rwandan Media Fraternity. 2011. *Code of Ethics Governing Journalists, Other Media Professionals, and the Media in Rwanda*. Kigali, Rwanda: Print, June.

Rwandan Parliament. 2009. "Law Number 22/2009 of 12/08/2009 on Media." Accessed eprint: http://aceproject.org/ero-en/regions/africa/RW/rwanda-law-nb022-2009-of-12-08-2009-regulating-the.

Rwandan Parliament. 2013. "Laws Published in 2013." Accessed eprint: http://www.parliament.gov.rw/uploads/tx_publications/Published_Laws_in 2013.pdf.

Schultz, Ida. 2007. "The Journalistic Gut Feeling: Journalistic Doxa, News Habitus and Orthodox News Values." *Journalism Practice* 1 (2): 190–207. doi:10.1080/17512780701275507.

Silberstein-Loeb, Jonathan. 2014. *The International Distribution of News: The Associated Press, Press Association, and Reuters, 1848–1947*. Cambridge, UK: Cambridge University Press.

Skjerdal, Terje, and Charles Muiru Ngugi. 2007. "Institutional and Governmental Challenges for Journalism Education in East Africa." *Ecquid Novi: African Journalism Studies* 28 (1–2): 176–190. doi:10.1080/02560054.2007.9653365.

Sobel, Meghan, and Karen McIntyre. 2018. "The State of Journalism and Press Freedom in Postgenocide Rwanda." *Journalism & Mass Communication Quarterly*. Advance online publication. doi:10.1177/1077699018782201.

Society of Professional Journalists. 2014. SPJ Code of Ethics. Web, September. eprint: https://www.spj.org/ethicscode.asp.

Stockmann, Daniela, and Mary E. Gallagher. 2011. "Remote Control: How the Media Sustain Authoritarian Rule in China." *Comparative Political Studies* 44 (4): 436–467. doi:10.1177/0010414010394773.

Thompson, Allan, ed. 2007. *The Media and the Rwanda Genocide*. Ann Arbor, MI: IDRC.

United Nations n.d. "Rwanda: A Brief History of the Country." United Nations. Accessed eprint: https://www.un.org/en/preventgenocide/rwanda/historical-background.shtml.

Vandevoordt, Robin. 2017. "Why Journalists Covered Syria the Way They Did: On the Role of Economic, Social and Cultural Capital." *Journalism* 18 (5): 609–625. doi:10.1177/1464884915620271.

Vergobbi, David J. 1992. "Journalist as Source: The Moral Dilemma of News Rescue." *Journal of Mass Media Ethics* 7 (4): 233–245. doi:10.1207/s15327728jmme0704_4.

Willig, Ida. 2013. "Newsroom Ethnography in a Field Perspective." *Journalism* 14 (3): 372–387. doi:10.1177/1464884912442638.

Wu, H. Denis, and John Maxwell Hamilton. 2004. "US Foreign Correspondents: Changes and Continuity at the Turn of the Century." *Gazette* 66 (6): 517–532.

Zeng, Yuan. 2017. "Detached Disseminator, Populist Watchdog and Facilitative Change Agent: The Professional Role Perception of Foreign Correspondents in China." *Journalism*. Advance online publication. doi:10.1177/1464884917724055.

The Development of Roles in Kosovo: From Fixers to Journalists

Abit Hoxha and Kenneth Andresen

ABSTRACT
Fixers and the journalistic labour they provide have been examined by many researchers. This research sheds new light into the practices of fixers during and after the conflict in Kosovo to show how their work contributed to the development of the journalism profession in that country. This study demonstrates how an examination of the interaction between international correspondents and fixers can be conducted by exploring news production phases, interventions, and capacity building. The researchers analysed qualitative interviews, which took place in 2018, with thirty journalists and editors in Kosovo who have experience as fixers. It discusses the various teaching/learning aspects in the complex relationships between fixers and international journalists. We conclude that fixers learn from international journalists by being exposed to journalism practice over extended periods of time. We reveal an eagerness from fixers to learn aspects of news production, as well as various challenges in the relationship. Additionally, we draw on studies of international journalists and parachute journalism to show how knowledge from foreign journalists who work with fixers and local journalists contributes locally to developing the professional role of journalists.

The Development of Roles in Kosovo: From Fixers to Journalists

Fixers are a special group of news professionals who connect international journalists with their subjects in the field; a go-between for journalists and interviewees. Fixers have traditionally been viewed as useful agents who provide solutions for journalists on the basis of cultural, political and social knowledge by identifying sources, translating cultural knowledge and providing contextual information to the journalists in the process of news gathering.

By working with foreign correspondents, fixers covering conflicts in the Balkans have obtained a considerable degree of respect. Their role has been essential because few foreign journalists are competent in the languages spoken in this region. This is also true for the Middle East, where traditions and particular cultural contexts meant fixers were especially vital to interpret elements of non-verbal communication. The same can be said to be the case in some reporting on Africa, where visiting journalists may encounter enormous variation in customs and languages (Andresen 2005).

However, this article will show that, besides serving as cultural translators and news gatherers, fixers are also the recipients of "hands on-training" while working, and that there is a mutual learning process between the fixers and international reporters. The fixers often deliver services to the foreign media as they prepare stories for a local newspaper; they do while benefiting from the resources of the foreign press. Above all, journalists working as fixers are trained by foreign international journalists on how to report conflict and war, how stories are balanced, and how to learn from the interactions with sources. But such interactions can give rise to controversy: the (often paid) interaction with visiting journalists may be negatively regarded as combining the values of the foreign journalists with local journalistic values.

A Historical View of Fixers in Post-War Kosovo

A study of the development of journalism as a profession in Kosovo (Andresen 2015) recorded Kosovo news editors describing how many young journalists were drawn to a career in journalism during the armed conflict there. Every time the daily newspaper *Koha Ditore*[1] announced openings, hundreds of young students applied. But many others started a journalistic career by joining international journalists as fixers. Many of today's journalists in the Kosovar media learned to report by observing foreign journalists at work. The period of war in Kosovo in the second half of the 1990s can be characterized as *emergency journalism*: journalists were recruited as youngsters lacking any professional education. It was "learning by doing", and a new form of journalism training developed in Kosovo through the practice of international reporters using local fixers. During 1998 and until the NATO war started in March 1999, the media scene in Kosovo consisted mainly of *Koha Ditore*, the Serbian service *RTP*,[2] and a few smaller publications. Increasingly, international journalists reported on Kosovo in cooperation with local fixers.

During this period, the Albanian population in Kosovo had virtually no access to their own media. The newspaper *Koha Ditore* published daily news, but it was very dangerous for its journalists to move around due to the many Serbian military checkpoints around Kosovo. At the same time, most foreign journalists that were covering the Kosovo developments used *Koha Ditore* as a base for information. From 1997 to the beginning of 1999, *Koha Ditore* journalists and foreign journalists travelled together in Kosovo, through Serb checkpoints. The Kosovar journalists identified themselves as translators for the international journalists, and at the same time, the visiting correspondents received valuable local information and guidance. Thus there developed a win-win situation, where Albanian and international journalists provided information both for the local and international audience (Andresen 2015).

When considering population, area and time span, Kosovo must be said to have experienced one of the most rapid media system developments in history. Within two years after the end of the NATO war, where there had been virtually no local media, 93 licensed local radio stations, 24 local TV stations and three nationwide TV stations were established. Since then, this number has remained fairly stable.[3] The high number of new outlets was the result of increased freedom of speech and broadcasting opportunities that had been denied for two decades to Albanians in Kosovo; but also a result of a rich Albanian tradition of self-organizing.

Today, the Kosovo media market is overwhelmingly privately controlled.[4] As in many other Eastern European countries since the fall of communism, Kosovo never experienced a traditional, staged, media development shifting from authoritative media, via public service media, to a private market (Siebert, Peterson, and Schramm 1963). As soon as the NATO war ended in 1999, many local business owners started media outlets, often in partnership with politicians. In many circumstances, business owners and politicians are one in the same, as demonstrated in the media overview below. Thanks to international funding, especially from the United States, European governments and western donors, the private sector has dominated the media market (Andresen 2015).

But recently the financial situation for the Kosovo media sector has worsened, as an (unnamed) editor in Kosovo confirmed in a report by the South East Europe Media Organization (SEEMO):

> After the war, it was a better time for media. There were a lot of tenders for the media. Now, the time has changed. People no longer get financing from NGOs and they have never invested money. They did not try to make business out of their media. They were used to getting money from the international community. Now this money is gone. (SEEMO 2012, 4–5)

Other recent reports on media in Kosovo confirm the difficult financial situation after international donations have reduced (IREX 2014; RSF 2010). Media owners are seeking other forms of financing. There are frequent accusations of corruption and deals being struck between owners and politicians, for example, in regard to government advertising. In its report on press freedom in Kosovo from 2010, Reporters Without Borders warned against the favouring of certain media outlets by the ruling party, PDK, who they claim was rewarding "positive" media coverage:

> Titles close to the majority parties (particularly the PDK) are clearly favored in the allocation of recruitment or tendering notices[...]This "indirect subsidy" also allows profits to be made by a number of influential decision-makers or company bosses who have turned part of the press into their "public relations officers". (RSF 2010, 5)

In Kosovo, there are also active local radio stations in minority languages, most of them Serbian. All are small and they struggle financially given that they have a very limited advertising market and the target groups are Serbian enclaves, where the living standards are among the lowest in Kosovo (UNDP 2014). The Kosovo Media Association (KOSMA) organizes the 27 Serbian radio stations in Kosovo, but several of these are one-person operations that only play music.

Between Journalist and Fixer: An Overview of Literature

Previous research on international reporters' dependence on local fixers has revealed how fixers contribute to the stories produced by international reporters. Studies from the Middle East (Murrell 2009, 2010, 2011, 2013, 2014, 2015; Palmer and Fontan 2007), Palestine (Bishara 2006) and Kosovo (Andresen 2005, 2009, 2015; Paterson, Andresen, and Hoxha 2012) have shown the unrecognized influence of local fixers on international news, and that, over the years, the labour of fixers is becoming more frequently researched. They have also shed light on various practical and cultural challenges within the practice of news fixing, depending on where it occurs. However, knowledge exchange processes between fixers and international reporters have not been significantly addressed.

Fixers can be said to be the invisible labour behind "parachute journalism". This term is a loaded one. It is used to describe journalism where international reporters are "dropped" into areas of complicated conflict; they work there a few days, then leave for the next conflict zone. Stories may be filed over a few hours or days with little research to support them. In their efforts to gather information quickly, parachute journalists are in danger of missing facts, aspects of culture and nuance in their stories (Hamilton 2004; Lundstrom 2001). The parachute journalist necessarily depends on local assistance, normally in the form of a temporarily hired local person with some knowledge of journalism, an ability to translate, and good local contacts. Palmer and Fontan (2007) define fixers as an additional relay point in the process of mediated communication. Globally, fixers have impacted the content and form of international news correspondents' work far more than the public has been aware (Murrell 2013, 2015; Witchel 2004).

Previous studies have shown that there is a tendency to treat fixers as helpers, doing the side-jobs, and not at the centre of news-making. This article suggests a *two-way approach* of explaining the capacity development for local journalists and fixers by the international and foreign international journalists through the provision of technical knowledge and skills that contribute to the professionalization of local journalistic practice. Our examination of the development of the roles of fixers and their learning from international journalists comes from the research strands of international journalism, parachute journalism and news production research.

In his study on foreign correspondents, Hannerz (2012) focused on routines, relationships and responses. However, his research on the relations of journalists with sources and interactions with other actors lacked an examination of the fixers' role. Similarly, Pedelty (2013) explored the culture of the international press corps, examining the institutions, practices, myths and rituals that shape the work of journalists. Willnat and Weaver (2003) examined professional norms and values, personal backgrounds and daily routines and work-related problems of foreign correspondents working in the United States; we used their research to shape our questioning of editors regarding work related learning.

Research on *parachute journalism* has noted the cultural clash between correspondents who go to the field ill-equipped with the necessary cultural, economic, social and political knowledge. Erickson and Hamilton (2006) proposed typologies that capture the complexity of the phenomenon. Wizda (1997) criticized such shallow approaches to knowing a community and the investigation of only the most obvious aspects of the location, neglecting potential journalistic insights. Similarly, Palmer and Fontan (2007) analysed journalists and fixers' role as translators in Iraq and saw this as "facilitating journalism", defining fixers as an additional relay point in the process of mediated communication. In his report for the Reuters Institute for the Study of Journalism Sambrook (2010, 51), concluded that

> there is a strong sense from international news organisations that they not only have the opportunity but the responsibility to train and employ more local journalists to report directly for them rather than simply act in support roles as "fixers" or translators. It is particularly acute for global services addressing international audiences'

He argued that collaboration by foreign correspondents should be more in the level of journalist-to-journalist and not involve fixers. But so long as there are conflicts and international events that international organizations send correspondents to cover, and as long as local journalistic capacity is not trusted to provide this coverage, there will be a need to use fixers.

The third strand of literature informing the current study is research on news production, particularly investigations of various influences on news production. Schudson's (1997) study of the construction of news indirectly pointed to the need for understanding the influence of fixers in the process of news production. Hoxha and Hanitzsch (2018) suggested a framework of news production divided into three stages: Ideation, narration and presentation of news. When combined with Clausen's (2004) research that looks at the "domestication" of processes in international news production, it brings to light the actual stages of the newsmaking process where such influences by the fixers may be located.

Turning to the practice of fixers in Kosovo, we see that the emergency reporting during the war in Kosovo (1997–1999) made the local journalists conscious of a *cause*, or a purpose, for their reporting, but their main concern was to bring news about the war to their audience. By travelling with international reporters, they were able to fill a need for information as to where the fighting took place and where the roadblocks were located. As the editor of *Koha Ditore* recognized, the combination of a cause and the reporting of events and facts transformed local journalists into eyewitness reporters (Andresen 2015). However, they had to do this under cover of being translators and drivers for the international reporters. Their own functions of being reporters for local Kosovar media had to remain secret at the Serbian checkpoints through the late 90s.

International journalists provided further benefits for the local journalists who were hired as fixers, both providing an inconsistent but important side income to the underpaid journalists and modelling international practices and standards of journalism. In this study we sought to determine:

- How is the profession of journalism developed through the interaction between local fixers and international journalists in Kosovo?
- How are the cultural and societal roles of local journalists as fixers influenced by the international journalists in Kosovo?

These research questions were addressed by analysing the experiences of current journalists in relation to their collaborative work; the position of fixers with such experience; and the roles that cultural, societal and lingual skills play in the context of news production in a transitional society (see Figure 1). As fixers are mostly cultural translators for international journalists, it is important to learn aspects of such skills. We found that many of the current editors and senior journalists in Kosovo were former fixers and journalists during the conflict years (Hoxha, Andresen, and Hoxha-Dobrunaj 2017).

As we elaborate in Figure 1, knowledge exchange between local journalists working as fixers and international journalists is influenced by the values each offers the other. Language skills and political knowledge, as well as privileged access to newsmakers through a better cultural understanding of context, enable international journalists to have local eyes and ears which enhance their news coverage. In a way, international journalists act as a filter for the local fixers. Fixers can provide information on regional power

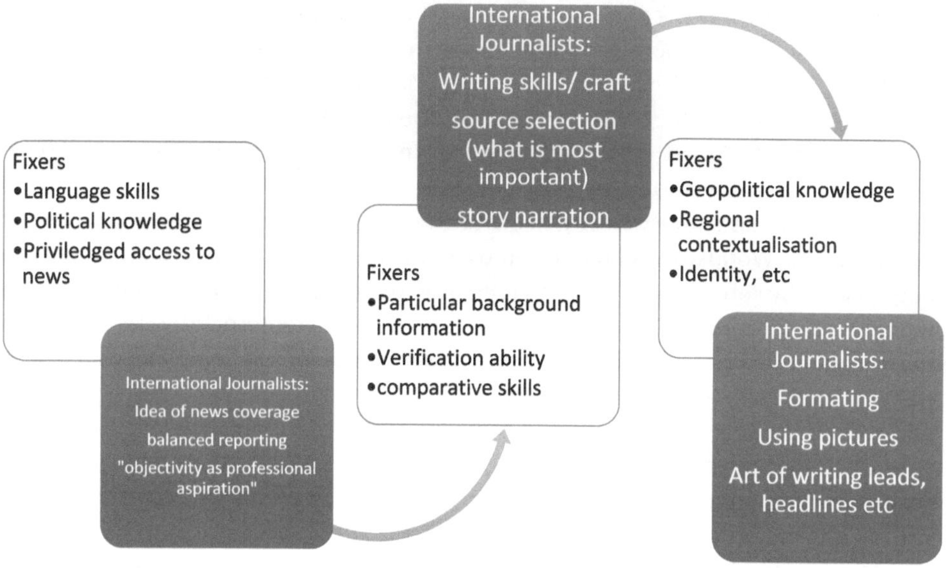

Figure 1. Knowledge exchange from fixers to international journalists during news production interactions.

issues, and local identity and culture, whereas international journalists bring the skills to report for their home (or global) audience.

Method

This project gathered qualitative data from selected journalists that represent Kosovar media. Our selection of interviewees required a fluid approach, given a small and vibrant community of journalists where it is nearly impossible to arrange meetings far ahead. Because media changes so rapidly in this area, journalists change news beats, media, and switch between media and public relations jobs depending on which generates better income. Similarly, fixer jobs are often held in addition to local reporter positions held by the journalists. Following journalists through their career is challenging because media in Kosovo often cease to exist as new media outlets emerge. It is normal for a journalist to quit working for a private television station and start working for an online news portal for a few months and then get back to a better paid television job. The profession of a journalist, as seen also in data from 2015 (Hoxha, Andresen, and Hoxha-Dobrunaj 2017) is not well-paid. For these reasons, a number of journalists would be engaged in "conflicting" jobs with their journalism work, e.g., public relations and communication for political parties or businesses.

Additionally, examining practices of journalists and detailed discussion of their role is often taken as unwelcome judgement. We reassured interviewees through explanation of why qualitative semi-structured interviews were vital. The interviews sought to provide a broad overview of journalistic culture and routines with an added discussion of the roles of fixers and experiences of learning from international journalists.

Interviews were conducted in Kosovo's capital Prishtina, where most of the media is concentrated. Kosovo, being a small nation where even the furthest border is located within two hours' drive, has its agenda setting media based in the capital. We asked journalists for meetings in coffee shops in town, outside their working environments, and the interviews were developed conversationally. Krosnick (1999) and Schober and Conrad (1997) argue that this type of interviews produces more accurate data.

Recruiting journalists for this research started initially from the list of the 206 journalists surveyed for the Worlds of journalism Study (WJS) in 2015. The first 10 were selected through the list by contacting every 10th journalist in the list and making the first 10 interviews in a random sample. As the first 10 interviews were not representative of the agenda setting media and popular journalists, we also undertook purposive sampling, choosing 20 journalists from prominent media who report on politics, justice and crimes (and, in particular, address aspects of the conflictual past). Interviewees from prominent media were also recruited through a "snowball sample" using the journalists' connections.

Kosovo media has emerged from conflict in 1999 into a western styled pluralistic media. Kosovo's Constitution guarantees media freedom but the application of relevant laws is weak, according to the Kosovo Journalist Association (Collaku 2018). Currently, according to the latest report of the Kosovo Independent Media Commission, a regulatory body, Kosovo has 20 TV stations and 83 radio stations (KPM 2017) and the Kosovo Press Council numbers 32 members which include web based newspapers and web news portals. Some newspapers are not members of the Press Council. There are five to six paper newspapers in Kosovo, including the prominent *Koha Ditore.*

The agenda setting media in Kosovo were decided by the media influence they have. Generally, Balkans Investigative Reporting Network (BIRN) is considered as an influential media outlet although it is registered as an NGO. Kosovo 2.0 is an NGO but with a regional and even international reach. Kosovo Public Broadcasting is the popular television channel, but trust has plummeted in the last few years despite the fact that citizens continue to watch it mainly for traditional reasons. Several privately owned televisions such as Klan Kosova were included in the sample because of their agenda setting role. The newly established T7 television was included due to its viewership among the younger generations. Although there is no useful data on viewership and audience in Kosovo, the sample includes all major media and news outlets and excludes some smaller regional radio and television stations because of their regional and limited reach.

The age of interviewees varied from 22 to 44 years old. The average age is 32.5 years, indicating that most of the interviewees experienced the war in 1999 as children, and not as journalists. In the end, we interviewed a wide range of journalists that cover newspapers, television, radio and online news portals ranging from private media and public media, as well as NGO, registered media. We also interviewed freelance journalists, full-time employees and journalists employed part-time. Two of the journalists are from the Kosovo Serb community. They both worked on the similar news beat of dealing with the past (see Table 1).

The data from the interviews were collected over a month of fieldwork. Transcriptions of interviews were done in the original language of the interviews (Albanian and Serbian) and translated into English. Impressions of emotions, background information and information that was spoken about after the end of interview were inserted as additional information in the analysis software to have a more thorough understanding of the data.

Table 1. Sample of interviewed journalists in Kosovo who worked as fixers.

	Journalists selected from WJS database of newsgatherers	*Agenda setting media and prominent journalists*
	10	20
Newspaper	3	5
Radio	0	2
Television	4	5
Online	3	7
Gender	5 female and 5 male	10 female and 10 male
Minority journalists		2 (1 male and 1 female)

The transcripts were coded through NVivo using an inductive approach. Codes were added as interviews were read. The first round of coding was based upon the interview guidelines which included questions about demographics, routines, freedom of the press, dealing with the past and news production as an overall framework. The particular coding regarding experiences with international journalists was done for those sections when journalists spoke about the collaboration with other journalists locally and internationally. Specific questions about working as fixers were coded further to understand experiences and learning processes. By coding from a wider perspective to more specific issues, we managed to have two levels of coding: a more general selection of codes and more specific codes that were linked to the particular experiences.

Findings

Journalists Learn from Mutual Interaction

Our interviewees noted that that their work is *influenced* by the work they have done with foreign journalists as fixers. An overwhelming proportion of the journalists have had such experience. Twenty-eight of the 30 interviewees have worked directly as fixers throughout their career. The two who lacked such experience said that they either didn't have the required language skills or were too young to have developed a network and the skills to provide services for international journalists. This indicates that many of today`s Kosovar journalists have direct experience as fixers aiding foreign journalists. They explained that their personal network of sources overlaps with those of their predecessors in their organizations, making their journalistic networks an inherited resource.

Regarding their knowledge exchange experiences, the interviewees' impressions were overwhelmingly positive. Twenty-four interviewees reported they had learned from international colleagues. The remaining six expressed the view they had learned little because they possessed equivalent knowledge to their international colleagues. A small portion felt that the international journalists were actually learning skills and cultural aspects of reporting from the locals.

Examples of Learning Journalism

Most of the journalists interviewed had some experience with foreign journalists. That contribution to international reporting by the local journalists has not always been attributed to them as by-line credit or acknowledgement of their collaboration, although they have been referred to as fixers and stringers. Their work often goes unnoticed and unannounced, but they still have two main benefits from this labour. The first significant benefit is *financial,* although the journalists do not speak explicitly about it. The positive financial side of the experience should not be underestimated as Kosovar journalists have very low salaries and have to cover many news beats.

The second benefit is that of *learning;* 24 interviewees reported that they observed their international colleagues in action during their work. Most stress that the learning aspect is very important. As one journalist recalls his work with a prominent economic journalist from an international magazine:

> I learned how to make an interesting feature, an analytic feature. As a journalist, you write and do analysis too. I learned from them (the international journalists) when you are writing a report along with economic analysis you are doing a political analysis where it means that if you do not have good politicians, you cannot have economic development. (Interviewee 1)

Learning from international journalists is evidently contributing to the professionalization of journalists in Kosovo and is mostly focusing on journalistic narrative building, whereas ideation of stories already has come with the international journalist. The journalist quoted above recalled that he did not have much experience in economic reporting and was hired as a language and cultural translator, but while working on many of the stories he also learned about economic and political reporting.

Another journalist echoed his colleagues in regard to learning from the international reporters. He was eager to learn more from an international colleague who hired him to arrange sources in Kosovo's capital. He recalled focusing on how the international journalist approached topics, how he reported and how he was being informed from his sources, keeping in mind that the international journalist was not in touch consistently with his contacts in Kosovo. In lacking consistent information, he recalls that; "lack of information is good after getting information from the beginning" (Interviewee 10). He explained this further by saying that he learnt how international journalists turn lack of information into an advantage to stay observant and distant from reporting, allowing them to report more independently on conflict and violence.

Journalists in Kosovo recognize that due to the difficult situation there, being local and reporting on local events can be exhausting and might weaken the recognition of what news is. The normalization of violence and thus familiarization of such events makes one think that they are not newsworthy. A journalist recalled his experience with an international journalist from a foreign public service broadcaster, and how he learned how to approach newsworthiness and reporting in a different way. He cooperated with this international journalist for several years but lately, his fixer work focused on providing information from the justice sector to gain insight on prisons and in particular, female prisoners. They produced reports of women who killed men and found that the "women who murdered men are sentenced to two or three times longer in prison than men who murdered women" (Interviewee 14).

Another journalist who worked as a fixer for BBC recalled how simple issues were made into stories and how he learned that everyday issues can be important:

> He literally made a good story in the street with a man … whom I pass every day and it did not occur me or I do not know, he saw something … next to the road and made a story about it, I do not know. He saw 30 gas stations from […] Podujeva to here (Prishtina) and he made a

> story about that. That for me, that was very normal to me and I did not notice it. So, those are the things from which I cannot say I have learnt, but it was quite interesting for me […] that the person has noticed something like that, which means that the news and the good story is all around us, we just need to use the imagination. (Interviewee 5)

An important aspect is the phenomenon of *mutual* learning between the journalists, shown earlier in this paper (Figure 1). One former fixer stated that the international journalist learned a lot from his experience with Kosovar Albanians and Serbs, and another explained that when his interests met with the international journalists', they joined forces to produce something together, although they come from different worlds:

> It was my story, but … international media wanted to tackle the same topic and I arranged the interviews. I think that they have more luxury and are slower. If we say we have completed this report for a week they say, "no we do not want to publish it until after 3 months". We (in the local media) do not have this comfort. (Interviewee 23)

Journalists in Kosovo recognize that working for more than one international journalist has its benefits. Working with multiple media outlets and journalists is strategic and better serves their own interest of getting published.

One Kosovar journalist who arranged interviews and translated for an international colleague spoke of how the experience caused him to re-evaluate his approach to interviewing:

> I worked with a German journalist in 2–3 cases and what I have professionally gained from them is the way or the idea of how to do an interview with a housewife or an elder. Often from negligence not every person we interview we treat the same way. What I have learned from foreign journalists is this aspect of human treatment of interviewees, persons regardless of whether she is prime minister or a housekeeper or housewife. They have the same approach as well in writing, we have found the deserved space for the interviewee. I tried to go to good trainings, I even tried to look online for training or interview method but I think that (work) helped me a lot during my career to balance information, […] always try to report the truth which even in a small case that can affect 10 or 15 people. (Interviewee 25)

A fixer who also works as a TV journalist said: "I think I have profited professionally, not just financially. We have a lot of unrestricted access to the way news is made" (Interviewee 28). This illustrates that, in addition to learning, journalists feel freer of pressures when working for foreign media.

The Importance of Practical Experience

Most of the experienced local journalists interviewed agree that there is no comprehensive training in Kosovo when it comes to reporting. This is confirmed by previous research (Hoxha, Andresen, and Hoxha-Dobrunaj 2017). Reporting well is a craft and is learned by experience. This learning experience is mutual between the fixers and international journalists.

Journalists constantly are seeking inventive methods of reporting and thus, Kosovar fixers benefit from associating and working with international journalists, as well as learn technological skills. A few journalists appreciated international journalists producing multi-format reporting singlehandedly, across audio-visual, text and visual media. One of the fixers was grateful for the experience of working with an international journalist and speaks what he had learned from a few days of work:

> For the 10th anniversary of Kosovo's Independence, I was a fixer of a journalist from Denmark. I set up interviews and meetings. From this I have learned the methods of work that they apply as a reporter as it is interesting for the journalists to know how to use the camera and to be able to do the entire story without technical assistance. (Interviewee 9)

The same journalist expressed interest in forms of human rights reporting which he would not previously have considered as a result of that experience of fixing, stating:

> I have learned a lot from a war journalist who has reported only about refugees, about methods of investigating in a refugee camp. We have not previously been familiar with this subject. (Interviewee 9)

Journalists who are fixers temporarily learn reporting techniques and how to handle sources, and they often publish stories related to their work as fixers. As journalists in Kosovo work on producing news with shorter turnaround time, they learn the importance of more comprehensive reporting and a longer investment of time in stories. A Kosovar journalist who worked with a Swiss team of journalists was impressed that the time invested for a story was about two weeks.

> The difference is the time ... they come for 1–2 weeks contacting dozens of resources to realize a subject; [they] are much more persistent than us in the sense of what to include ... if we go to [report] a topic in another country [we] are much more dedicated to having much more resources involved. (Interviewee 26)

Different *storytelling techniques* are also something that Kosovar journalists learn while working with international journalists. A photojournalist was covering Kosovo when he started publishing photos in a Kosovar newspaper while using the journalists of that newspaper as fixers. The fixer who followed him in the field and translated for him says he adopted the technique of storytelling through photographs: "He (the international photojournalist) follows the story through photography and also [writes text] that fits [the] photos" (Interviewee 10). The fixer is a senior reporter and often employs that technique in storytelling. This particular newspaper now publishes online only and is estimated to be the most popular web-based media in the Balkans.

Experiences of fixers are very colourful, and mistakes happen. Not all fixers felt international journalists they worked with were sufficiently professional or produced quality journalism. One journalist recalls how a week's work was lost when the journalist he worked for lost her notes. He suggested that a glorified view of international journalists does not always live up to the reality. In his words,

> We, local journalists have had a greater expectation from them [but] they make fast food journalism. They come for 3 days in Kosovo to drink two beers here and two there and collect our stories, [do] some interviews with people who are more accessible and just [write] a review of what we already know. (Interviewee 29)

This fixer who works continuously with international journalists explained "fast food journalism" as stories prepared quickly but with artificial ingredients which just appear appealing.

Conclusions

Our interviews indicate that in general, younger journalists in Kosovo have learned the craft of journalism from older journalists and through education. All thirty journalists interviewed for this study had a university degree in communication and media related studies, or on a subject related to the beat, they cover. In other words, they are highly educated but with little experience. This was similarly seen in the Worlds of Journalism Study (WJS) survey in 2015, in which 96.2 per cent of the 206 respondents held a university degree and 67.0 per cent had specialized in journalism and/or communication (Hoxha, Andresen, and Hoxha-Dobrunaj 2017). Furthermore, journalists in Kosovo have short working experience on average, compared to other countries in the WJS. According to the same report, Kosovar journalists have 7.5 years of experience in average.

Knowledge exchange and professionalization of fixers is a dynamic process between them and the visiting journalists they work with. Although previous scholarly work on fixers focuses on their influence on news content, the process of learning and adaption of a journalist identity amongst fixers are important aspects that can help deepen our understanding of their work. In previous research, fixers also have been connected to `parachute journalism` but our findings show that most international journalists need collaboration when they are outside their home environment. This collaboration does not necessarily need to be viewed negatively. As Murrell (2015) has discussed, arguments in favour of parachute journalism argue that as a practice it allows the quantitative breadth of coverage of news from places that might not otherwise see any reportage.

Practically, it is impossible for an international journalist to understand the languages and cultural aspects of all the countries they are expected to cover. Fixers are part of almost all news production and usually uncredited for the work they provide (Paterson, Andresen, and Hoxha 2012). In this article, we have shown how fixers in Kosovo learn skills of reporting by using resources and knowledge of seasoned international reporters. At the same time, international journalists utilize the local skills and cultural interpretations of fixers who are either local journalists of some capacity or aspire to become journalists in the future. Hence, the work of fixers is of immense importance to coverage of news and media production both locally and internationally.

We have found that the practices of news production, learning processes, and outcomes from fixers' work are similar to those of journalists researched by Hannerz (2012) and Pedelty (2013). Fixers do not represent an anomaly of journalism's normal practice but rather an enhancement, an added value and asset for better coverage of events and more effective news production for both local and international news media. There is an increased role for fixers associated with increased conflicts and decreasing budget for foreign news coverage (Sambrook 2010). Fixers are finding a new field of operation by becoming more professional and in the words of Clausen (2004) are domesticating the international news but also internationalizing the domestic news. This process of influence and exchange of knowledge deserves further research in other reporting contexts.

Finally, it is worth noting that most journalists in Kosovo act with two hats. They are journalists—and fixers—and sometimes both; co-producing stories with international journalists while fixing sources and translating for them. It is important for them to switch between positions in an attempt to present themselves and the media they work for as professionally as they can. As soon as the journalists in Kosovo are contacted by international journalists to collaborate on stories, they often do not hide it from editors but rather try to make good use of the opportunity both financially and practically to produce similar news reporting. Like international journalists, local journalists and fixers are "parachuted" into the global news cycle by providing news for millions and they are aware of the importance of their job.

Notes

1. *Koha Ditore* (translated as *Daily Time*) is the leading daily newspaper from Kosovo.
2. Radio Television of Prishtina was the public television of Prishtina, and ceased to function in July 1990 as part of measures by Serbia to control Kosovo.
3. In 2006, the number of radio stations in Kosovo was at its peak with 116 (Kyrke-Smith 2007).
4. With the exception of Radio Television Kosovo (RTK), which is Kosovo's only public service media organization.

Aknowledgement

The authors also want to aknowledge the contribution of Prof. James A. Sweeney, Lancaster University Law School (UK) (j.sweeney@lancaster.ac.uk) and the Worlds of Journalism Study Project (www.worldsofjournalism.org).

Disclosure statement

No potential conflict of interest was reported by the authors.

Funding

This work was supported by the British Academy International Challenges Programme 2017 (grant number: IC2\100044).

ORCID

Abit Hoxha http://orcid.org/0000-0001-9722-493X
Kenneth Andresen http://orcid.org/0000-0001-6151-7394

References

Andresen, K. 2005. "Ethnography in News Production Research in Kosovo Newsrooms." Paper presented at the Nord Forsk Seminar "Problems of the News Media: Focuses, Methodologies and Innovations in Journalism Research" at Tampere University, September 2005(Unpublished Material), 1–19.

Andresen, K. 2009. "Producing 'Protocol News' in Kosovo's Public Broadcaster: Journalism in a Transitional Risk Society." *Conflict & Communication* 8 (2): 1–19.

Andresen, K. 2015. "Journalism Under Pressure." University of Oslo.

Bishara, A. 2006. "Local Hands, International News." *Ethnography* 7 (1): 19–46. doi:10.1177/1466138106064590.

Clausen, L. 2004. "Localizing the Global: 'Domestication' Processes in International News Production." *Media Culture & Society* 26 (1): 25–44.

Collaku, P. (2018) "Treguesit e nivelit të lirisë së mediave dhe sigurisë së gazetarëve [KOSOVA]: Përmbledhja e të gjeturave." Western Balkans Regional Platform for Advocating Media Freedom and Journalists' Safety.
Erickson, E., and J. M. Hamilton. 2006. "Foreign Reporting Enhanced by Parachute Journalism." *Newspaper Research Journal* 27 (1): 33–47.
Hamilton, J. 2004. "All the News That's Fit to Sell: How the Market Transforms Information into News." Princeton University Press.
Hannerz, U. 2012. "Foreign News: Exploring the World of Foreign Correspondents." University of Chicago Press.
Hoxha, A., K. Andresen, and A. Hoxha-Dobrunaj. 2017. *Journalists in Kosovo: Country Report*. Worlds of Journalism Study. https://epub.ub.uni-muenchen.de/31986/7/Abit_Hoxha_Kenneth_Andresen_%26_Arbesa_Hoxha-Dobrunaj__Journalists_in_Kosovo.pdf.
Hoxha, A., and T. Hanitzsch. 2018. "How Conflict News Comes Into Being: Reconstructing 'Reality' Through Telling Stories. *Media War & Conflict* 11 (1): 46–64.
IREX. 2014. *Media Sustainability Index (MSI) 2013-Europe & Eurasia*. Washington: IREX.
KPM. 2017. "Raporti Vjetor I Punes për vitin 2017 drejtuar Kuvendit të Republikës së Kosovës."
Krosnick, J. A. 1999. "Survey Research." *Annual Review of Psychology* 50: 537–567.
Kyrke-Smith, L. 2007. "Information Intervention and the Case of Kosovo: Realizing the Responsibility to Protect." *Knowledge Politics Quarterly* 1 (1): 1–48.
Lundstrom, M. 2001. "Parachute Journalism: The Damage Wrought by Regional Stereotypes." *Poynter Online*. https://www.poynter.org/archive/2002/parachute-journalism/.
Murrell, C. 2009. "Fixers and Foreign Correspondents: News Production and Autonomy." *Australian Journalism Review* 31 (1): 5.
Murrell, C. 2010. "Baghdad Bureaux: An Exploration of the Interconnected World of Fixers and Correspondents at the BBC and CNN." *Media War & Conflict* 3 (2): 125–137.
Murrell, C. 2011. "Foreign Correspondence and Fixers: The Missing Link." Audio from the 2011 Reuters Institute Seminar Series. Reuters Institute for the Study of Journalism.
Murrell, C. 2013. "International Fixers: Cultural Interpreters or 'People Like Us'?" *Ethical Space* 10 (2/3): 72–79.
Murrell, C. 2014. *Foreign Correspondents and International Newsgathering: The Role of Fixers*. New York: Routledge.
Murrell, C. 2015. "Fixers, the People Behind the Foreign Correspondents." "Fixers, the People Behind the Foreign Correspondents," 1–1.
Palmer, J., and V. Fontan. 2007. "Our Ears and Our Eyes." *Journalism: Theory, Practice & Criticism* 8 (1): 5–24.
Paterson, C., K. Andresen, and A. Hoxha. 2012. "The Manufacture of an International News Event: The day Kosovo Was Born." *Journalism: Theory Practice & Criticism* 13 (1): 103–120. doi:10.1177/1464884911400846.
Pedelty, M. 2013. *War Stories: The Culture of Foreign Correspondents*. New York: Routledge.
RSF. 2010. *Kosovo Still Not Too Late for Press Freedom*. Report. Paris: Reporters Without Borders (Reporters Sans Frontières).
Sambrook, R. 2010. "Are Foreign Correspondents Redundant?" Reuters Institute for the Study of Journalism, Department of Politics and International Relations, University of Oxford.
Schober, M. F., and F. G. Conrad. 1997. "Does Conversational Interviewing Reduce Survey Measurement Error?" *Public Opinion Quarterly* 61 (4): 576.
Schudson, M. 1997. "The Sociology of News Production." In *Social Meanings of News: A Text-Reader*, edited by Daniel A. Berkowitz, 7–22. Thousand Oaks, CA: Sage.
SEEMO. 2012. *Report on the SEEMO Press Freedom Mission to Kosovo Nov. 23-25 2011*. Report. Vienna: South East Europe Media Organization (SEEMO).
Siebert, F. S., T. Peterson, and W. Schramm. 1963. *Four Theories of the Press*. Urbana-Champaign: University of Illinois Press.
UNDP. 2014. *Human Development Report Kosovo 2014*. Prishtina: UNDP (United Nations Development Programme).

Willnat, L., and D. Weaver. 2003. "Through Their Eyes." *Journalism: Theory, Practice & Criticism* 4 (4): 403–422.
Witchel, E (2004) "The Fixers." Committee to Protect Journalists. https://cpj.org/reports/2004/10/fixers.php.
Wizda, S. 1997. "Parachute Journalism." *American Journalism Review* 19 (6): 40–45.

One Foot in Prison and One Foot Out: State-Appointed Local Journalistic Labor in North Korea

Soomin Seo

ABSTRACT

Foreign correspondents are often required to work with government-appointed fixers or minders in authoritarian regimes. This article is a case study of these frequently overlooked journalistic workers in North Korea and the structure of surveillance and social control they work within. Interviews with foreign journalists show that many of these locals are much more than mere government spies. The competing desires Pyongyang has for its fixer-minders—to both control and woo the correspondents—and a news environment increasingly open to Western media have led to a further diversification of roles among these journalistic workers. While minders from the State Security Ministry surveil journalists without directly interacting with them, English-speaking locals who work as photographers or writers contribute by taking pictures and writing stories. Foreign correspondents gradually form collegial rapport with the locals, which in turn makes them suspect in the eyes of the North Korean state despite the impeccable ideological credentials that earned them the posts in the first place. This makes the locals "Marginal Men" (Park 1926), people who belong to multiple cultures that are at odds with each other, people who have "one foot in and one foot out of prison."

Introduction: Putting Minders in Center Stage

There is a growing interest in the work of locally hired journalistic labor, who are variously labeled "fixers," "stringers," or simply "local journalists." These individuals offer a wide array of services to the foreign press, from logistical support to editorial assistance. While their work has been discussed by scholars of international reporting (Hannerz 2004; Palmer and Fontan 2007; Pedelty 1995), it is only in the last decade or so that these local journalists have taken a central place in research, rather than as serving supporting cast for stories about Western correspondents (Murrell 2015; Palmer 2018b; Paterson and Sreberny 2004; Seo 2016). Murrell (2015) established the importance of fixers in TV journalism, showing how their everyday work makes them much more than the logistical aides that their title suggests. But fixers working amidst wars and disasters are underappreciated, and, not coincidentally, under-protected from dangers. Furthermore, fixers are often frustrated by foreign correspondents' lack of cultural understanding regarding the countries they cover (Palmer 2018a). Such scholarly recognition comes amidst a similarly increased appreciation from the practitioner side, as budget cuts and bureau closures mean that locals are doing most of the newswork for Western outlets in many countries (see, e.g., Sambrook 2010). Much of the original reporting—which is increasingly delegated to news agencies like AP and AFP—is done by locals, with staff foreign correspondents parachuting in for short durations (Murrell 2015; Paterson and Sreberny 2004).

Largely missing from the research, however, are local journalistic workers who operate in more restricted settings. Many authoritarian and dictatorial regimes continue to tightly control foreign media access. Press visas are issued intermittently and strategically, typically only to journalists working for major outlets and/or those deemed friendly to the ruling regime, and only during carefully chosen occasions like elections and festivals (Committee to Protect Journalists 2015). Once foreign correspondents enter these countries, they are invariably required to work with state-appointed locals, who are called "minder," "guides," "translators," or "fixers" (Jerreat 2017). While similar roles exist in different contexts—think about the military public affairs officers who accompany embedded American journalists in Afghanistan—they are most commonly found in authoritarian regimes in Central Asia, the Middle East, and the Horn of Africa (Bunce 2011; Palmer 2007; Palmer and Fontan 2007; Wright 2018).

This article is about an even less explored subset of these local journalistic workers in a uniquely controlled and repressive setting, North Korea. The goal is not only to understand the role the local journalistic workers play in journalism, but also to make sense of the greater structure of surveillance and social control in North Korea. By exploring the multiple, often conflicting roles the state-appointed individuals play in journalism, I hope to fill in the gap in scholarly research about news practices in this and other heavily censored countries of the world.

The Case of Journalism in North Korea

It would be difficult to find a harsher news climate than North Korea. Consistently ranking near bottom in global free press rankings, the country stands out with the exceptionally tight grip it exercises on the movement and communication of its citizens and visitors alike (Committee to Protect Journalists 2015; Freedom House 2017). All news outlets are owned by the government, and the general public do not have access to the Internet, a privilege reserved for senior party elites and foreigners (Koh, Lee, and Hong 2012). Similarly, there is no meaningful independent journalism to speak of, with the exception of underground dissident press which operates mostly from outside North Korea, which sometimes gets passed on to those inside in USB sticks and SIM cards (Lerner 2015).

Although North Korea is one of the least-visited countries in the world for foreign correspondents, tensions over its nuclear and missile programs have led to a major increase in a global demand for news from the nation. The presence of foreign correspondents itself is something of a novelty in the capital city of Pyongyang. Doors to the foreign media began to crack open around the year 2000, when North Korea began to establish diplomatic relationships with Western countries like Britain, Canada and Germany. In this spirit of increased openness, the AP's TV subsidiary APTN was permitted to launch the first Western media bureau in Pyongyang in 2006, which resulted in exceptional—and often exclusive—access to images from North Korea (Paterson 2011). This was followed by Japan's Kyodo News Agency (2006), an official AP bureau (2012), and Agence France Presse (2016). Out of these bureaus, the official establishment of the AP bureau was perhaps the most significant due to the symbolic nature of the flagship American news agency moving into a city where state-issued banners still prominently display anti-American slogans.

In addition to these new entries, the foreign press corps in Pyongyang also includes the long-timers at state news outlets from Russia (ITAR) and China (Xinhua News Agency and *People's Daily*)—whose historical Communist bona fides allowed them a head start. The South Korean media also enjoyed preferential treatment during the presidency of Kim Dae-jung (1998–2004). At the time, South Korean journalists visited North Korean factories in the border city of Kaesong and attended family reunions, tours, and sporting events in Pyongyang and Mt. Kumgang. In his study of South Korean reporters who visited North Korea in the early 2000s, Chon (2002) found that the Pyongyang regime was extremely selective and strategic in issuing entry permits to foreign journalists, giving preferential treatment to progressive and liberal media outlets. On the other hand, Seo (2009) showed that reporters' nationalities—American, South Korean, and Chinese—led to different perspectives in their coverage of discussions regarding North Korea's nuclear programs.

Still, research about the complicated nature of the surveillance journalists encounter in North Korea or the sociology of various actors involved has rarely been attempted. Journalists and scholars often portray the government-appointed guides primarily as spies, performing surveillance and censorship roles, or sees them primarily as technical, non-journalistic labor doing mechanical work (e.g., see S. Kim 2015; Sweeney 2013). What these works overlook is the complicated reality on the ground, where the individuals play multiple, often conflicting roles including that of a journalist. So how should we understand the structure of surveillance and the role of local journalistic labor in North Korea? This is the first question this article seeks to answer:

> RQ1: How do the state-appointed journalistic labor work with the foreign correspondents in North Korea, and what is their relative position between the regime and the international media outlets?

As more journalists visit North Korea, the conditions surrounding their work—and the concessions they are willing to make—have come under scrutiny. In a content analysis of AP articles datelined from North Korea, Seo (2018) showed that the Pyongyang bureau avoided sensitive subjects like diplomacy and the nuclear program and focused its energy on capturing photographs of everyday lives and covering state-sanctioned events such as sports competitions. Criticism of the facile reporting and self-censorship among the foreign press often comes from the journalists themselves. Evan Ramstad, who visited North Korea for the *Wall Street Journal*, pointed out the lack of Korean language skills among foreign journalists allows them to be easily manipulated by the North Koreans. Additionally, most of them parachute into North Korea for short trips, allowing them little time to absorb the historical, cultural, and political context of North Korea. For example, Ramstad (2018) described how during his 2008 trip with New York Philharmonic, reporters had 40 hours of tightly packed schedule. Others have alleged that in order to retain access to the country, journalists abandon pillars of their professional ethics like independence and balance when they follow the predetermined itinerary dictated by the North Korean government (Kim 2008). Given the controversies, this article is also interested in how the foreign correspondents themselves navigate the complicated terrain in North Korea, with all its restrictions and dangers. How do they do their work, when they themselves are newcomers and utterly unfamiliar with the country? Do they apply the same set of moral, ethical standards in the process or are there are concessions they make? These are the second set of questions this article hopes to explore through the following research question:

> RQ2: How do the foreign correspondents in North Korea negotiate with the surveillance structure in their daily work?

Data and Method

This article employs interviews with journalists who have been to North Korea ($N = 17$) as the primary method. The foreign journalists were chosen because there was no way to safely interview North Korean minders and fixers. Interviews were conducted from 2017 to 2019 in South Korea and in the United States. This was a time when news about North Korea appeared frequently in Western outlets due to rising tensions surrounding its nuclear program as well as the resumption of high-level diplomatic activities between the North Korean leader Kim Jong-un and Donald Trump of the USA, Moon Jae-in of South Korea, and Xi Jinping of China.

In selecting interviewees, I tried to locate representatives of all news outlets with a track record of sending a reporter to North Korea more than once. A list compiled by the author showed at least 60 outlets belonged to this group, meaning nearly one third of such outlets which visited North Korea are represented in this article. On an individual level, most of the interviewees ($N = 14$) were foreign correspondents from Western or neighboring Asian countries who had worked in North Korea or had colleagues working there. Two interviewees are not foreign correspondents per se, but rather North Korean defectors who have worked as journalists from the South Korean side. One interviewee is not a reporter but works as a consultant for Western news outlets when they seek to gain entry to North Korea. The three non-foreign correspondents were included because their unique experiences provided them with a deep understanding of North Korea's handling of news media. Overall, interviewees were senior figures in their profession, with an average of 17 years of experience as journalists or in related jobs such as intelligence. A majority of interviewees considered themselves North Korea specialists, having spent the majority of their careers focusing on the country. But even the self-professed generalists—such as foreign correspondents covering both Koreas for international outlets—reported spending much or most of their time working on North Korea-related issues. Eleven were male and six female. Interviewees worked for US, South Korean, British and Japanese news agencies, newspapers, and TV stations. Most of the interviewees (12 out of 17) asked to remain anonymous, citing possible repercussions for their outlet and the North Korean locals they have worked with. Others asked to omit statements that would identify their specific news organization. Those who agreed to be identified include Jean Lee and David Guttenfelder (formerly Associated Press), Jang Yong-hoon (Yonhap News Agency), Kim Hyun-kyung (MBC), and Chad O'Carroll (NK News). (Table 1).

Table 1. Typology of North Korean local hires working with foreign media.

	Low Commitment to Surveillance	*High Commitment to Surveillance*
Low Commitment to Journalistic Quality	Guides (generic or location-specific guides including translators)	State Security minders
High Commitment to Journalistic Quality	Photographers, videographers and writers (long-term or recurring partnership with foreign media)	Stringers (short term, event-specific work with parachuting or first-time foreign media)

The interviews were part of a larger project on journalists covering North Korea. Separate from this article, I conducted content analysis on the themes and formats of their work and also looked into their sourcing practices, both of which informed this research by providing the context of the overall social climate and news environment in North Korea. This context helped me to formulate interview questions about work routines and news values involving the North Korean minders, such as: Who were the North Koreans you worked with? What do you know about their training, qualifications, and other relevant background information? To what extent were the North Koreans similar to—and different from—fixers and stringers you worked with in other countries? And what changes you have witnessed over time, if any?

Nevertheless, the interviews are inherently limited in several ways. First and foremost, there are the inherent challenges of interviewing people about their work, which can lead to distorted depictions rather than the more objective portraits required in social science research (Geertz 1973). For example, journalists may have underplayed their own lack of preparedness in covering North Korea, as well as their own practices deemed unethical or unprofessional. To retain their access to North Korea, they may have avoided mention of censorship or surveillance by the North Koreans. Most fundamentally, the actual views of the North Korean journalistic labor or government officials are not represented, as there was no way those in North Korea could be contacted and safely interviewed for academic research. To overcome this problem, I have also used published first-person accounts from journalists and non-reporters who have visited North Korea or who have expertise on the matter. This includes both those critical of and sympathetic to the regime. Further, I obtained an English-language copy of the rule book North Korea hands out to all foreign journalists, which contains relevant regulations and rules of conduct. I also used research reports and analyses from South Korea's Unification Ministry and global NGOs whenever possible to triangulate findings made during the interviews.

A Typology of North Korean Journalistic Labor

The North Korean system of allocating government minders/fixers to journalists reflects the conflicting desires of the Pyongyang regime: to control and surveil, and at the same time, to win favorable coverage and improve the country's profile in the global arena. Little is left to chance in these assignments, with factors like social rank, nationality, and temperament taken into account as the government matches minders to foreign journalists. Officially, all of these individuals working with foreigners are given the generic title of "guide" (*bojang seongwon* in Korean) by the North Korean government but I identify four types who exhibit significant differences along two axes: (1) their commitment to surveillance and control, and (2) their commitment to quality journalism. The former is a domestic value, referring to Pyongyang's primary goal of in pairing locals with journalists, which is to surveil and monitor journalists' activities and intervene if necessary. The latter, journalistic quality, is more global in nature, referring to commonly accepted definition which includes accuracy, context, and comprehensiveness (Anderson 2014). Those with a high commitment to surveillance and a low commitment to quality journalism are officials selected from the country's intelligence agency, whose primary role is to surveil. In contrast, the professionally-oriented local staffers with a sustained relationship with the foreign journalist or outlet who take pictures and obtain quotes for foreign correspondents have less interest in surveillance and more interest in producing quality content.

For the purpose of this article, I adopt four proprietary titles to match them to the four subcategories of local journalistic labor depending on their position on the two axes. I use the term "guide" (low journalistic quality, low surveillance) to refer to multipurpose locals focused on providing basic assistance, "minder" (low journalistic quality, high surveillance) to refer to the more control-oriented locals, "stringer" (high journalistic quality, high surveillance) to refer to locals who offer more professionalized journalistic support such as arranging interviews and fetching quotes, and "local reporter" (high journalistic quality, low surveillance) to refer to those with journalistic credentials. In North Korea, the same title (*bojang seongwon*) is used for the them, and in the field, there is much overlap across the different categories. However, the four categories show how the work of North Koreans has diversified in recent years with the increase of foreign correspondents. As we will see below, locals who work for prolonged periods of time with foreign journalists are developing a deeper understanding of Western journalistic norms, and they increasingly internalize these values as they take photos and write stories alongside foreigners. This, however, contributes to their precarious status within North Korean society.

The Minder: Surveillance and Control

North Korea has built one of the world's most extensive human surveillance networks, at the top of which is the State Security Ministry. This government organ reports directly to Kim Jong-un, and its 100,000 employees are granted extrajudicial powers like imprisonment and even execution (Unification Ministry 2018). This ministry is also tasked with monitoring foreign journalists. To do so, it employs workers I will call "minders," to emphasize their role in "minding" foreign journalists as opposed to providing linguistic or logistical assistance.

To make sense of the minder system, one must understand the rationale behind social control in North Korea. Like the former Soviet Union, China, Cuba, and other communist countries, North Korea resists the liberal media model, preferring to use it for propagandistic ends. Accordingly, North Korea has been critical of the news media in capitalist countries, alleging that its sensationalism leads to decadence and ignorance among the public. North Korea's media policies took an even more insular—and repressive—turn with the adoption of the Juche ideology in the early 1970s. Translated into "self-reliance," Juche emphasized a self-sustaining economy and the nationalistic leadership of Kim Il-sung. Unlike in the Soviet Union, where independent journalism continued despite political oppression, there was no meaningful dissident or independent press to speak of in

North Korea (Koh, Lee, and Hong 2012; Shafer and Freedman 2010). This insularity is still reflected in Pyongyang's handling of the foreign media, where the top goals are to control, monitor, and to censor. First-time visitors or those from major Western outlets are assigned to at least one State Security minder as part of their entourage. On assignments, a North Korean may introduce himself or herself as one of the generic "guides" working alongside other state-appointed individuals, when in fact he or she is part of the State Security. They may come across as rigid and strict individuals, especially in the beginning, as David Guttenfelder of the AP recalled:

> When I first arrived in North Korea, their assumption was that whenever I pointed my camera, they'd automatically assume it was a bad thing. So they were racking my brain to see what could be bad about [the picture of] people waiting for a bus. They were questioning my every move.

The minders also see foreign correspondents as sources of valuable intelligence, asking lots of questions to gather information from the well-traveled and well-informed reporters. They have a reputation of grilling journalists for seemingly minute and trivial details on their past experience and life back home, with reporters saying it was obvious they were gathering material for their nightly report to the government (J. Kim 2015). However, genuine curiosity is also part of the motivation. A British journalist who visited North Korea in 2017 recalled that many of the minders apparently did not have access to the Internet and were thus unable to see the final coverage of the foreign correspondents they worked with. He said he wondered whether the inquisitiveness and the frankness of his North Korean minder was genuine:

> One of the [minders] was my age, and I don't know if he was deliberately doing this, or whether it was due to naivete, but quite often we'd talk about negative things like the power shortages, how poor North Korean news is, lack of data.... When I showed him some stories I had written about North Korea, he was like, "This is really good, I would love it if you could share your story every day while you are here."

In cases where multiple North Koreans are assigned to work with foreign journalists, the division of labor among the locals becomes obvious, with the State Security minder keeping a distance or even lurking in the background. This may be because the minder is focusing his energy on surveillance, producing detailed records, including verbatim quotes, which will be submitted to the spy ministry at the end of the day. Often times, the minder pays just as much attention to the North Korean translators and guides working closely with the foreigners, as well as to any civilians with whom the journalist may come in contact. This has the effect of keeping North Korean translators on their toes, incentivizing them to control the foreign journalist in order to keep them both out of trouble.

The all-powerful nature of the State Security Ministry means its employees often have the final say in granting journalists access to non-landmarks, towns, and factories. More importantly, the minders have the ability to act aggressively when things go wrong, for instance if a foreign reporter sneaks out of the hotel or openly criticizes the regime while still in North Korea. This was the case for BBC reporter Rupert Wingfield-Hayes, who visited Pyongyang with two colleagues in 2016. Covering the visit of Western dignitaries, the reporter and his team clashed with the five North Korean guides assigned to them. The minders took issue with the use of adjectives like "grim-faced" and verbs like "barked" in Wingfield-Hayes' stories, so they interrogated his group for ten hours and demanded a written apology (Wingfield-Hayes 2016).

The nationality and ethnicity of journalists affects the way minders treat them. The North Korean regime is acutely aware of the different perspectives held by news outlets of different national origins, and treats them accordingly. For example, foreign correspondents from Russia and China, countries deemed friendlier to North Korea, are given minimal surveillance compared to Western ones. Those with permanent Pyongyang bureaus—AP, AFP and Kyodo—work primarily with local journalists and translators rather than with State Security minders. In contrast, South Korean journalists are kept on a shorter leash, as they speak the same language and can blend in more easily with the locals to dodge surveillance.

Treatment is also contingent on the political climate, with minders sometimes making unreasonably rigid demands for journalists, knowing too well the foreign correspondents could not afford to go back home empty-handed. Kim Hyun-hyung of MBC, who has logged more than 20 visits to North Korea since the 1990s, recalled some of the lowest moments in her interaction with the minders:

> Much depends on individual character. I've worked with those who have stopped us in every step, whisking the driver or car away and leaving our team stranded or unable to transmit footage via satellite when they were unhappy. One [minder] even asked [foreign] reporters to write a letter of apology addressed to the regime [when something went wrong]. This was so that he could leave a paper trail to absolve their own responsibility.

It is common for the minders to "ask" if certain elements—for example, the partial exposure of Kim Jong-un or Kim Il-sung's faces rather than showing their entire face in videos—can be avoided. Still, outright censorship of text content is becoming rare, as North Korea increasingly understands conventions of press in the Western world. More often, it is the foreign reporter who engages in self-censorship to filter out material considered outside of permissible coverage. A South Korean TV journalist once filmed an elderly North Korean citizen openly begging for change from her team, unaware that they were journalists on assignment, but said she did not use it. "Honestly, I was not planning on using that clip because I feared for the safety of the old man."

The Guide: Help and Negotiation

> Travel to local areas, in principle, shall be made [*sic*], attended by guides at all times. (*Regulations for the Activities by Foreign Journalists in the Territory of Democratic People's Republic of Korea*, Chapter 2, Article 19)

If minders are people who keep a distance and can lurk in the background, guides are the ones working directly alongside foreign correspondents at all times. At least one government official is assigned to monitor each journalist. This person can serve multiple roles—censor, translator, tour guide, and editorial helper. The "helper" component is not insignificant, as correspondents are in genuine need of guidance in an unfamiliar country. Most Western correspondents working in North Korea do not speak the Korean language, and English is rarely understood as Russian had been the preferred foreign language in North Korea until the 1980s. Even if foreign correspondents were granted the freedom to move freely in North Korea, they would be unlikely to get far as they attempted to navigate dilapidated roads and chronic energy shortages. Within Pyongyang, journalists at the

AP and other news outlets with physical bureaus are kept on a longer leash and travel unaccompanied within city parameters, but even these journalists said it would be difficult for them to talk to "regular" North Koreans, as civilians are suspicious of outsiders. In a police state, the assumption is that everyone is being surveilled.

The North Korean guides recruited to help foreign journalists are trusted elites within the country's political system. Those assigned to Western reporters are first screened for their language skills, with many holding degrees from the Pyongyang University of Foreign Languages, where the intense training allows many to speak with a British accent despite never having set foot outside North Korea. (The American accent—previously shunned for historical and political reasons—is becoming more popular, however). In addition to their linguistic fluency, an unblemished record of loyalty and ideological soundness is a job requirement for those working with foreigners. Nearly all guides are residents of Pyongyang, a relatively affluent city somewhat removed from the extreme poverty that afflicts the rest of the country. They are likely to have family members who are military officers or diplomats. Chad O'Carroll of NK News said many of the North Korean guides he met were young, aspirational men who are very smart and in possession of very good language skills, and who often work other day jobs, as bureaucrats for government agencies dealing with international affairs or global business. Few of them had received journalistic training:

> The Information Committee pulls people from normal jobs for the foreign press, so it's quite an interesting class of characters. I recognized some of them from my tourist days, from tour guides to professor to an interlocutor who works with an American NGO.

The guides typically herd their charges through a pre-determined itinerary including the Juche Tower, the Pyongyang Institute of Arts and the People's Library, Munsu Palace, the USS Pueblo, and the Pyongyang subway. Some even get to visit the mausoleum containing the caskets of Kim Il-sung and Kim Jong-il. There, foreign visitors will be pressured to respectfully bow to the deceased leaders like everyone else. While the usual propaganda landmarks do offer interesting tidbits, the tight scheduling often means the foreign correspondent has little time to pursue new story leads. Foreign journalists thus spend a lot of time negotiating with the guides for better access to less visited sites as well as more logistical support. Kim Hyun-kyung of MBC said that she tried hard to break from the tightly choreographed itinerary:

> North Korea leaves nothing to chance. Entering North Korea, we usually have a broad outline of an itinerary, but all the details have to be worked out on site via the fixers, so it's endless negotiations. Where do we go? Who do we talk to? After that they [fixers] have to get the approval of officials there, clean and prep the place. They work very hard to make sure everyone is prepared.

Foreign correspondents said their interactions with the North Korean guides—especially junior, low-ranking ones—were transactional in nature. As agents of a regime, they make it clear that North Korea wants to be compensated for providing access with positive (or at least not negative) coverage. Intense negotiations over the day's itinerary—with whom the journalist can meet and where he or she can visit—often become a daily ritual. Some guides expect gifts and even ask openly for cash, asking higher sums from TV journalists, as they are assumed to have deeper pockets compared to print reporters

(Ha 2006). None of the interviewed foreign correspondents openly admitted bribing North Koreans, but said they "heard" of other people who did so. Still, foreign correspondents in North Korea have been known to make their share of Faustian bargains. While such admissions are rarely published in the journalists' own accounts, *The Wall Street Journal*'s Evan Ramstad, who was a member of the 80-person press corps organized by the US State Department to cover a Pyongyang performance by the New York Philharmonic as part of a cultural exchange event, said that while the Pyongyang government imposed "draconian" controls on media access, the journalists themselves were hardly free from blame (Ramstad 2018):

> [North Korea] also benefits from the willingness of competitive news organizations to lower their reporting standards in return for access to a place that is exotic, scary, bizarre and even entertaining. Unfortunately, often enough, it has been able to count on journalists' shortcuts and short memories for some extra polishing of its reputation in the world.

Despite the transactional nature of the relationships, journalists often become friends with the guides after spending long hours on the road with them. David Guttenfelder, who visited North Korea over 40 times during his time as the chief photographer at the AP's Pyongyang bureau, said the guides were invaluable for providing insight into North Korea and its people:

> The guides are often seen as people who are there to invalidate the work we do .... Yes, they're never going to let me go to prison to take pictures, but I learned a lot of other things through them. I would ask, 'How did you meet your wife, when did you meet first? What's your relationship with your dad?' ... I came to really like and care about them.

The Stringer and the Local Journalist: Exploring New Journalistic Boundaries

> Foreign journalists and journalists of representative offices shall ensure objectivity and impartiality in their respective activities. (*Regulations for the Activities by Foreign Journalists in the Territory of Democratic People's Republic of Korea*, Chapter 3, Article 21)

Although journalists continue to use adjectives like "reclusive" and "hermit" in describing North Korea, the quantity as well as quality of journalistic access to North Korea has improved greatly since 2000. In the spirit of increased openness, a handful of Western outlets successfully established Pyongyang bureaus. As noted previously, the AP was the first to open a bureau, launching a TV subsidiary APTN in 2006 followed by full-fledged bureau in 2012. Kyodo News Agency opened a bureau in 2006, and in 2016 Agence France-Presse joined the press corps (Seo 2018). In 2018, South Korea's JTBC announced they also reached an agreement with North Korea to open a Pyongyang bureau, joining the aforementioned long-established outlets from Russia and China (Park 2018).

Opening a new bureau in Pyongyang meant foreign news outlets were inevitably paired with local, North Korean staffers doing journalistic labor. The identity and allegiance of these individuals—and whether the Western outlets compromised their journalistic integrity by hiring ones vetted by the North Korean government, became a subject of contention. When a draft of the AP's agreement with the North Korean counterpart KCNA was leaked in 2014, critics pointed out key journalistic principles the AP abandoned by agreeing that the North Korean side will "nominate" the full-time staffers who will work with the

AP, as well as agreeing that changes to North Korean journalistic content to be distributed via the AP will be made with "full consultation" between the North Koreans and the AP staff (Hudson 2012).

But Jean Lee, the AP's first bureau chief in Pyongyang, strongly denied such allegations. While the candidates had indeed been vetted by the North Korean government, she pointed out the AP had the final say in selection, with the North Koreans receiving extensive training in AP's journalistic practices afterwards. While both of the AP stringers—text and photo—had previous journalism experience working for North Korean and Japanese media, she spent time to introduce them to the AP's multidimensional fact-checking processes, with staffers from different continents working on putting together a big story:

> A major part of my job as a bureau chief was to show the values, impart the values. ... As a bureau chief I was teaching them how to be part of the larger news operation, to tap each person to play a role in the larger puzzle, pulling together information. For one story, I would seek information from the [US] State Department, while they [North Koreans] would pull information [from North Korean government].

The AP's North Korean stringer Pak Won-il, a veteran reporter with fluent English and multimedia skills, initially wrote short pieces based on government statements and press releases. As time went on, however, he came to play a bigger role in the agency's Pyongyang operation by stepping up and taking on more reporting duties when bureau chiefs were away in Seoul or Tokyo. Gradually, he and the photo stringer Kim Kwang Hyon began to pitch more stories to their AP colleagues from the US.

Although the American AP correspondents had to be accompanied by their North Korean colleagues wherever they went, they stressed the normalcy of their assignment there. For Lee, the longer, more regular stays allowed her to visit villages no foreigner had visited before and write about sensitive subjects such as poverty and economic reform. For Guttenfelder, the collegial bond he formed with the North Korean photographers and videographers was absolutely crucial. He said the conversations he had with the stringers and local journalists came to constitute the very core of his photographic reporting:

> The most interesting conversations I had were with the North Korean colleagues. My work was based on the relationship I had created over time with the minders and guides, and I felt that while it was certainly not perfect [in terms of journalistic independence] ... I felt strongly that I could defend the access, the version of the reality I was showing because it was the reality of those people I had observed over time, the insight I got from the country.

Photo and video is a particular case in point. Demand for visual images from North Korea has been particularly strong in the West as fears over North Korea's nuclear program arose. In working to meet these demands, foreign photographers and TV journalists said that their North Korean counterparts were becoming increasingly professional, going as far as to exhibit an appreciation of factually-driven, in-depth journalism that is also polished in style. Increasingly, they reported, the locals exhibited professional pride, internalizing some of the norms and values of the foreigners they work with. They became more competitive, even developing a competitive streak typical of the commercial press in their everyday reporting, as Kim Hyun-kyung recalled:

> When we worked with the North Korean TV crew in spring of 2018, I was very impressed with the professionalism of the North Korean cameramen and the producer. When we asked for equipment or software, they would reply promptly that of course they have it. They were

> so proud, boasting about the quality of their shots, and I could see how competitive they had become.

In 2019, the South Koreans have accumulated nearly two decades of working in North Korea. For the AP, this is the eighth year in Pyongyang. As time went on, foreign correspondents said their relations with the local guides/minder/fixers matured, with the locals taking on an`increasingly proactive role in reporting by, for instance, fighting for better access of the visiting foreign correspondents. The North Koreans and foreigners regularly bond over drinks and karaoke, a common way of socializing in North Korea.

If anything, some became too close, leading to self-censorship by foreign correspondents. Foreign correspondents who worked in Pyongyang conceded that these relationships with the locals sometimes complicated journalistic efforts to provide balanced and in-depth coverage.

Publishing even slightly critical stories becomes personally and morally fraught for the foreign reporters. In addition to getting themselves banned from the North, the choice to write such stories, for instance on human rights or rumors about Kim Jong-un, could come at great cost to their local colleagues. Self-censorship extended to outside North Korea, with journalists in Seoul, Tokyo or Washington worrying about the possible repercussions of their stories. A Seoul-based correspondent whose outlet also has a Pyongyang bureau said its journalists often thought twice about writing stories that could bring down the wrath of the regime:

> We once had a good scoop about Kim Jong-un, which we got from sources outside North Korea. But we couldn't tell the North Koreans that! ... Since so many people worked hard to set up our Pyongyang bureau, we became too cautious, reluctant to run the story which had a high likelihood of shutting down the bureau.

While both the foreign journalists and the North Korean minders face such ethical and epistemological challenges, the practical and physical challenges are not symmetrical: Whereas the foreign journalists can clash with the regime and move on to the next beat, open disagreement with the government is not an option for the North Koreans who may face severe punishment. Furthermore, their proximity to the foreigners renders them suspicious in the eyes of the regime. The locals become insider-outsiders, stuck between their countrymen and the foreign correspondents they work with. This became increasingly apparent to an American journalist, who noted a marked change in the North Koreans he worked with in recent years. Many of them not only understood, but secretly embraced Western journalistic standards on objectivity and transparency:

> I feel like they are stuck between [us Western journalists] and [the regime-controlled entity] they worked for, between a rock and a hard place, especially as their job was first to facilitate our work. In a country where the entire idea of what a journalist does is completely different, they [also] have to answer to authorities within the country. And I think ultimately there was a big difference between how much they [the North Koreans who worked as stringers] got it [Western journalism] and how much the Foreign Ministry minders got it.

The dynamics between the foreign correspondents and North Korean locals thus offers a unique opportunity to see the locals engaging in transformative work of "domesticating" foreign news. In discussing foreign correspondents, Gurevitch, Levy, and Roeh (1991) sought to connect the identity of journalists with the news they produce, which often results in "domestication," turning unfamiliar and foreign stories into something their audience back home can understand and digest. While working with foreign correspondents, the locals help "domesticate" what is already domestic to them. Furthermore, the locals inevitably become familiar with global news and perspectives, resulting in a secondary domestication process of their own. The nature of this journalistic partnership requires both sides to understand—and possibly internalize—each other's norms and values, or no meaningful work can be completed.

As scholars have noted, the insider-outsider relationship is a dialectical one that is constantly being informed by an individual's self-perception (Ergun and Erdemir 2010).

For all the talk about reform, change, and liminality of the local journalistic labor in a changed news environment, it is still unclear if the North Koreans genuinely feel the same way about their working relationships with the foreigners, and are embracing different journalistic values of the West. Furthermore, working with insiders does not necessarily facilitate good work, as such can lead to bias and cronyism (Adams 1999).

Conclusion: Journalists in a Changing North Korea

Academic studies of news media in Communist countries have increasingly shown that few—if any—of them have been able to maintain absolute control over news and information over a prolonged period of time. In particular, research shows that even in fiercely patrolled police states like East Germany or Soviet Union, the treatment of foreign media has been a sound indicator of the regime's willingness to open up to the outside world during years of political transition (Jakubowicz and Sükösd 2008).

Even in North Korea, what we have seen so far indicates that the system of surveillance and information control is becoming more porous. Although the size of the international press corps allowed into North Korea pales in comparison with other countries, the numbers have increased steadily. Since 2017, the regime let in a wide range of Western news organizations including the *New Yorker*, the *New York Times*, the BBC, the *Los Angeles Times*, the *Washington Post*, the *Financial Times*, Reuters, CNN and NPR. Unlike his reclusive father, Kim Jong-un has been seen thanking foreign journalists and suggesting unplanned photo sessions. This was shown again during a recent visit to meet with Vladimir Putin, when Kim gave his first-ever impromptu interview with a Russian TV station Rossiya 1 (Choe 2019).

And even with surveillance and other restrictions, the increased presence of the international media is resulting in coverage that is more diverse and colorful. Previously, researchers found the international media's coverage of North Korea—often with Washington, Seoul or Tokyo bylines—to be steeped in negativity (Choi 2010, 2018), based mostly on government officials and diplomats of Western officials (Kim and Jahng 2016). Thematically, stories leaned heavily on hard subjects like politics and diplomacy. One of the ironies of the strict restrictions Pyongyang imposes on foreign correspondents is that it has led journalists to be creative, for instance producing softer news about the everyday lives of North Koreans such as the marketplace economy and fashion trends.

The local guides, minders and stringers who work with foreign correspondents are at the forefront of these changes in North Korea. As we have seen, the relationship between the foreigners and the locals is dynamic one which has evolved over time. Although the locals are usually assigned by the North Korean government to keep tabs on foreigners while offering limited assistance with language and/or logistics, the locals increasingly—and inevitably—become useful as teachers of local politics and culture. As highly educated, elite individuals, some of the locals are assuming on even more proactive roles in journalism, taking pictures and pitching stories that can help the outside world understand North Korea. The locals' work would be impossible if they did not understand Western perspectives or grasp the idea of journalistic balance and objectivity which contrasts greatly with the norms of the news media in North Korea.

For this reason, any North Korean working with foreigners is constantly being surveilled, questioned, and even forced to receive periodic ideological instruction (Chon 2002). Such liminality is reflected in the joke in Pyongyang that people who work with foreigners have "one foot in prison and one foot outside." They may be rich from the material compensation from their work with foreigners who often bring in goods, but it is telling that although there have been over 30,000 defections by North Koreans from all walks of life, there is no known record of a single North Korean guide, minder or stringer defecting while on international assignments with foreigners including journalists (Ministry of Unification 2018).

Consequently, the North Koreans who engage in various journalistic labor as guides and stringers are at once insiders and outsiders, akin to the "Marginal Man" used by sociologist Robert Park to refer to a person who exists at the juncture of cultures and histories, belonging to two societies with conflicting allegiances. According to Park, the marginal man is a "cultural hybrid, a man living and sharing intimately in the cultural life and traditions of two distinct peoples ... a man on the margin of two cultures and two societies, which never completely interpenetrated and fused." (Park 1928, 892). He makes a good journalist, because he possesses divided selves and embodies the very conflict that led to his creation.

A major limitation of this article is that it was unable to get the North Koreans' side of the story, as all of the interviewees were foreigners. As a result, the journalists' own lack of preparedness—which led them to rely more on the North Korean locals—was rarely discussed directly. Also missing is the admission of the professional and ethical lapses. In her memoir, Suki Kim—an American who lived in Pyongyang for six months as a college instructor—criticized that the foreign correspondents from major international outlets were rarely prepared for the Pyongyang assignment, and were easily manipulated by the regime (S. Kim 2015).

What do these findings suggest about the future of journalism in North Korea? Some think liberalization and the embrace of more pluralistic values—including the relaxation of surveillance and the connection to the World Wide Web—may be in order (Seliger and Schmidt 2014). Many look to the trajectories of other Communist countries. In Cuba, Internet access has been granted to the general public since 2017, albeit with Chinese-style government firewall.

Although Cuba does not allow independent, private press, there has nevertheless been a growth of investigative journalism by bloggers and underground news outlets (Committee to Protect Journalists 2016). In China, North Korea's strongest ally and a role model, the regime lifted travel restrictions for foreign journalists (Zhang 2012). Others, however, warn against such optimism and point out the North Korean regime may adopt the technology-driven surveillance model to increase surveillance, stifle dissent and strengthen their grip on power, a route taken by other dictatorships around the world (Morozov 2011; Warf 2015).

Findings—and lessons—from North Korea could be useful if compared with other countries with tightly controlled political systems such as Azerbaijan and Eritrea, where few foreign correspondents have been able to report from. It would help to understand the different desires the authoritarian regimes have of the global media, as well as the locals who themselves embody different, often conflicting identities and values. Comparative, cross-cultural and cross-national research will be particularly valuable for not only global media scholars, but also for other social scientists looking into processes of democratization and liberalization, where changing media systems are part of the picture. If the optimists are right and relations between North Korea and the outside world improves, future researchers should strive to visit North Korea and interview the guides, minders, fixers and local journalists directly and conduct on-site fieldwork. Research could also investigate the education and training of North Korean journalists as well as the handlers and the social and political structures supporting journalism in North Korea.

Disclosure Statement

No potential conflict of interest was reported by the author.

Funding

This research was supported by the Provost's Research Award at Temple University.

ORCID

Soomin Seo http://orcid.org/0000-0001-8095-6958

References

Adams, Laura L. 1999. "The Mascot Researcher: Identity, Power and Knowledge and Fieldwork." *Journal of Contemporary Ethnography* 28 (4): 331–363.

Anderson, Peter J. 2014. "Defining and Measuring Quality News Journalism." In *The Future of Quality News Journalism*, edited by Peter J. Anderson, Michael Williams, and George Ogola, 7–34. New York: Routledge.

Bunce, Melanie. 2011. *The New Foreign Correspondent at Work: Local-National 'Stringers' and the Global News Coverage of Conflict in Darfur*. Oxford, UK: Reuters Institute for the Study of Journalism.

Choe, Sang-Hun. 2019. "Kim Jong-un Arrives in Russia for Meeting with Putin." *New York Times*, April 24.

Choi, Jinbong. 2010. "The Representation of North Korean National Image in National Newspapers in the United States." *Public Relations Review* 36 (4): 392–394.

Choi, Jinbong. 2018. "National Image of North Korea in South Korean News Media." *Journal of Public Affairs* 18 (4): e1710.

Chon, Shi-yong. 2002. "A Study on the Patterns of North Korea's Restrictive Policy toward Foreign Media." Unpublished master's thesis. Yonsei University, Seoul.

Committee to Protect Journalists. 2015. "10 Most Censored Countries." *Attacks on the Press*. https://cpj.org/2015/04/10-most-censored-countries.php.

Committee to Protect Journalists. 2016. "Connecting Cuba." https://cpj.org/reports/2016/09/connecting-cuba-castro-bloggers-laws-internet-websites-webzines-press-freedom.php#Bloggers.

Ergun, Ayca, and Aykan Erdemir. 2010. "Negotiating Insider and Outsider Identities in the Field: 'Insider' in a Foreign Land; 'Outsider' in One's Own Land." *Field Methods* 22 (1): 16–38.

Freedom House. 2017. "Freedom of the Press." https://freedomhouse.org/report/freedom-press/2017/cuba.

Geertz, Clifford. 1973. *The Interpretation of Cultures*. New York: Basic Books.

Gurevitch, Michael, R. Mark Levy, and Itzhak Roeh. 1991. "The Global Newsroom: Convergences and Diversities in the Globalization of Television News." In *Communications and Citizenship: Journalism and the Public Sphere in the New Media Age*, edited by Peter Dahlgren, and Colin Sparks, 159–216. New York: Routledge.

Ha, Taewon. 2006. "Money for Massage, Please: Rampant Corruption among North Korean Guides." [Anmabi jom daejusirayo]. *Dong-A Ilbo*, February 15. http://news.donga.com/List/3/00/20060215/8275491/1.

Hannerz, Ulf. 2004. *Foreign News: Exploring the World of Foreign Correspondents*. Chicago: University of Chicago Press.

Hudson, John. 2012. "How the AP Selected Its North Korea Reporter." *The Atlantic*, March 15. https://www.theatlantic.com/international/archive/2012/03/how-ap-selected-its-north-korea-reporter/328194/.

Jakubowicz, Karol, and Mikös Sükösd. 2008. *Finding the Right Place on the Map: Central and Eastern European Media*. Chicago, IL: University of Chicago Press.

Jerreat, Jessica. 2017. *Supervised Access*. Committee to Protect Journalists, April 10. https://cpj.org/2015/04/10-most-censored-countries.php.

Kim, Suki. 2008. "A Really Big Show." *Harpers*, December.

Kim, Jieun. 2015. "North Korean Tour Guides Express Interest in South Korea." [Bukhan gwangwang annaewon hankuk e gwansim nopwa]. *Radio free Asia*, October 20. https://www.rfa.org/korean/in_focus/ne-je-10202015095226.html.

Kim, Suki. 2015. *Without You, There Is No Us: Undercover among the Sons of North Korea's Elite*. New York: Broadway Books.

Kim, Yonghan, and Mi Rosie Jahng. 2016. "Who Frames Nuclear Testing? Understanding Frames and News Sources in the US and South Korean News Coverage of North Korean Nuclear Testing." *Journal of International Communication* 22 (1): 126–142.

Koh, Yuhwan, Jucheol Lee, and Min Hong. 2012. "North Korean News Media and Its Functions." [Bukhan eonron hyeonhwang gwa ginung e gwanhan yeongu]. Seoul, Korea: Korea Press Foundation.

Lerner, Mitchell. 2015. "Markets, Movies, and Media: The Growing Soft Power Threat to North Korea." *Journal of East Asian Affairs* 29 (1): 41–70.

Ministry of Unification. 2018. "Number of North Korean Defectors Entering South Korea." *Policy on North Korea Defectors*. Seoul, Korea: Ministry of Unification.

Morozov, Evegeny. 2011. *The Net Delusion: The Dark Side of Internet Freedom*. New York: Public Affairs.

Murrell, Colleen. 2015. *Foreign Correspondents and International News Gathering: The Role of Fixers*. New York: Routledge.

Palmer, Jerry. 2007. "Interpreting and Translation for Western Media in Iraq." In *Translating and Interpreting Conflict*, edited by Myriam Salama-Carr, 13–28. Amsterdam: Rodopi.

Palmer, Lindsay. 2018a. *Becoming the Story: War Correspondents Since 9/11*. Champaign, IL: University of Illinois Press.

Palmer, Lindsay. 2018b. "'Being the Bridge': News Fixers' Perspectives on Cultural Differences in Reporting the 'War on Terror'." *Journalism* 19 (3): 314–332.

Palmer, Jerry, and Victoria Fontan. 2007. "Our Ears and Our Eyes: Journalists and Fixers in Iraq." *Journalism* 8 (1): 5–24.

Park, Robert. 1928. "Human Migration and the Marginal Man." *American Journal of Sociology* 33 (6): 881–893.

Park, Sisoo. 2018. "Officials of South Korean Broadcaster JTBC to Visit North Korea to Discuss Pyongyang Bureau." *Korea Times*, July 7. http://www.koreatimes.co.kr/www/nation/2018/07/103_251872.html.

Paterson, Chris. 2011. *The International Television News Agencies: The World from London*. New York: Peter Lang.

Paterson, Chris, and Annabelle Sreberny. 2004. *International News in the 21st Century*. Ann Arbor, MI: University of Michigan Press.
Pedelty, Mark. 1995. *War Stories: The Culture of Foreign Correspondents*. New York: Routledge.
Ramstad, Evan. 2018. "The Dilemmas Facing Reporters Who Write About North Korea." *Columbia Journalism Review*, February 14. https://www.cjr.org/first_person/north-korea-olympics.php.
Sambrook, Richard. 2010. *Are Foreign Correspondents Redundant? The Changing Face of International News*. Oxford: Reuters Institute for the Study of Journalism, University of Oxford.
Seliger, Bernard, and Stefan Schmidt. 2014. "The Hermit Kingdom Goes Online ... Information Technology, Internet Use and Communication Policy in North Korea." *North Korean Review* 10 (1): 71–88.
Seo, Hyunjin. 2009. "International Media Coverage of North Korea: Study of Journalists and News Reports on the Six-Party Nuclear Talks." *Asian Journal of Communication* 19 (1): 1–17.
Seo, Soomin. 2016. "Marginal Majority at the Postcolonial News Agency: Foreign Journalistic Hires at the Associated Press." *Journalism Studies* 17 (1): 35–56.
Seo, Soomin. 2018. "Covering the Hermit Regime: A Comparison of North Korea Coverage at the Associated Press and NK News." *Journalism: Theory, Practice and Criticism* 19 (9/10): 1363–1379.
Shafer, Richard, and Eric Freedman. 2010. "An Overview of Contemporary Central Asian Mass Media Research." *Media Asia* 37 (2): 112–119.
Sweeney, John. 2013. *North Korea Undercover*. London: Bantam.
Unification Ministry. 2018. "State Security Ministry." [Gukgwa anjon bowi bu] North Korea Information Portal. http://nkinfo.unikorea.go.kr/nkp/term/viewNkKnwldgDicary.do?pageIndex=3&koreanChrctr=&dicaryId=15.
Warf, Barney. 2015. "The Hermit Kingdom in Cyberspace: Unveiling the North Korean Internet." *Information, Communication & Society* 18 (1): 109–120.
Wingfield-Hayes, Rupert. 2016. "Detained and Interrogated for 10 Hours in North Korea." BBC, May 20. http://www.bbc.com/news/magazine-36200530.
Wright, Kate. 2018. *Who's Reporting Africa Now?* New York: Peter Lang.
Zhang, Di. 2012. "How China-Based Foreign Reporters' Aggressiveness Changed: The Honeymoon Effect of the Chinese Government's Media Relation Strategies." *Asian Journal of Communication* 22 (5): 525–548.

Appendix 1. List of interviewees

1. David Guttenfelder, former chief photographer of AP's Pyongyang bureau, interviewed January 2019
2. Jean Lee, former Pyongyang bureau chief of AP, interviewed January 2019
3. Chad O'Carroll, NK News, interviewed January 2019
4. Kim Hyun-kyung, Munhwa Broadcasting Station reporter, interviewed January 2019
5. Jang Yong-hoon, Yonhap News Agency reporter, interviewed July 2017
6. Anonymous correspondent for a US newspaper, interviewed August 2017
7. Anonymous correspondent for a US newspaper, interviewed August 2017
8. Anonymous correspondent for a US broadcasting station, interviewed July 2017
9. Anonymous correspondent for a UK outlet, interviewed December 2018
10. Anonymous correspondent for a UK outlet, interviewed July 2018
11. Anonymous correspondent for a Japanese news agency, interviewed August 2017
12. Anonymous correspondent for Hankyoreh, interviewed December 2017
13. Anonymous correspondent for a South Korean TV station, interviewed July 2017
14. Anonymous correspondent for a South Korean news agency, interviewed August 2017
15. Anonymous defector journalist, interviewed August 2017
16. Anonymous defector journalist, interviewed August 2017
17. Consultant for international media seeking entry to North Korea, interviewed January 2019

Hierarchies of Editorial Power in International NGOs

Muganzi M. Isharaza

ABSTRACT

International non-governmental organisations (INGOs) have long been recognised as major contributors to the construction of Africa's image in the West through their impact stories, fundraising and advocacy campaigns. Yet although there has been considerable academic inquiry into these messages, research focusing on the editorial processes that produce them is still limited. Moreover, the few studies that exist tend to focus on the finished products as seen at the INGOs' Western headquarters. This is particularly curious, given that most of these stories originate from the INGOs' fields of operation in the Global South and are initially collected, written and edited by communication staff in national offices. This paper explores the various editorial power centres in the INGO story production process from the perspectives of global South staff. Based on data collected from five INGOs operating in East Africa, the paper draws three key conclusions; that INGO editorial processes are dynamic, contested and heterogeneous, field office staff possess underappreciated agency in the story editing process, and the extent to which INGOs can be said to speak on behalf of those they claim to help is in part linked to the amount of agency that communication staffers in the global South possess.

Introduction

International non-governmental organisations (INGOs) have long been recognised as major contributors to the construction of Africa's image in the West. Since the latter half of the twenty-first century when African countries gained independence from colonial rule, INGOs have gained traction in international politics, acting as conduits through which Western publics get to (partly) understand or perceive the African continent. Through their fundraising drives, impact stories and advocacy campaigns, INGOs share stories about beneficiary communities with their Western audiences that not only shape their perspectives on Africa, but also influence Western governments' policies towards the continent. These policies, ranging from reproductive health funding priorities to the ways in which humanitarian aid is delivered, both affect and are affected by INGOs' operations in Africa. Together, they constitute what Dogra has aptly dubbed the West's "stock of knowledge" of the rest of the world (Dogra 2012, 1) or in the case of Africa, what is known or understood about the continent by Western audiences.

However, these INGO stories and narratives are in themselves mediated constructs, put together and decided upon by editors and managers at various levels of the INGO hierarchy. A story about an INGO's work in Africa published in a newspaper in the UK will typically have been shaped by least two of four hierarchies within the organisation; the media liaisons department in the UK, the INGO's country director in the African country from which the story originates, the communications manager or officer (sometimes both) who decided that it was the story that best represented the issue being written about and the organisation's social worker that helped organise for the communications team to interact with the community or beneficiary about whom the story is written. At each of these levels, decisions have to be made about the structure, form and substance of the story. By the time the story is read by the final audience in London, significant amounts of editing have taken place at several levels of the story production process.

Curiously, although there has been considerable academic research around the published stories, their origin and their effects on the reading audience, INGO beneficiaries, the INGOs themselves and Western governments' policies, very little research has been done about the editorial processes that produce them. Even the few attempts at researching these processes (Dogra 2012; Franks 2013; Wright 2018) focus either on the finished products as seen at the INGO's Western headquarters or the interaction between them and the media. What is seldom acknowledged and even less researched, is the fact that these stories often originate from the INGOs' fields of operation in the Global South[1] and are initially collected, written and edited by communication staff in national offices.

This paper explores the various hierarchies of editorial power in the story production processes of INGOs from the perspectives of INGO staff based in the Global South. In the cases I present here, it is from them that many of the stories published and read in the West originate and as such, media and communications scholarship would benefit from understanding the practices, politics and processes that affect these primary sources of INGO news.

Scope and Methodology of Research

Although development and communication researchers have approached the subject of INGO narratives about their work in Africa from various perspectives, two significant gaps in research exist. First, many researchers on this subject tend to conceptualise INGOs as homogenous entities. Dogra (2012) for instance, conducts an exhaustive content analysis of press adverts and inserts by selected INGOs in the UK as well as audiences' reactions to them. What this study does not capture however, are the various voices, perspectives and opinions of the communications staff of these organisations' offices abroad, in places like Uganda, Kenya or Sudan who—although not expressly acknowledged in the press adverts—contribute to them by way of taking the photos, writing the stories or shooting the videos being used by their UK counterparts. In other words, it is assumed that the views expressed in the UK/Head offices of the INGO are necessarily those of the entire organisation. This may be true, but it may also be untrue. There has been some related research, such as Bunce, who explored the influence local journalists have on news production processes of international media, concluding that "the dominance of Western views and 'traditional' news values in the newsroom continues without major challenge" (Bunce 2010, 527). In a study about how Western journalists write about Africa, Nothias

(2018) comes to the nuanced conclusion that Africa isn't portrayed as negatively as many post-colonial scholars assert but also notes that although African sources make up half or more of the directly quoted voices, the manner in which they were quoted undermined their agency and authority as compared to the Western voices quoted. Both works, however, are focused primarily on story production processes of journalists and not those of INGOs. Kothari (2018) explores the ways in which NGOs in Tanzania use financial incentives and media training opportunities to influence media coverage of HIV/AIDS and the resultant ethical questions. Although this does link to INGOs' media and advocacy strategies, it does so only in relation to journalists and news organisations and not the internal story production processes of the INGOS. In the absence of empirical data on the issue, assertions about it are mere assumptions. This gap in knowledge is seen in major research on INGO communication (see Yanacopulos 2015; Enghel and Noske-Turner 2018a; Orgad 2015; Krause 2014).

Related to this absence of knowledge about the extent of homogenous thought within INGOs' various offices, is the amount of agency staff based in African offices have in the story production process. Here once again, most researchers conceptualise INGOs as being Western, on account of the location of their headquarters, major source of funding or history. In reality, INGOs' field offices are legally semi-autonomous entities, operating in varying contexts and hiring diverse groups of employees. It would therefore be important to understand the extent to which staff operating in countries like Uganda or Kenya for instance, get to influence the stories shared with audiences of the INGO in the UK. This is particularly important given that these staff tend to be nationals of the countries receiving INGO assistance recruited locally and therefore, their involvement (or lack thereof) can be linked to local participation.

It is widely accepted that stories INGOs tell about their work in Africa directly influence Western audiences' perceptions of the continent and existing research supports this view (Achebe 1977; Hawk 1992; Nothias 2016; Khor 2010; Keim 2012; French 2016; Bunce 2010; Dogra 2012). What remains under-researched, is the process through which these stories get to be produced and the political economy therein.

The Conceptualised vs. the Actualised: What Is Communicated?

The primary goals of INGO communication to Western audiences, are to inform or educate them about what the charities are doing, the progress or challenges being faced and the ways in which they (Western audiences) can contribute towards predetermined solutions or development objectives (Dogra 2012; Najam 1996; Madon 1999; Waisbord 2011; Stroup and Wong 2016). In some cases, this communication is also intended as an advocacy tool to influence Western governments' policies or public opinion (Enghel and Noske-Turner 2018b; Franks 2013; Bunce, Franks, and Paterson 2016). As a result, unlike regular journalistic stories which tend to be instigated by an occurrence, INGO stories tend to be conceptualised and produced to fit an already established narrative or funding objective and are intended to do more than just inform or entertain the audience.

This distinctive feature of INGO stories is an important one, seeing as they tend to be embedded in foreign/Africa news reports in the media (Wright 2017; Jacobs 2016; Badawi 2016). For instance, in an extensive research on the Ethiopian famine of 1984–1985, Franks (2013), concludes that international aid policy on the part of Western governments was quite often influenced by the media's portrayal of the disaster as well as public opinion. And because INGOs work closely with media, providing them access to places they (the media) would otherwise be unable to reach, the media was often too eager to accept INGO narratives without question. In the end, she argues that because "our awareness of nearly all disasters is defined by the media" (Franks 2013, 13) and the media is both uncritically trusting of INGOs and has a short attention span, Western audiences tend to receive an oversimplified, depoliticised narrative of development efforts.

Normative Narratives vs. Contextualised Stories

Enghel and Noske-Turner (2018a) note that for many INGOs, there is a constant tension between focusing their efforts on "doing good" or on "looking good". In communication terms, this boils down to choosing between these two; on the one hand, stories that help in creating, sustaining or regaining a particular public image (which ultimately results in successful fundraising) and on the other, using communication tools to improve programme outcomes, empower beneficiary communities to speak out on their own behalf (with no guarantees about how the organisation would be spoken of or portrayed by the empowered communities). Wilkins (2018) notes that "when the performance of development becomes more a matter of looking good (other than doing good), then the goal of doing well may be sacrificed". While balancing the two extremes may seem like the obvious thing to do, doing so isn't always straightforward, not least because the economic value of looking good far outweighs that of doing good. Negative media coverage of INGOs can have significant and long-lasting implications to the organisation concerned. A case in point is the explosive story that broke in February 2018 of senior Oxfam and Save the Children officials hiring prostitutes in Haiti and Central African Republic respectively. Within a week, Oxfam had lost 7094 individual donors, accounting for up to 3.5% of such benefactors (Elgot and Mcveigh 2018). Similarly, Save the Children has been forced to engage in damage control over its staff's alleged conduct in Central African Republic (Elgot and Mcveigh 2018). Several governments halted funding for the organisations and lawmakers demanded more accountability from them.

On the other hand, positive news coverage of Invisible Children's *Kony 2012* documentary raised over 30 million dollars, got several US politicians' and celebrities' backing and thrust the organisation into the limelight in mere days (Goodman and Preston 2012; Nothias 2013).

In both instances of positive and negative publicity for the INGOs, media attention over the ideals the organisations stand for took the centre stage as opposed to what was happening on the ground. It was this focus that led Mark Goldring, Oxfam's Chief Executive, to insist that the negative reactions to the news was unfair and disproportionate to the organisation's culpability (BBC 2018). He insisted that the overwhelming majority of the organisation's staff were honourable people and that the loss in revenue was going to hurt the poorest most.

In view of the above, this research is particularly concerned with three areas of inquiry. First, to identify and understand the various points along the story production process at which editorial decisions are made. Second, the extent of agency possessed by locally based INGO staff and the ways in which institutional authority and individual initiative interact to affect and influence INGO story narratives and perspectives. Lastly, I try to gauge the extent to which the agency of these INGO staff reflects the claim by most INGOs that they speak on behalf of and represent the interests of communities in Africa that are deemed poor, vulnerable and excluded.

Methodology

Because they have a presence in multiple countries across the globe, INGOs often operate in vastly contrasting political, economic and social contexts, all of which influence the way they deliver their programmes. Advocacy against human or child rights abuse for instance, is much more vigorous in countries like Uganda and Kenya that have relatively open media and civil society laws (Wiegratz 2016) than say Sudan or Rwanda whose governments maintain heavy control on both the media and civil society activities (Gready 2010; Christensen and Weinstein 2013). However, as will be seen from the organisational profiles of the selected INGOs, the bulk of their work and investments are focused on Africa, with the East African region in particular benefiting most from their programmes (financially).

For practical purposes as well as data consistency, the research looks at INGOs that have their headquarters or origins in the UK and operations in East Africa. The data is collected from five INGOs working in the East and Central African countries of Uganda, Kenya, Rwanda, Sudan, South Sudan, Tanzania and Burundi while interviews with staff members are from field work conducted in the country offices of 3 out of the 7 nations: Uganda, Kenya and Sudan.

Uganda was chosen due to its highly publicised humanitarian and development programmes. Over 3 million refugees have fled to the country from South Sudan, Rwanda and Democratic Republic of Congo over the past 30 years (Rutinwa 2017; Meyer 2006), attracting billions of dollars in aid and the presence of many INGOs. Similarly, the country's successful battle against HIV/AIDS in the early nineties was made possible by heavy donor funding both directly to government and through INGOs (Okware et al. 2001; Biesma et al. 2009). Kenya too has historically had significant aid investment due to crises such as the Ethiopian Famine of 1984–1985, the decades-old instability of neighbouring Somalia and the consequent creation of Africa's largest refugee settlement in Dadaab (Montclos and Kagwanja 2000). Also, all the five INGOs selected have their East Africa regional offices located in Nairobi, Kenya. As the study is aimed at getting a continental view of the organisations' structures and practices, a combination of data from country and regional offices provided both strategic and operational perspectives. Sudan was selected to cater for situations in which these INGOs collected, edited and produced stories almost entirely off-site or remotely.

Furthermore, although INGOs are often grouped into categories such as development, humanitarian or human rights organisations, the reality is that most engage in more than one—often all these activities (Demars 2005; Cooley and Ron 2002). Taking note of differences in the technical categorisations of these INGOs is therefore neither the goal nor within the scope of this research. Instead, because these organisations all communicate their work in Africa to audiences in the West, the research focuses on the similarities and differences in the story production processes and editorial hierarchies.

The five INGOs this research focuses on are Christian Aid, Save the Children, World Vision, Plan International and Action Aid. Brief descriptions of each INGO are included below:

World Vision: World Vision (WV) is a global Christian relief, development and advocacy organisation dedicated to working with children, families and communities to overcome poverty and injustice (World-Vision 2018). The organisation employs over 45,000 people working in "nearly 100 countries" and had a total budget of 2.4 billion dollars in 2014 (World Vision 2014b57). A significant portion of this—47.9% is spent on programmes in Africa (World Vision 2017).

Save the Children: Save the Children (StC) describes itself as the world's leading INGO for children, consisting of 29 member organisations that work in 120 countries to deliver change for vulnerable children (Save the Children 2015a). The organisation employs over 25,000 staff worldwide and in 2015, had a revenue of 2.1 billion dollars, 13% of which was spent on fundraising and marketing. They too spent the largest part of their budget—41%—on Africa programmes with 20% of that allocated to East Africa (Save the Children 2015b). The organisation has its headquarters based in London, UK.

Action Aid: Founded in 1972 to sponsor poor children and communities in Kenya and India, Action Aid (AA) is currently a federal INGO headquartered in South Africa and with operations in over 40 countries, mostly in Asia and Africa (Action-Aid 2018). The organisation's work focuses on developing local communities' capacity to exercise their civil and human rights as well as tackle root causes of poverty and address humanitarian needs. In 2016, over 37% of its £229 m annual budget was spent on programmes in Africa with East Africa taking the lion's share (38%) of it (Action-Aid 2017).

Christian Aid: Christian Fund (CA) was founded by a collection of Churches in the UK in 1945 to help refugees after the Second World War (ChristianAid 2018). Since then, it has grown into a network of British and Irish Churches supporting humanitarian and development programmes mainly in Africa and Asia. Almost 60% of its 2016 budget was spent on programmes in Africa, with East Africa taking up 16.4% of the budget (ChristianAid 2017).

Plan International: Founded in 1937, Plan International (PI) works in 76 countries to advance the rights of children and girl empowerment (Plan-International 2019). 36% of the organisation's 2017 global budget was spent on programmes in Africa as compared to 21% in Asia and 11% in Central and South America. 54.6% of the Africa budget was spent in East and Central Africa (Plan-International 2018).

Given the consistently high amounts of investment in East Africa by these organisations, a study of their story production processes in the region would provide important insight into their general operations. The primary data discussed in the article was collected in three main ways: extended interviews, non-participant observation and professional experience.

Interviews

A total of 25 individuals who worked with these organisations in Uganda and Kenya were interviewed. All but one were citizens of the countries in which they worked, with the lone exception being a Ugandan working at the regional office based in Kenya. Of the 25, 6 were communication managers, responsible for national office communication teams and reporting directly to the organisations' country directors. Ten of the interviewees were communications staff, tasked with the actual collection and initial writing of stories and reported to the communications managers. I also interviewed two country directors as well as four communications staff that were employed at the organisations'

East Africa regional offices. Three of the interviewees were former communications staff with these organisations and at the time of collecting the data, were either working as independent consultants or on short-term contracts with similar INGOs. They were included in the study to help provide the kind of context and insight current employees of the INGOs may be constrained to give as well as to test the variability of some of my observations. The interviews were semi-structured and were conducted in 30–60 min intervals, sometimes over several days.

Non-Participant Observation

These interviews were complemented with non-participant observation (Liu and Maitlis 2010). Over the data collection period of four months, I spent a total of six weeks embedded in two of the INGOs' communications offices. These were World Vision Uganda and Plan International Kenya. I was allowed on field trips with the organisations and observed first-hand, the collection of basic information from beneficiary communities that was to be used in generating stories. I also sat in departmental meetings in which tasks were allocated to individuals and assignments were discussed. Some of the observations I made during this period were discussed further with the participants to gain better understanding of their perspectives or state of mind at the time while in other instances, no discussions were held. In all instances, field notes were taken.

The decision to adopt a non-participant approach was made for two reasons. Logistically, it allowed the organisations to host me while avoiding the legal and labour implications of my involvement in their work. From a methodological perspective, it helped maintain some professional distance from the actions I was observing (Jerolmack and Khan 2014) and minimise "attitudinal fallacy" (Paterson 2016, 109).[2] This was particularly important for me given my previous work as an INGO communications officer with one of the organisations and the inherent danger of implicit bias.

Professional Experience

Between 2008 and 2013, I worked as a communications staff for two INGOs: World Vision and Compassion International. During this time, I was responsible for conceptualising, writing and editing impact stories of the organisations' programmes in Uganda, Democratic Republic of Congo and Mali. For a year, I was a member of World Vision's Regional Disaster Management Team (RDMT). The RDMT is a specially trained group of staff from all sectors of the organisation's workforce that is depended upon to deploy on site within 48 hours of a humanitarian emergency occurring anywhere on the continent. My training, as well as eventual deployment in three crises, not only uniquely equipped me with comprehensive understanding of INGO story production processes but was also a great resource when interviewing and observing staff from the selected organisations. It also helped to significantly reduce the observer effect during my non-participant observation.

Parallels with Journalism and the Newsroom

INGO Communications departments can—and often do—look strikingly similar to newsrooms. A typical example of this would be World Vision Uganda's communications department. It is a space measuring approximately six by three metres in size, with two sections. In the first, the larger of the two-three desks are laid out in an open office set up, each with a telephone, paper tray, and pencil holders. A metallic filing cabin in one corner contains copies of newspaper clippings, compact discs and even albums of events and stories produced, commissioned by or featuring the organisation's work in Uganda. One cabin also contains communication equipment; three Nikon D5000 cameras, a video camera, camcorder, two tripod stands, detachable microphones and long-range lenses. A log of which communications staff has taken what equipment is also stored there. Atop the cabin is a 20-inch flat-screen television that is switched from one local station to another depending on the time of day, news events taking place and the person in charge of the remote control. The open-office is where the two communication officers, one senior communication officer and—for two to four months each year—the communications intern work from, producing impact stories for the organisation, designing and putting together the national office's annual report and responding to any communications and public relations-related requests. One of the staff's explanation for this arrangement confirms the correlation between a newsroom and the office layout:

> As the communications team, we need to be constantly informed about what is going on and that is why we are the only ones in the office with a television ... we are like journalists, but instead of documenting news, we document World Vision. (Interview A3, 2018)

To the left of the office is a door that leads to a partitioned office. In there, just as in a newsroom with the editor, is the Communications Manager's office. In it, are more filing cabins a worktop and a computer. When the manager is in, the door to her office is almost always open and every now and then, conversations or instructions to her team are shouted out, without any of them leaving their desks.

The set at Plan International Kenya is a little different. The space is considerably smaller and there is no partition. Still, it would be hard not to draw parallels with a newsroom. The Manager and Communications Coordinator occupy the window area. The Communications Assistant and the intern occupy the space closest to the entrance. Here too, communication is largely done without leaving their desks.

Even beyond physical set up, INGO communications departments operate like newsrooms. 16 of the 19 communication staff I interviewed started out their careers as journalists. At these INGOs, the bulk of the work they are engaged in is heavily journalistic. A staffer at one of the INGOs describes the department as a support function, tasked with showing the impact of the organisation's work through stories, photographs and videos.

This description is similar to that of staff at Plan International, who described their role as follows:

> My role primarily is to sort of be the contact person between the fields and Plan Kenya in communications ... understanding what projects they are doing, being able to profile their work and being able to now showcase their work to the different national offices, locally and also internationally. (Interview A7, 2018)

The communications staff working with the other INGOs involved in the study also look at their work as essentially writing or producing journalistic stories about the organisation that essentially inform audiences of the work being done.

In their study of journalism and its roles in both political and everyday life, Hanitzsch and Vos (2018, 153) usefully identify 18 ways in which journalism addresses six political needs. These are; advocative-radical, developmental-educative, collaborative-facilitative, informational-instructive, analytical-deliberative and critical-monitorial.

When describing their work, INGO communication staff identified strongly with most of these roles. Fifteen of the eighteen roles listed by Hanitzsch and Vos were identified by communications staff in all the four INGOs identified as part and parcel of their work. For instance, owing to their work with children, StC staff constantly talked of advocacy as a key objective that is regularly achieved through collaborating with, educating and informing the communities in which they operate. As one staffer put it, "Our role is to use the power of storytelling to advocate for children's rights and to showcase the organisation's efforts towards doing this" (Interview A14, 2018). WV's and CA's Christian/evangelical roots mean that staff view their work not simply as development work, but also as missionary. In fact, the Christian Aid Kenya Country Director puts it this way:

> Christ's love is transformational. As an organisation, we take the view that our Christian faith compels us to advocate for the poor, just as Christ did, and fight for the rights of those who happen to occupy the lowest of our social ladder. Development work is ultimately a consultative process that is aimed at not just eradicating poverty, but achieving equality among all peoples. (John Kitui, Christian Aid)

Significantly, the only roles that the staff did not universally accept as a part of INGO communication were those within the critical-monitorial section. INGO communications staff go beyond journalism and into the realm of promotional industries of public relations, marketing and advocacy. Where journalists strive to maintain for independence (or appear to do so) as a critical aspect of their credibility (Wright 2016; Council of Europe 2015; Cooper 2009), INGO communications staff aim for the opposite-gaining credibility by being (or appearing to be) passionately involved boots on the ground.

> Our job is to make the world see the work our organisation is doing and how important it is. And the best way to do this is by not only understanding (the organisation) but also being a part of it. The more you embrace the organisation's mission, vision and values, the more likely you are to successfully tell its story. (Interview A12, 2018)

INGO Communication Hierarchy and Editorial Structure

Communications staff at national level view their role as primarily supporting the country office's branding and public relations needs as well as fulfilling demands from the Western offices for impact or visibility stories. Consequently, while the office set up and departmental structures resemble those of a news organisation (with the communication officers—like journalists—churning out stories while the manager provides the strategic leadership similar to that of an editor), these promotional objectives also mark significant structural differences.

Because their work is seen as a support function rather than an editorially independent enterprise, the success of an INGO communications department is based on how evocative its stories are of the organisation's work, values or advocacy objectives. In this regard, the department draws far more parallels to a public relations department of for-profit corporations than a newsroom. It is precisely because of this that most INGOs have their communications department situated within the Country Director's office, facilitating, rather than questioning power.

The typical editorial hierarchy of INGOs could easily be correlated to newspapers or agencies. In both contexts, those who source and put together the stories are at the bottom of the editorial chain. However, unlike the news agencies in which the editorial process is entirely managed by professional journalists, INGOs tend to put the communications department under non specialist leadership. In the case of WV for instance, the Communications Manager reports to the Country Director (CD). However, unlike all the other positions that report to the CD, the Communications Manager is not part of the Senior Leadership Team. This is the same for StC Uganda and PI.

What this ultimately means is that communications within these INGOs is overseen by leaders that are not primarily employed for their technical expertise in communication. Because most INGOs' organisational culture is focused on "doing good", Country Directors tend to be chosen based on experience in programme delivery, supply chain management and other such functions seen as core to the organisation's work (Jayawickrama 2011, 10). Consequently, while in practice many of them defer technical decisions to their communications team, Country Managers and their (non-technical) leadership team ultimately bear the responsibility of the kind of stories that come out of the organisation's national office. This can pose communications staff with huge operational challenges in which their professional advice is challenged or even overridden by non-technical staff based on non-technical reasons. An interviewee remembered getting really frustrated after a photo and story they took of children fetching water from a borehole was used in the organisation's report on their programmes on Water, Sanitation and Health (WASH).

> The problem wasn't the photo. It was the context (in which it was used). The text seemed to suggest that we had built the borehole as part of our programme. In fact, that particular borehole had been built by another organisation and my focus had been on the child, who was one of our sponsored children. I tried to explain to the programmes people that it was misleading, but they had the final say on the report! (Interview A13, 2018)

What such experiences reveal, is that INGOs are not institutions of homogenous thought in which all involved agree with each other about what to say and how to say it. Instead, competing interests and agendas influence what stories are successfully published. These agendas not only impact the kind of stories that make it through the production process, but also those that get into it in the first place. Partly as a result of the child's photo being used the way it was in the organisation's report, the said communication staff decided that in the future, they would simply focus on getting great photos rather than the context.

> At some point, I realised that sometimes in our work, context is not as important as the quality of the photo. That is why most INGOs have stockpile photos that they can go back to and use over and over again in different contexts. As a former journalist, I thought it was wrong. But ... we are communicators for the organisation, not journalists. So while for a journalist, the photo has a single story behind it, for us, a smiling child could mean he or she is well fed, or happy about going to school, or safe from harm. (Interview A13, 2018)

While this tendency to use generic images with more emphasis on quality than context is generally on the rise within visual communication industries (see Frosh 2001; Aiello et al.

2016), the transformation of the staff's way of thinking was also a result of this constant conflict in agendas and the fact that their perspective(s) where constantly overridden by other staff's views. This is consistent with the argument that INGOs are sites of "dynamic cooperation and conflict among (their) partners" (Demars 2005, 45). While the communications staff member and colleagues in the programmes department generally agreed with and worked towards the same organisational goals, their personal perspective about how to do this and agendas while doing it conflicted. The report in question and accompanying photo were constructed as a result of the merging of one perspective into another.

Sometimes, however, the influence goes the other way round. National office communication staff can, and in several instances do change the story direction. In one of the INGOs' Kenya office, communications staff once escorted a Media Team sent by one of the organisation's donor offices to the field. As part of their field visit, they met children within the beneficiary community, some of whom were naked and playing in a muddy pond. The Media Team, eager to highlight the plight of the community and scarcity of clean water sources, moved to take photos of the playing children. At this point, the national communications team interjected, insisting that such photos would not be consistent with their understanding of respecting the dignity of beneficiaries, a core communications value within most INGOs (Dogra 2012; Crewe and Harrison 2002).

> Photos of naked children are a no, no for me personally. Their argument was that this was the reality and in a sense, they were right. But there are different ways to show that reality without compromising on the beneficiary's dignity. For me personally, it was a big no. I know some people in the office who would have agreed with the Media Team, but I was in control and ultimately, it was me to make the call. And I said no. (Interview B15, 2018)

Eventually, the Media Team relented and took photographs of the children fully dressed and fetching water from the muddy pond as they would normally do. The communications staff indicated that they viewed this particular incident as an example of how local staff can exercise their agency in the story production process. This view was shared by several communications staff member from other INGOs, with some even saying they stopped media teams from publishing entire stories months after the team had visited beneficiary communities.

Another way that staff felt they had some form of agency over the story production process of stories collected by Western media teams was through the initial preparations. As hosts to the media teams, the locally based staff members get to organise for the team's visit beforehand. This includes selecting which community or individual beneficiary to visit and which projects will be the focus of the media team's field trip.

> They give us a general idea of what kind of story they want, but we are the ones who get to choose who they will interview to get that story. So if for instance I feel that there is a success story is better than the one they initially had in mind, I can influence them towards it. Sometimes their requirements are very specific and there's no room for this, but often times, they are very quick to defer choices of who to interview to us who are on the ground. (Interview A13, 2018)

There were, however, two important caveats to local staff agency in such situations. First, explaining the extent of their control, one communication staff member noted that although they have some control over what these teams from donor offices write about, film or photograph, they do not have that much control on how the stories are written. In other words, their ability to influence the story narrative in cases where a Western office sent a media team was limited. This was especially true because the general direction or theme of the story was predetermined by the visiting media team from the very start and formed part of the parameters given to local staff members to select potential subjects of the story. So while the local communications staff member was able to stop the media team from taking photos of naked children playing in dirty water, the story still focused on those children and the dirty water they were playing in.

Secondly, the ability of locally based staff members to stop or change the focus of the media team is largely dependent on the social relationships and trust they build with the senior leadership. In cases where the communications manager or officer had a strong collegial relationship with senior management, particularly the national director or programme director, they were more assertive and confident in exercising their editorial power or agency. This was usually attained through intentionally socialising at various functions in and outside office. This ultimately meant that those with greater social skills tended to gain more agency than those that didn't, regardless of whether or not their technical competencies were better.

However, there were cases in which the locally based communication staff members felt they did not have the full support or backing of management and therefore, were not as assertive.

> Here, staff employed in the programme implementation departments see themselves as the real engine of the organisation. We in communications are seen as just supporting them or as cameramen … They call us "paparazzi", as if we are not part of the organisation but just journalists who are called upon to take photos here and there, then leave the big people to do the real work! (Interview A12, 2018)

Being categorised as a support function, therefore, seems to be interpreted by both the communication teams and other staff members to imply that communications is not core to the organisation. As a result of this and the reporting structures that have them under non-technical staff, communications staff appear to lose a significant amount of agency over their work.

Interestingly, this is in direct contrast to what senior management would like to think or even what some communications managers believe the communications function to be. One communications manager, responding to this observation was very defensive of the organisation's structure:

> Communications is part of the programmes department, advocacy department, human resources and so on. At the end of the day, all those would like to showcase what we are doing and we are the ones that help do this. Most of the campaigns we are doing, Communications is at the heart of showcasing. Before, we were on the fringes, but we have raised our voices as a department and become involved in all branches of the organisation's work. (Interview, 2018)

Still, there was an acknowledgement that communications was at some point viewed as being on the organisation's "fringes" and change only came after a conscious, concerted effort on the part of the department.

Regional/West-based Communication Staff and Protocol in INGOs

As earlier seen, most INGOs, like corporate organisations, assign National/Country Directors (CDs) with the duties of Communicator-in-Chief. This was certainly the case in all the five organisations studied, with communication departments situated under the CDs. In practice, however, national communications staff have several matrix or dotted-line managers. Matrix/Dotted-line managers are people within the organisation other than the direct line managers, that have an indirect form of supervisory authority over the employee or his/her function (Sy, Beach, and D'Annunzio 2005) There are two main dotted-line management levels national office communications staff have; the regional communications staff (who in all five organisations were based at their East African Regional Offices in Nairobi) and the global communications managers who usually are based in the UK or in some cases, the United States. Sometimes, there is also a clash of expectations from communications staff working for a donor office (for example the UK office of the INGO) and communications staff working at the headquarters of the organisation (also based in the UK, but distinct from the UK national office). Both may make contradictory demands or requests to the national office in Uganda or Kenya. Each of these relationships impacts on the story production process in ways that are under-researched.

Regional communications staff are usually highly skilled professionals. In the case of the INGOs included in the research, all regional communication staff had over 7 years' experience as either communication managers or senior communications officers in national offices. Like their national office counterparts, they usually have some journalism experience and get employed at the regional offices as a result of stellar performance at the national level. They exist to provide technical support and mentorship to national office communications staff. Significantly, all the regional communications staff interviewed emphasised that they viewed their roles merely as providing support to national offices and not direct supervision. They described their roles as primarily advisers to national offices, with no power to commission story assignments.

This view, however, was not always shared by national office staff. The majority of the national office communications staff tended to view the regional office staff as not only their seniors but also their bosses. Indeed within three of the five organisations, regional communications directors had dotted-line management responsibilities to national communications managers. The job description for World Vision's Regional Communications Director, expects the incumbent to among other things, "guide and support national communications staff recruitments, orientations, trainings, annual performance agreements and reviews, and specific hiring/firing decisions when so required" as well as "Lead national communications managers for their success and development, as their matrix functional leader" (World Vision East Africa Job Advert 2017). Save the Children too, hires Regional Communications Directors that are charged with supervising "regional media and communications staff, ensuring they have the capacity and tools to deliver high quality products" as well as "provide necessary support to Country Offices on advocacy, media and communications during key global moments or surges of activity" (Save the Children Job Advert, 2016)

In practice, therefore, the "support" referred to by the regional staff member tends to translate into indirect, sometimes even direct oversight of national offices, meaning that yet again, the agency of national communications staff is subjected to further editorial oversight.

At the global level, communication directors and managers hired by the INGO headquarters provide overall leadership to the organisations' communication efforts, ensuring consistency in branding, advocacy and messaging among all national and regional offices. Like their regional counterparts, global office staff tend to view their jobs as providing support to the national offices, even though in reality, this "support" translates into oversight. In fact, their influence is so significant that it could determine which national office staff gets their story published, gains prominence within the organisation or not. A national office communications staffer put it this way:

> Those people at headquarters are tricky. I think they have their favourites. If they like you, they really market you and your work. Just one good story can get you promoted or assigned the big tasks. If they don't like you, you can write all the stories you want but all you will hear is "received". It is all politics. (Interview A7, 2018)

Conclusion

This article has explored the various editorial power centres in the INGO story production process. Observations of locally based communication staffers about the extent and limits of their agency and involvement in the editorial process were presented and discussed within and the impacts of these views analysed. From the data collected, three conclusions can be made about the hierarchies of editorial power in INGOs.

First, the INGO story production is a dynamic process in which competing agendas converge, conflict and emerge. This is an important conclusion, as it highlights the heterogeneous nature of INGOs, calling into question the tendency among researchers to conceptualise INGOs as homogenous entities. When conducting studies about INGO stories, therefore, media, communications and development researchers would do well to take into account the various, sometimes conflicting individual, departmental and national agendas that are constantly at play in the story production process and how these agendas interact to form the eventual narrative.

Secondly, this article demonstrates that South-based communication staff both impact and are impacted by this dynamic process. While individual INGOs may have a globally consistent missions, vision and core values, the interpretation of these at national office, departmental and individual level may differ. As a result, communication staff in one country may approach a story from a totally different perspective than those from another or different departments within the same national office may differ. As communication staff are compelled to adopt a view of their role that is different from what they initially thought it to be, their choice of stories, story angles and focus also changes. Similarly, in cases where their perspectives get adopted by the organisational leadership, the story choices, angles and focus change. For researchers, this conclusion would mean that individual staffers' perspectives are as important a consideration as the organisation's official perspective.

Lastly, this findings presented in this article suggest that communication staffers in the Global South gain and wield editorial agency over the story production process by building alliances and relationships with both the country office senior leadership and global communications leadership. Those who succeed at gaining the trust and confidence of senior leadership are more likely to have more editorial power than those who don't. Researchers therefore ought to strongly engage with and include INGO communication staffers' relationships with their superiors in any analysis of the organisation's editorial hierarchy. Also, the extent to which they succeed at gaining and utilising their agency has a direct impact on whether or not it can be said that INGOs' stories published in the West reflect the perspectives and realities of those in the Global South.

As this article has shown, South-based INGO communications staff are not passive, powerless actors in a West-driven development process. For better or worse, they are active participants in producing stories of INGOs' work in Africa and therefore hold a measure of responsibility for the ways in which the continent is portrayed to audiences in the West.

Notes

1. The term "Global South" has been used by academics over the past two decades as a replacement of terms such as "Third World", "Developing World", "Underdeveloped" or "Poor" countries, all of which are used to denote divisions along geographical, political or economic constructs (Dogra 2012) as well as to demean, orientalise, belittle and other non-European or non-American parts of the world and their products. The term Global South itself is problematic and arguments have been made against its usage (Comaroff and Comaroff 2015). While I acknowledge the seriousness of these discussions, alternative terms that can be used to mean the same thing are not without similar contestations. In this paper therefore, the term is used in reference to what are also known as "less-developed countries" in which INGOs implement their development programmes, with particular emphasis on East Africa. Likewise, while the term "West" is often used in reference to Europe and United States of America, this paper's use of the term is mostly focused on Europe generally and the United Kingdom in particular. For in-depth discussions of the terms and their meanings, see Comaroff and Comaroff (2015) and Dogra (2012, 20–22).
2. Paterson (2016, 109) applies the concept of Attitudinal fallacy to journalism studies as "the resilient but naïve faith that what (respondents) say about their work (in interviews with researchers or in surveys) explains a significant amount about the manufacturing of the stories" I extend the concept to this study of INGO story production processes.

Disclosure Statement

No potential conflict of interest was reported by the author.

ORCID

Muganzi M. Isharaza http://orcid.org/0000-0002-6478-4591

References

Achebe, C. 1977. "An Image of Africa." *The Massachusetts Review* 18: 782–794.
Action-aid 2017. "Annual Report 2016." Accessed January 10, 2018. http://www.actionaid.org/sites/files/actionaid/aai_ar_2016_final_low_res.pdf.
Action-aid. 2018. "About Us." Accessed January 10, 2018. http://www.actionaid.org/what-we-do.

Aiello, G., F. Bardelli, S. Chiarini, G. Flaim, S. Boas, E. Brussaard, J. Colombari, R. Estermann, O. Piquer, and J. Schelling. 2016. "Taking Stock: Can News Images Be Generic?" Accessed June 20, 2018. https://wiki.digitalmethods.net/Dmi/TakingStock.

Badawi, Z. 2016. "Media Perspectives: Television Reporting of Africa: 30 Years on." In *Africa's Media Image in the 21st Century*, edited by M. Bunce, S. Franks, and C. Paterson, 101–103. London: Routledge.

BBC 2018. "Attacks are out of Proportion, says Oxfam's Mark Goldring." Accessed November 11, 2018. https://www.bbc.co.uk/news/uk-politics-43095679.

Biesma, R. G., R. Brugha, A. Harmer, A. Walsh, N. Spicer, and G. Walt. 2009. "The Effects of Global Health Initiatives on Country Health Systems: A Review of the Evidence From HIV/AIDS Control." *Health Policy and Planning* 24: 239–252.

Bunce, M. J. T. R. T. 2010. "'This Place Used to be a White British Boys' Club': Reporting Dynamics and Cultural Clash at an International News Bureau in Nairobi." *The Round Table* 99 (410): 515–528.

Bunce, M., S. Franks, and C. Paterson. 2016. *Africa's Media Image in the 21st Century: From the "Heart of Darkness" to "Africa Rising"*. New York: Routledge.

Christensen, D., and J. M. Weinstein. 2013. "Defunding Dissent: Restrictions on aid to NGOs." *Journal of Democracy* 24: 77–91.

Christianaid. 2017. "Annual Report." Accessed January 10, 2018. https://www.christianaid.org.uk/sites/default/files/2018-05/christian-aid-annual-report-2016-2017-september-2017.pdf.

Christianaid 2018. "About Us." Accessed January 10, 2018. https://www.christianaid.org.uk/about-us/our-history.

Comaroff, J., and J. L. Comaroff. 2015. "Theory from the South: Or, how Euro-America is Evolving Toward Africa." *Anthropological Forum* 22 (2): 113–131. doi:10.1080/00664677.2012.694169.

Cooley, A., and J. Ron. 2002. "The NGO Scramble: Organizational Insecurity and the Political Economy of Transnational Action." *International Security* 27: 5–39.

Cooper, G. 2009. "When Lines Between NGO and News Organization Blur. *Harvard University*." *Nieman Journalism Lab* 21. Accessed June 20, 2018. *The Round Table* 99 (410): 515–528.

Council of Europe. 2015. *Journalism at Risk: Threates Challenges and Perspectives*. Brussels: Council of Europe.

Crewe, E., and E. Harrison. 2002. *Whose Development? An Ethnography of aid*. London: JSTOR.

Demars, W. E. 2005. *NGOS and Transnational Networks: Wild Cards in World Politics*. London: Pluto Press.

Dogra, N. 2012. *Representations of Global Poverty: Aid, Development and International NGOs*. London: IB Tauris.

Elgot, J., and K. Mcveigh. 2018. "Oxfam Loses 7,000 Donors Since Sexual Exploitation Scandal." *The Guardian*, February 20.

Enghel, F., and J. Noske-Turner. 2018a. *Communication in International Development: Doing Good Or Looking Good?* London: Routledge.

Enghel, F., and J. Noske-Turner. 2018b. *Introduction. Communication in International Development: Towards Theorizing Across Hybrid Practices. Communication in International Development*. New York: Routledge.

Franks, S. 2013. *Reporting Disasters: Famine, aid, Politics and the Media*. London: Hurst.

French, H. W. 2016. "Media Perspectives: How Does Africa Get Reported? A Letter of Concern to 60 min." In *Africa's Media Image in the 21st Century: From the "Heart of Darkness" to "Africa Rising"*, edited by M. Bunce, S. Franks, and C. Paterson, 38–39. London: Routledge.

Frosh, P. J. M. 2001. "Inside the Image Factory: Stock Photography and Cultural Production." *Culture & Society* 23: 625–646.

Goodman, D., and J. Preston. 2012. "How the Kony Video Went Viral." *The New York Times* 9.

Gready, P. 2010. "'You're Either with us or Against us': Civil Society and Policy Making in Post-Genocide Rwanda." *African Affairs* 109: 637–657.

Hanitzsch, T., and T. P. Vos. 2018. "Journalism Beyond Democracy: A New Look Into Journalistic Roles in Political and Everyday Life." *Journalism* 19: 146–164.

Hawk, B. 1992. "Introduction: Metaphors of African Coverage." In *Africa's Media Image*, edited by B. Hawk, 3–14. London: Praeger Publishers.

Jacobs, S. 2016. "Media Perspectives: New Media and African Engagements with the Global Public Sphere." In *Africa's Media Image in the 21st Century: From the "Heart of Darkness" to "Africa Rising"*, edited by M. Bunce, S. Franks, and C. Paterson, 190–192. London: Routledge.

Jayawickrama, S. S. 2011. "Developing Managers and Leaders: Experiences and Lessons from International NGOs." Hauser Center-Harvard Humanitarian Initiative Special Report.

Jerolmack, C., and S. Khan. 2014. "Talk is Cheap: Ethnography and the Attitudinal Fallacy." *Sociological Methods & Research* 43: 178–209.

Keim, C. A. 2012. *The Image of Africa*. Oxford: Oxford University Press.

Khor, L. 2010. "Whose Image of Whose Africa? Problems of Representation in Ryszard Kauscinski's 'The Shadow of the sun.'" In *Facts, Fiction and African Creative Imaginations*, edited by T. Falola and F. Ngom, 23–47. New York: Routledge.

Kothari, A. 2018. "NGOs and Health Reporting in Tanzania." *African Journalism Studies* 39 (2): 42–60.

Krause, M. 2014. *The Good Project: Humanitarian Relief NGOs and the Fragmentation of Reason*. Chicago: University of Chicago Press.

Liu, F., and S. Maitlis. 2010. "Nonparticipant Observation." *Encyclopedia of Case Study Research* 2: 610–612.

Madon, S. 1999. "International NGOs: Networking, Information Flows and Learning." *Journal of Strategic Information Systems* 8: 251–261.

Meyer, S. 2006. *The "Refugee Aid and Development" Approach in Uganda: Empowerment and Self-Reliance of Refugees in Practice*. Geneva: UNHCR.

Montclos, M.-A. P. D., and P. M. Kagwanja. 2000. "Refugee Camps or Cities? The Socio-Economic Dynamics of the Dadaab and Kakuma Camps in Northern Kenya." *Journal of Refugee Studies* 13: 205–222.

Najam, A. 1996. "NGO Accountability: A Conceptual Framework." *Development Policy Review* 14: 339–354.

Nothias, T. 2013. "'It's Struck a Chord we Have Never Managed to Strike': Frames, Perspectives and Remediation Strategies in the International News Coverage of Kony2012." *Ecquid Novi: African Journalism Studies* 34: 123–129.

Nothias, T. 2016. "Mediating the Distant Other for the Distant Audience: How do Western Correspondents in East and Southern Africa Perceive Their Audience?" In *Africa's Media Image in the 21st Century*, 91–100. Routledge.

Nothias, T. 2018. "How Western Journalists Actually Write About Africa: Re-assessing the Myth of Representations of Africa." *Journalism Studies* 19 (8): 1138–1159.

Okware, S., A. Opio, J. Musinguzi, and P. Waibale. 2001. "Fighting HIV/AIDS: is Success Possible?" *Bulletin of the World Health Organization* 79: 1113–1120.

Orgad, S. 2015. "Underline, Celebrate, Mitigate, Erase: Humanitarian NGOs' Strategies of Communicating Difference." In *Humanitarianism, Communications and Change*, edited by S. Cottle and G. Cooper, 117–132. New York: Peter Lang.

Paterson, C. 2016. "The Ethnography of Digital Journalism." In *The Routledge Companion to Digital Journalism Studies*, 108–116. London: Routledge.

Plan-international 2018. "Directors' Report and Combined Financial Statements." Accessed January 10, 2019. file:///C:/Users/cs10mmi/Downloads/annualreview-financialstatement-2018.pdf.

Plan-international. 2019. "About Us." Accessed January 10, 2019. https://plan-international.org/organisation.

Rutinwa, B. 2017. *The end of Asylum? The Changing Nature of Refugee Policies in Africa. International Refugee Law*. London: Routledge.

Save the Children, I. 2015a. "Annual Review 2015" Accessed June 20, 2018. https://www.savethechildren.org.uk/content/dam/global/reports/annual-report-2015.pdf.

Save the Children, I. 2015b. "Global Accountability Report 2015" Accessed June 20, 2018. https://www.savethechildren.de/fileadmin/user_upload/Downloads_Dokumente/Berichte_Studien/Archiv/global-accountability-report-2015.pdf.

Stroup, S. S., and W. H. Wong. 2016. "The Agency and Authority of International NGOs." *Perspectives on Politics* 14: 138–144.

Sy, T., L. Beach, and L. S. D'Annunzio. 2005. "Challenges and Strategies of Matrix Organizations." *Human Resource Planning* 28 (1): 39–48.
Waisbord, S. 2011. "Can NGOs Change the News?" *International Journal of Communication (19328036)* 5: 142–165.
Wiegratz, J. 2016. *Neoliberal Moral Economy: Capitalism, Socio-Cultural Change and Fraud in Uganda.* London: Pickering & Chatto Publishers.
Wilkins, K. G. 2018. *Communication About Development and the Challenge of Doing Well: Donor Branding in the West Bank. Communication in International Development.* London: Routledge.
World Vision, I. 2014. "Impact and Resilience: World Vision International Annual Review." Accessed June 20, 2018. https://accountablenow.org/wp-content/uploads/2017/01/2016-World-Vision-International-Accountability-Report.pdf.
World Vision, I. 2017. *2016 Annual Review.* London: World Vision.
World Vision 2018. "Our Work: How We Protect Children." Accessed February 20, 2018. http://www.worldvision.org.uk/our-work/child-protection.
Wright, K. 2016. "'These Grey Areas' How and why Freelance Work Blurs INGOs and News Organizations." *Journalism Studies* 17 (8): 989–1009.
Wright, K. 2017. *It was a "Simple", "Positive" Story of African Self-Help (Manufactured for a Kenyan NGO by Advertising Multinationals).* New York: Routledge.
Wright, K. 2018. *Who is Reporting Africa Now? Journalists, Non-Governmental Organisations and Multimedia.* Bern: Peter Lang.
Yanacopulos, H. 2015. *International NGO Engagement, Advocacy, Activism: The Faces and Spaces of Change.* Springer.

"Translating" Russia: News Fixers and Foreign Correspondents in an Era of Political Uncertainty

Lindsay Palmer

ABSTRACT

This article examines the work of news fixers based in Moscow, in hopes of better understanding the risks and challenges that they face as they "translate" Russia for foreign journalists. Drawing upon the theoretical concept of "cultural translation," which understands interpretive work as vastly exceeding the merely linguistic register, this study will analyze the complex—and sometimes, risky—processes through which Moscow-based news fixers render Russia intelligible to their foreign clients. Using qualitative, in-depth interviews with 16 news fixers, the study explores news fixers' perceptions of their clients' representations of Russia, as well as investigating the fixers' feelings about the risks they face in the field. The article finds that news fixers in Moscow sometimes find their clients' representations of Russia to be reductive and, in some cases, biased. In order to combat this problem, fixers say that they try to "translate" Russia for their clients, filling in the gaps in foreign journalists' knowledge about the culture. They ultimately say that while their work can subject them to political and financial risk, they do not believe themselves to be in the same level of physical danger as that faced by journalists working in conflict zones.

News "fixers" are the locally-based media workers who help foreign correspondents secure good interviews with sources, safely navigate challenging geographical terrain, and interpret the languages with which the correspondents are unfamiliar. Because news fixers act as mediators between foreign journalists on the one hand, and the societies these journalists scrutinize on the other hand, they can end up in a precarious position within their own communities. It is the very act of "translating" back and forth between different world views that often places fixers on dangerous footing. This article examines the work of news fixers based in Moscow, in hopes of better understanding the risks and challenges that they face as they "translate" Russia for foreign journalists. Drawing upon the theoretical concept of "cultural translation," (Italiano and Rössner 2012) which understands interpretive work as vastly exceeding the merely linguistic register, this study will analyze the complex—and sometimes, risky—processes through which Moscow-based news fixers render Russia intelligible to their foreign clients.

Though Moscow is not situated within an active warzone, and although the Russian media were liberalized after the fall of the Soviet Union, there is much evidence to suggest that Russia is a complicated place to work as a news employee in the twenty-first century. This is not simply because the Russian media have, over the past decade, seen "the marriage of liberalism and authoritarianism," where the state increasingly instrumentalizes and controls even the commercial media in a variety of different ways (Ramaprasad et al. 2018b, 78). Russia is also a complex place to be a journalist because of the high demand for the news product to be economically profitable (Nygren and Degtereva 2012; Nygren and Stigbrand 2014), the growing tendency for Russian media organizations to hire employees on temporary contracts (Pasti et al. 2018), and the ambivalent industrial attitudes towards ethics and professionalization that surfaced in the 1990s when young media outlets started springing up overnight (Roudakova 2017; Ramaprasad et al. 2018a).

This particular blend of commercialism and state control makes Moscow an important site for the study of domestic journalism in the region, let alone for the study of international journalism. But I focus here on the collaboration between local and international media workers because I am interested in the cultural collisions that can occur when professional journalists find themselves depending so heavily on their "translators"—not only to translate words, but also cultural contexts and histories. Fixers working in Moscow indicate that this broader cultural translation is a vital part of their labor. They need to engage in this complicated practice, partly so that they can help their clients get the story, and partly so that they can show their clients that Russia is a more layered and nuanced place than some of its critics might realize.

There is reasonable evidence to suggest that foreign correspondents hailing from the West have a long history of viewing Russia as "Other" to themselves—a history of which Russian authorities and journalists are all too aware. There is also a tendency in Western scholarship to understand Russian news organizations and Russian journalists more specifically as either "dupes" of the political system or as hard lining dissenters, with little care for the nuance of Russian journalists' political roles or for the way that their values and ethics have changed over time (Roudakova 2017).

This same attitude could easily be applied to Moscow-based news fixers, many of whom are journalists themselves. It might also be rather tempting to assume that Moscow-based news fixers' work is inevitably perilous, especially in the context of rising tensions between Russia and the West in recent years ("M16 Chief Warns Russia: Don't Underestimate the West" 2018; "Twelve Russians Charged with 2016 Elections Hack" 2018). Yet, my goal in this study is to understand news fixers' *own* perspectives on the challenges involved in collaborating with foreign correspondents in Russia—an approach that has rarely been taken in scholarly studies of news fixers. Before I analyze these perspectives, I first give some background on the concept of cultural translation and its relationship to the role that local fixers play in helping their clients to cover international news.

Local Journalists and Cultural Translation

The news fixer's role as cultural translator inspires some ambivalence on the part of foreign correspondents. This observation especially surfaces in the research conducted by Palmer (2007) and Palmer and Fontan (2007), where some of the correspondents interviewed on the topic of news fixers voiced the fear that their news fixers might try to "slant" what would otherwise be an "objective" news story, either by mistranslating something at the linguistic level, or in a broader sense. Colleen Murrell's 2015 book on news fixers also points to this concern, as does my own 2018 study of western journalists' discourse on news (Palmer 2018b). Though some foreign correspondents have very famously formed tight bonds with their news fixers in the field, there does seem to be at least an occasional tendency toward distrusting these local media workers (Palmer 2018a; Palmer 2019).

Yet, the very idea of distrust suggests that foreign correspondents tend to believe that their own understanding of a given story is the "true" and "neutral" understanding, while the fixer's is potentially biased. This is part of the reason why it is vital for journalism scholars to conduct research that focuses not only on foreign correspondents' perspectives, but also on news fixers' *own* perspectives. Examining news fixers' unique viewpoints on the act of cultural translation can be particularly revealing, since it can complicate the assumption that there is only one "right" or "wrong" version of every story.

Federico Italiano and Michael Rössner define cultural translation as "a concept including all those processes which … make [possible] communication between varied groups—be they linguistically, religiously, socially, generationally, or otherwise defined" (2012, 11). Following the growing tradition in translation scholarship of seeing translation as an inherently *active* process of *negotiation* (Venuti 1998; Bielsa and Bassnett 2009; Tymoczko 2010; Bassnett 2014), they argue that engaging in this task necessarily means making creative choices, rather than serving as a passive medium for someone else's message. In other words, these scholars follow post-structuralists and postcolonial theorists in asserting that there is no possibility of a direct substitute or a faithful reproduction of "original" meaning in the process of translation, because the entire idea of the "original," "correct" meaning is biased in favor of whichever "varied group" has the most power. Instead, cultural translation involves the perpetual negotiation and recreation of meaning, since the collision of cultural difference reveals meaning itself to be multiple, layered, and messy (2012).

Italiano and Rössner also suggest that cultural translation involves much more than linguistic exchange; to "make communication between varied groups" possible, the cultural translator must be able to mediate between multiple registers of meaning—meaning that has to do with different world views, different social mores, and different lived experiences. Because cultural translation exceeds the translation of specific words and instead gets at this need to comprehend (and respect) cultural difference, Italiano and Rössner suggest that cultural translation not only makes communication possible, but it also creates the possibility for "different traditions of discourse" (2012, 11) about "other" cultural communities.

Alongside the many tasks that news fixers complete, it could be argued that they also regularly engage in cultural translation, drawing upon their knowledge of multiple cultural discourses in order to make "different traditions of discourse possible" (Ibid.). But for news fixers working in Moscow, this is potentially a very difficult task. There is much research to suggest that, rather than communicating the objective "truth" about Russia, the journalistic discourse coming from the US, the UK, and, to some extent, Western Europe has tended to situate Russia as "Other" to Western liberal ideals, though the way of understanding this "Otherness" has shifted over time and has taken on different guises depending on the country where it originates (Krylova 2000; Malia 2009; Golubev 2013; Vartanova 2014; Roudakova 2017; Mitrofanov, Promyslov, and Prusskaya 2016; Laqueur 2018). The notion of "Eternal Russia" first as a wealthy (but sleeping) neighbor gave way to the image of Russia as a barren and backward empire, languishing under the control of a despotic czar (Vartanova 2014). This image then eventually gave way to an understanding of the

Soviet Union as a totalitarian, barbaric place that was the opposite of the "free" and "enlightened" West, while rather paradoxically still drawing upon the earlier representations of Russia as barren and backward (Malia 2009).

Yet, it is important to note—most especially, in order to avoid taking a simplistic and equally biased approach toward the West—that the Western narrative of Russian "Otherness" has been complicated at different points in history. Indeed, the historian Martin Malia argues that at different times, the West has shown an attitude of kinship and admiration toward Russia (2009). During the earlier years of the Soviet Union, for example, some Western intellectuals (and journalists) heavily identified with the nascent socialist experiment (Vartanova 2014). And during World War II, U.S. government officials saw the merits of maintaining strong diplomatic ties with the Soviet Union, an attitude that many journalists also displayed (Folkerts 2015). But even these more positive attitudes were hardly neutral in their orientation. And even in these particular moments, there was a second, more "Russophobic" narrative emerging (Vartanova 2014; Folkerts 2015), one that reached a fever pitch during the Cold War (Malia 2009). This phobia appeared within some U.S journalism during this time (Dorman and Hirsch 2006; Lane 2010), with highly respected correspondents like Harrison Salisbury "naturaliz[ing] the American-Soviet confrontation" in their reporting (Fainberg 2015, 153).

Though the fall of the Soviet Union might have temporarily assuaged this xenophobia (Tsygankov forthcoming 2019), the end of the Cold War has arguably not ended this tendency to situate Russia as the "Other" to Western ideals (Malia 2009; Roudakova 2017; Tsygankov forthcoming 2019). Instead, alongside the optimism about the liberalization of the former Soviet Union, the West has also revealed new fears about imperialism in the region as well as fears about dangerous new nationalisms (Malia 2009). The increasing consolidation of state power over the 2000s contributed to this unease. According to Andrei Tsygankov's study of US media coverage of Russia in the first decades of the twenty-first century, "leading U.S. newspapers and TV networks presented a view of Russia in which an authoritarian police state was systematically eliminating political opposition, harassing foreigners and minorities, and aggressively vilifying the United States. Those developments inside Russia that did not fit this binary narrative received little media coverage" (forthcoming 2019). Other scholars have identified a similar tendency within Anglophone news coverage of Russia (Le 2006; Macgilchrist 2011; Goss 2015), perhaps especially in the news coverage of the recent conflict in Ukraine (Ojala and Pantti 2017; Boyd-Barrett 2016, 2017).

Some scholars suggest that this "Othering" of Russia has not gone unnoticed by Russian officials. Indeed, Russian officials have invoked the problem of Russophobia in their own political rhetoric—rhetoric which can, at times, be just as driven by stereotypes and general distrust as the discourse found in the West (Feklyunina 2013; Golubev 2013). This is only one of many reasons why it is necessary to be aware of the discursive legacy that undergirds the vexed relationship between western journalists and Russian sources, especially when investigating the labor of the news fixers who mediate between these two entities.

Yet, it is also important to note that news fixers in Russia do not merely engage in cultural translation with journalists from the U.S. and the U.K. Though the fixers I interviewed all said that they primarily spoke English with the journalists who hired them, they still listed a variety of nations from which their clients traveled to Russia. These nations included the U.S., the U.K., and Canada, but they also included France, Germany, Spain,

Italy, China, South Korea, Singapore, and India, among others. In every case, news fixers must adapt their "translating" skills and find creative ways of building bridges between the foreign journalist on the one hand, and Russian officials and citizens on the other hand. Cultural translation not only exceeds linguistic registers, in other words, but it also potentially exceeds the binary oppositions that both *create* and *are created through* discourse.

Though cultural translation is a highly discursive process, translation scholars suggest that there is a staunchly material element to engaging in this task. Translators have long faced the suspicion, surveillance, and even the persecution of powerful people who expect them to act merely as passive mediums (Tessicini 2014, 4; Cronin 2003), or who do not want them to share information with cultural "outsiders" (Roland 1999; Amich 2013; Kwan and Wong 2014; Lan 2016). This history of suspicion and persecution is relevant to news fixers in the present moment, since they so often serve as translators.

Clearly, the task of cultural translation is complicated for news fixers. With these insights in mind, I pose the following research questions, in an effort to better understand the perspectives of news fixers working in Moscow:

(1) How do news fixers based in Moscow feel about foreign correspondents' representations of Russia in their news reports?
(2) How do news fixers in Moscow describe the process of culturally translating Russia for their foreign clients, as well as translating their foreign clients for local authorities and citizens?
(3) What unique risks do these news fixers say that they face in the process of doing their work?

Methods

In order to answer these research questions, I conducted in-depth, semi-structured interviews with 16 Moscow-based news fixers. The sample was selected purposively, although a few of my interviewees were also selected through "snowball sampling," when certain news fixers felt comfortable connecting me with their colleagues. It was necessary to take this purposive approach to building my sample because of the highly specialized nature of the work that news fixers do. Using the websites "World Fixer" and "HackPack," I located a number of people who were advertising their services as fixers, often alongside other media skills that they possessed.

Each of my interviewees had some kind of background working in the Russian or Eastern European media industries. A few of them not only worked with traditional journalists but also with documentary crews, many of whom were making films that were meant to air on television. One of my interviewees explained to me that especially European documentary crews tend to work for television networks and to create nonfiction stories that target a mass audience—much like broadcast journalists do. Because of this, I included my interviewees' stories about working with documentarians in my data set.

12 of my 16 interviewees were male and only 4 were female. While I noticed a number of female fixers advertising their services online, I was only able to speak with four women, while the rest of my sample was comprised of men. In order to diversify the sample as

much as possible, I did try to speak with people of different ages and social backgrounds. For example, one of my interviewees had started working in the Russian media industry when Russia was still a part of the Soviet Union. Others had broken into the business in the heady days of the 1990s, when countless new media organizations were springing up around the former Soviet bloc. Still others had only just recently graduated from university and begun their careers in the media at the time of our interview. They differed in terms of their levels of experience, their perspectives on journalism in and outside of Russia, and even their ethnic backgrounds. Though my interviewees were all based in Moscow, not all of them were "native" to Russia. Some came from other countries in the former Soviet bloc, one was British, and one had spent a large part of her childhood living in the United States.

These interviews were all conducted in person during my January 2017 research trip to Moscow. They were conducted in English, although one interviewee spoke with me through the use of a professional translator. Four of my interviewees asked to be anonymous in this study and one of them gave me an alias that I could use. The other 11 told me that they were comfortable with me using their names, but I ultimately opted to keep them all anonymous in order to avoid bringing any potential risks to the people who kindly shared their stories with me.

The interviews were typically about one hour in length, although sometimes they went longer than 60 min. In each case, I asked the interviewee a few predetermined questions, but I mostly allowed the conversation to flow organically from one topic to another, without attempting to control the order in which each topic was discussed. In taking this semi-structured approach, my goal was to encourage spontaneity and specificity in my interviewees' responses, allowing me to gather a much more complex data set than might otherwise have been possible (Weiss 1995; Hesse-Biber 2013).

It was my intention to approach this research from the "ground up," even at this early stage. I also took this flexible approach when I analyzed the completed transcripts of my interviews. Though I coded the data with an eye toward my three broad research questions, I made a point of allowing more specific themes and anecdotes to emerge on their own. This qualitative approach to analyzing interview data can be seen as an attempt to let the interviewees speak for themselves; this approach also arguably yields "thicker" and thus, richer insights from the stories that people tell about their lives (Weiss 1995).

Representing Russia: R1 Findings

My data shows that there was a sense among my interviewees that foreign journalists do not always represent Russia in a very nuanced fashion, although there are certainly some exceptions. For example, speaking specifically about foreign coverage of the conflict in Ukraine, one of my interviewees recounted an instance where a Dutch crew deeply impressed him by making sure to interview Russians as well as Ukrainians. This was important in his view, because without speaking to both sides, it might be very easy to decide that one group was a simplistic aggressor while the other was an equally simplistic victim. Another news fixer I interviewed noted that a number of freelance journalists had traveled to Ukraine because "they wanted to understand … [they] were like, 'in my country, they cover the whole conflict from one side, and I want to see the different side, and that is why I am here'."

Yet, in other cases, my interviewees described a much more reductive approach to representing Russia. For instance, a man who had worked as a news fixer during the 1990s told me about the stream of foreign journalists coming into Moscow after the fall of the Soviet Union. According to this fixer, many of these journalists were searching for dramatic stories about topics such as the Russian mafia—something that he personally found to be problematic, since it failed to account for the intricacies of what was happening in Russia at the time. On a similar note, another fixer told me about a much more recent instance in which a news team came into Moscow with only five days to spend on the story, demanding that their fixer find them a Russian "drug den." And one of my interviewees who works with news reporters but also with television documentarians recounted an occasion where the crew wanted to produce a television documentary called "Putin's Propaganda Machine."

In each of these cases, the news fixers found themselves face to face with a particular "tradition of discourse," (Italiano and Rössner 2012, 11) one that situated Russia as a backward place full of stock characters who could easily serve as the "villains" of the news narratives. Conversely, in the cases where they witnessed foreign correspondents trying to understand the nuance of the story and speak to multiple types of sources, the news fixers implied that they saw the potential for new discursive traditions, for new opportunities to translate the complexity of Russia to the foreign correspondents' audiences. While my interviewees did occasionally see this more productive type of discourse already informing the work of their clients, they also said that the more deeply entrenched traditions of simplifying and villainizing Russian society continued to impact many of their clients' story ideas.

Some of my interviewees seemed to think that the habit of seeking these types of stories could very well be a product of journalists' need to address a particular audience —and thus, to draw upon an angle that would already be recognizable to news viewers and readers. For example, a fixer who also works as a photographer told me that he was in a conversation with a news team covering the conflict in Ukraine, and the journalists very frankly told him, "We have an American angle. We have to keep it in mind that we have an American angle." According to this fixer, the foreign journalists arrived in the field with a keen sense of the "angle" that they needed to take, an insight that calls into question the notion that foreign correspondents trained in the US are always neutrally seeking the objective "truth."

The "American" angle was especially pressing for a news fixer who worked full time with the foreign bureau of a major newspaper based in the United States. She told me that she sometimes spent too much time in the office, because "you have to listen to Putin today … And you have to listen to Putin tomorrow … and you have to be in Moscow because Jim Carey's coming." For this particular fixer, who was hired under the title of "translator-fixer," it was vital that she help the correspondents to produce news content that would ostensibly be of interest to the US-based readers of this particular newspaper.

The imperative to cover stories that would be interesting to US audiences was arguably informed by the broader discursive traditions in the United States, traditions that required US journalists to construct familiar narratives about Russia. In a similar vein, other news fixers also noticed that their clients were seeking familiar images or faces to share with their audiences. One of my interviewees told me that the most common places that his clients wanted to photograph were St. Basil's Cathedral and the Kremlin Wall. Another fixer told me about some clients who were adamant that they had to get an interview with Mikhail Gorbachev:

> I tried to tell them, "Oh, he's very old. He very seldom meets the media now because he's very ill." ... They say, "We want Gorbachev. We want Gorbi. We want Gorbi. Please, please, please."

Eventually this particular fixer had to flat out tell his clients, "no," that it simply would not be possible to get an interview with "Gorbi."

In each of these circumstances, the news fixers found that their clients were actively seeking the elements of a news narrative that was already skewed in a very specific direction: a direction that would, first and foremost, appeal to news audiences who were enmeshed in certain traditions of discourse about Russia. From the fixers' perspectives, then, these journalists were not at all trying to neutrally report an objective truth, an assumption that underscores the anxieties of journalists, news editors, and scholars who worry that fixers might add a previously non-existent element of bias to the correspondent's story (Palmer 2007; Palmer and Fontan 2007). Instead, my interviewees suggested that some of their clients arrived in the field with their own very obvious biases, which were informed by certain traditions of discourse that had long circulated in those correspondents' regions of the world.

Interestingly, the news fixer whose clients wanted an interview with Gorbachev also told me that he understood where the journalists were coming from in this case:

> Well, it's natural because [Gorbachev is] very famous ... well, we [Russian media] usually do the same thing. So, yeah, we are looking for celebrities or someone well known.

Since this news fixer also worked for Russian broadcast television, he was able to understand the pragmatic side of foreign news reporting. It made sense to him that foreign journalists would seek a "well-known" face to put in their story. Indeed, this fixer suggested that Russian journalists also tended to seek certain angles on a news story, due to their own traditions of discourse.

Some of my other interviewees revealed a similar sense of pragmatism when they reflected on foreign journalists' representations of Russia. Speaking about the angles that foreign media might take on the conflict in the Ukraine, one fixer said:

> I think it is kind of normal. If you have the *New York Times* for democrats, liberals and so on ... I mean everyone knows that they cover it from their *New York Times'* angle. If you have, I don't know, Breitbart, they have another angle, and everyone is aware. I mean they are the same, basically, in that kind of way.

Yet, this fixer also told me that he finds these representations to be "lame," while another news fixer called these types of stories "BS." One interviewee told me that the tendency for Western journalists specifically to privilege the accounts of Russian officials who opposed the ruling party has led to a vicious cycle where members of the ruling party now are quite reluctant to speak with members of the Western media even when their opinions are wanted. In turn, this fixer suggested that this leads to more of the same biased coverage. And another news fixer said that if she were the one ultimately in charge of these stories, she would try to include much more depth.

This ambivalence on the part of Moscow-based news fixers points to their complicated role as cultural translators. Because they must act as mediators between local sources and foreign correspondents, news fixers often find themselves making compromises (Palmer 2019). What the majority of my interviewees all had in common was their assertion that they are ultimately *not* the ones who are in charge of the story, and that, at the end of the day, they feel that their job is to help their clients get the story they want. The next section of this article discusses the ambivalent work of "explain[ing] the context" of Russian culture and politics, while still helping the correspondent get the story. This ambivalent work is quintessentially the work of cultural translation—a process that, in its most ideal form, can potentially encourage new "traditions of discourse" (Italiano and Rössner 2012, 11).

Strategies for Mediating: R2 Findings

My interviewees described the labor of mediating between foreign correspondents and local sources in a variety of ways. The first and most obvious aspect of this work is the act of translating the Russian language for correspondents who are unfamiliar with it. Each of my interviewees asserted that they had, at some point, acted as a linguistic translator on behalf of their clients. They also noted that even if their clients did not speak English as a first language, English was typically the mediating language in which the fixers and the clients worked together. Though it would be easy to read this as an example of the hegemonic hold of the English language in the age of globalization (Crystal 2012; Pennycook 2017), it should be noted that there are other communities of fixers in Moscow who specialize in different languages—such as French—and they tend to work with journalists who are more comfortable operating in those languages. Either way, news fixers say that one of their most important tasks is translating, on the most basic linguistic level.

Yet, as Italiano and Rössner argue, cultural translation involves much more than helping people to communicate verbally. My interviewees also discussed the need to serve as a kind of interface between foreign correspondents and Russian news sources, even when the foreign correspondents could speak Russian. For instance, two fixers who often work together told me about a correspondent with whom they once collaborated, who was fluent in Russian, and thus, who felt comfortable launching very directly into her questions at the beginning of an interview. But according to the news fixers, this direct approach is not acceptable in Russian culture. "That was the problem because she just rushed into it," the fixers told me. "And, they [the sources] became really scared and they didn't want to [do the interview]. They just said, 'No, no, no, we won't be on your cameras'."

In this particular circumstance, the foreign correspondent could speak the local language, in a literal sense. Yet, she did not have the broader understanding of the social mores governing how strangers are expected to talk to each other and to seek information from each other in Russia. Because the journalist lacked this broader knowledge, she could not easily succeed in getting the interview material she needed for her story. Instead, she had to rely on her fixers, who could fill in the blanks in the correspondents' knowledge about the best ways of communicating with Russian news sources. By educating the correspondent on these social mores, the news fixers were engaging in the type of cultural mediation that Italiano and Rössner describe (2012).

Some of my interviewees also discussed an even deeper level of cultural translation, where they felt compelled to adequately convey the complexity of Russian culture and politics to the client. This was especially the case for those news fixers who found that their clients were drawing upon problematic discursive traditions to guide their entire conceptualization of Russian society. When these news fixers saw their foreign collaborators glossing over such complexity or drawing upon stereotypes to tell their stories about Russia, the fixers tended to assume that the clients were ignorant about the region. In turn, my interviewees appeared to believe that they could help "translate" Russia for their clients by providing them with some of the context that the news fixers felt the foreign correspondents were missing.

For one fixer I interviewed, this could be a matter of "showing" his clients that there are "incredibly beautiful and naturally, architecturally and historically diverse territories" in the region that makes up the former Soviet Union. For another, it could involve "explain[ing] everything" about a given conflict, or, at the very least, "send[ing] some links [for the client] to read." Both of these fixers described a type of cultural translation that was not merely about linguistic exchange, but that was also about helping foreign journalists learn more about the region they were trying to cover. In sharing this extra information with clients, these news fixers implied that they could contribute to "different traditions of discourse" than the impoverished traditions upon which they saw their clients relying (Italiano and Rössner 2012, 11).

However, some of my interviewees also seemed to be aware of the tendency for foreign correspondents to distrust cultural translators, and they made a distinction between giving the client more background information and telling the client what to think. For instance, the same news fixer who told me that he might send links to articles that his clients should read also asserted that "you cannot say [to your clients], 'those are the good guys and those are the bad guys.' It is not ethical." Rather than directing the client toward a particular angle on a story, this individual asserted that his job is merely to provide the nuance that his clients might be lacking. In this sense, the interviewee overtly disassociated himself from the image of the translator as a biased individual, while at the same time accentuating his own active role in helping his clients to understand the complexity of Russia. For this particular news fixer, engaging in an active process of cultural translation is not the same as "slanting" the objectively "true" news story.

But another news fixer I interviewed did appear to feel comfortable telling his clients how to interpret the political leanings of certain Russian officials:

> My duty as a fixer is to explain that this expert is quite a left party person, he's quite communist, or he's quite right wing. Or he's quite oppositional, or he's extremely oppositional.

According to this fixer, part of his "duty" was to help foreigners to better understand how to "read" Russian politicians, especially when conducting interviews with them: "Because the expert could be a liar. Could be." Interestingly, this news fixer told me that even if the correspondent happened to speak Russian, he or she would still need a fixer to help translate these deeper systems of meaning, pointing again to the broader implications of cultural translation.

Since, as translation theorists have argued, translation is a process of active *negotiation*, it is also important to note that Moscow-based news fixers must do more than make

Russian society legible to foreign correspondents. Alongside that important task, fixers also have to make foreign correspondents more legible to the people who live in Russia. This task is necessary almost from the very beginning, when the foreign journalist wants to contact a local person to set up an interview. According to one Moscow-based news fixer,

> you can't call a Russian expert and say, 'Hi, I'm a journalist from Denmark, and I'd like to have an interview with you, in a couple of days, in Moscow.' Such an attempt would likely fail, because of the tension. The international, political tension we have between the West and Russia.

Because of this tension, my interviewee said that the journalist from Denmark

> needs to have a fixer, for example, me, who can call some politician and say. … My friend from Denmark need to have an interview. Needs to have an interview with you. Could you? That's it, just one call.

In other words, foreign journalists working in Russia—and especially those hailing from Western nations—seem to benefit from the mediating role that news fixers can play. The fixer is the person who can present the journalist in a way that makes him or her seem less like a threat and more like a "friend of a friend." This type of cultural translation makes the foreign correspondent more intelligible, and ultimately, less threatening, to potential news sources.

The fixer can also represent the journalist's story in a way that will be less threatening to local authorities. This is why, as one fixer told me, "on an intellectual level, I have to understand what they are doing, you know, and how to interpret it. How to present the project inside of Russia in a way to have less shock angles." Another interviewee told me that with one American client, he felt it was best to keep the news team as "out of the scene" as possible, because the content of their story would be controversial to people in Russia. So this fixer decided to speak to the source himself, and his clients chose to trust his translation of what that source said. In yet another situation, the client was stopped by the police for shooting video without a proper permit; the client immediately handed the situation over to the fixer, who eventually provided an explanation that convinced the officer to give permission for them to shoot.

In each of these cases, the news fixers had to work on multiple registers to make communication "between varied groups" possible (Italiano and Rössner 2012, 11). In some circumstances, the news fixers worked to render Russia intelligible to their clients, who the fixers read as lacking the necessary background information on the complexity of Russian culture and society. In other instances, the news fixers had to speak on their clients' behalf, portraying the foreign journalists in a way that would open more doors and help them get the story. My interviewees ultimately suggested that the complex work of cultural translation was not easy. They said that at times, this work could even put them at risk, although they were cautious about asserting themselves to be in any directly physical danger.

Risks of Mediating: R3 Findings

Despite the longstanding Western stereotype of Russia as a "perilous" place for journalists, only a couple of the people I interviewed overtly said that news fixers working in the region might potentially be injured or killed. These individuals were referring to fixers who work with journalists covering the conflict in Ukraine or in the North Caucasus. Some mentioned that at certain points in the past few years, it has been dangerous for Russian citizens to go into specific parts of Ukraine, and it has also been dangerous for Ukrainians to go into Crimea at certain moments. But even with these more active conflict zones nearby, many of my interviewees said that they did not typically feel as though they were in physical danger. For example, one news fixer said: "I don't think there are many scary places right now in Russia, not really." Another asserted that Moscow specifically is not the kind of place where a fixer would need to be provided with a flak jacket or health insurance. And another told me that she has never worried about her own safety, since she has never "had to travel somewhere which I wouldn't feel very safe about."

There are a few important things to note about these remarks. First, these interviews were conducted in January of 2017, before many of the most recent events that have contributed to a greater sense of tension between Russia and the Anglophone West ("M16 Chief Warns Russia: Don't Underestimate the West" 2018; "Twelve Russians Charged with 2016 Elections Hack" 2018). It could be possible that the dangers of working with especially Western journalists has increased since the time that these interviews were conducted. It is also possible that my interviewees were downplaying the dangers of working in Moscow because they felt at risk in even naming those dangers.

But it is also possible that my interviewees did not want to play into the long tradition of Western discourse that represents Russia—especially, the Russian government—as inevitably violent, especially since this discourse assumes that Russian journalists must either be hard line dissenters or dupes of the system (Roudakova 2017). In turn, it is vital to remember that Moscow-based news fixers do not only work with journalists from the UK or the US. They engage in cultural translation on a much broader scale, which means that their labor might not always even be that controversial to the powerful people in Moscow. By examining Moscow-based news fixers' own perspectives on the potential danger of their work, a number of complex possibilities emerge, possibilities that add more nuance to the knee-jerk assumption that it is always, inevitably perilous to be a journalist in Moscow.

Crucially, though, the interviewees did seem to make a distinction between physical danger and a subtler kind of political or social risk. Perhaps this is why some of them instead said that, if they didn't feel themselves to be in danger, this was because they intentionally avoided dangerous stories, or they worked to protect their identities. For example, one of the interviewees told me that when he works on politically sensitive topics, he uses a different name or asks his name to be kept out of the story altogether—not a difficult thing to achieve since foreign correspondents only rarely give official credit to their fixers anyway (Murrell 2015; Palmer 2019). Others suggested that they just don't do "those stories" because they have to keep living in Moscow after the stories run. And another person told me that he specifically avoids military assignments, "because of my family." Instead, he said that working with foreign (and in his case, especially "American") news crews is "maybe not wise, but not dangerous."

In most of the interviewees' stories, there was a marked sense of political and social pressure, a pressure that could potentially lead to trouble. For example, one person had received death threats from a criminal on whom he had helped to do a story, while another had been placed under surveillance by intelligence officers. Several of the news fixers conveyed a sense that if they chose to work on the "wrong" kind of story, or if they were found with a news crew in the wrong place at the wrong time, they might at the very least end up paying a fine or falling out of favor with the government offices that held a great deal of sway over their other jobs in the Russian media industries. Some of them voiced the concern that they could get called in for questioning by law enforcement or intelligence officials, while others told of more minor issues where they got arrested because their clients did not have the correct permit to shoot video in a specific area.

One thing that emerged in this discussion was the sense that news fixers working in Russia can sometimes get into a bad situation directly because of their foreign clients. For instance, one individual told of a time when he was briefly detained because his clients from BBC Sport were shooting video in Red Square without permission. The authorities made the fixer, who was also shooting video, delete his footage. Another interviewee told me that it is important for fixers to choose their clients very carefully because if these journalists upset the authorities or the people in the field, "maybe [the authorities will] just send you to local security services. And say [the security officer] is kind of a crappy person." Along similar lines, one individual told me very frankly:

> The risk is that you're going to get in trouble for negotiating something that was not supposed to happen. Say they [the journalists] are getting to some military facility, let's say. … So you could potentially get in trouble and then get a call from the Secret Service.

In each of these cases, the interviewee invokes the risk of displeasing local authorities, displeasure that comes as a result of the fixer working with foreigners who might be pushing the limits of what local laws and customs allow. As the last interviewee intimated, the fixer's job as cultural translator is to negotiate for the foreign journalist; yet, it is possible to "negotiate something that was not supposed to happen." Thus, the labor of cultural mediation does indeed seem to hold certain risks for news fixers working in Moscow, even if those risks are not quite as direct as the risks they might face in a war zone. The potential for detainment and surveillance loom large in the lives of the people who try to build a bridge between Russian society and the foreign correspondents who represent that society to distant news audiences.

The fixers I interviewed suggested that they experience a low level of physical danger in their work—but they do still experience *risk*. This risk emerged in the interviewees' stories as a disturbing byproduct of the labor of cultural translation. In the process of "mak[ing] communication between varied groups" possible (Italiano and Rössner 2012, 11), fixers also risk the ire of powerful people who do not want this communication to happen at all. In this sense, the work of cultural translation is not only discursive; it also has a staunchly material element, since it can have a concrete impact on the social, financial, and emotional well-being of the people who act as translators.

Conclusion

My interviewees' testimonies highlight some important insights about the journalistic practice of covering Russia, and about the profession of international correspondence more generally. The first insight is related to the question of whether or not news fixers feel that foreign correspondents ever misrepresent Russia in their stories. As my findings showed, news fixers do indeed feel that some correspondents come to Moscow with simplistic and stereotypical story ideas that they want to pursue. Though my interviewees mostly took a pragmatic approach to this problem, asserting that they understood the time constraints on journalists and the target audiences that journalists and television documentarians must appease, the issue that they raised is troubling from the standpoint of critical journalism studies.

While scholars have increasingly moved away from arguing that journalism can and should be entirely objective, there is still a need for journalists to fairly and accurately represent the people and the places they cover in their pieces. If foreign correspondents are traveling to Russia with dramatic and sensationalizing stories already firmly in their minds, then this focus on fairness and accuracy is falling by the wayside. What is more, if Western journalists especially are simplistically representing Russia as "backward," "barren," or "dangerous," then they are arguably bolstering a "tradition of discourse" (Italiano and Rössner 2012, 11) that has long situated Russia as cultural "Other" to the ostensibly "free" and "enlightened" West.

The second insight that surfaces in these news fixers' accounts is the suggestion that the labor of foreign correspondence is actually far more collaborative than many international journalists tend to admit. Though correspondents in the Anglophone West have long been lauded as the authoritative eyewitnesses who go where their audiences cannot and who tell the stories that no one else can tell (Zelizer 2007), the very existence of news fixers subtly destabilizes that heroic narrative. The fact is that many foreign correspondents working in Russia are heavily dependent upon their news fixers—not only to translate the unfamiliar language, but also to translate cultural difference on a deeper level. Whether they always realize it or not, foreign correspondents are also quite dependent on their fixers' ability to "translate" the correspondents' own words and actions to the people who live in the region, a mediating capacity that often keeps the foreign journalist out of trouble. In other words, international journalists are not necessarily the self-sufficient mavericks they and their news organizations portray themselves to be; instead, they have to pay these cultural translators to help them function in the field.

The last insight that emerges in the interviewees' stories has to do with the question of risk. It is vital to note the distinction that news fixers make between physical danger—which they say they rarely face, working in Moscow—and a subtler type of political and social risk. Though Western discourse has a long history of portraying Russia as a "dangerous" and violent place, the news fixers I interviewed did not overwhelmingly argue this to be true. Yet, they simultaneously suggested that there are a number of social and political risks that they face in their work, pointing to the material ramifications of working as a cultural translator. Ultimately, this study has revealed the complexity of conducting media work in Moscow and in the broader region—complexity that needs more careful consideration from journalism scholars and from journalists themselves.

Disclosure Statement

No potential conflict of interest was reported by the author.

References

Amich, María Gómez. 2013. "The Vital Role of Conflict Interpreters." *Nawa Journal of Language and Communication* 7 (2): 15–28.

Bassnett, Susan. 2014. *Translation Studies*. 4th ed. New York: Routledge.

Bielsa, Esperança, and Susan Bassnett. 2009. *Translation in Global News*. New York and London: Routledge.

Boyd-Barrett, Oliver. 2016. *Western Mainstream Media and the Ukraine Crisis: A Study in Conflict Propaganda*. New York: Routledge.

Boyd-Barrett, Oliver. 2017. "Ukraine, Mainstream Media and Conflict Propaganda." *Journalism Studies* 18 (8): 1016–1034. https://doi.org/10.1080/1461670X.2015.1099461.

Cronin, Michael. 2003. *Translation and Globalization*. New York: Routledge.

Crystal, David. 2012. *English as a Global Language*. Cambridge: Cambridge University Press.

Dorman, William A., and Daniel Hirsch. 2006. "Chernobyl —The U.S. Media's Slant." *Media Development* 53 (4): 25–28.

Fainberg, Dina. 2015. "A Portrait of a Journalist as a Cold War Expert." *Journalism History* 41 (3): 153–164.

Feklyunina, Valentina. 2013. "Constructing Russophobia." In *Russia's Identity in International Relations: Images, Perceptions, Misperceptions*, edited by Ray Taras, 91–109. New York: Routledge.

Folkerts, Jean. 2015. "Report on the Russians: The Controversy Surrounding William Lindsay White's 1945 Account of Russia." *American Journalism* 32 (3): 307–328. https://doi.org/10.1080/08821127.2015.1064684.

Golubev, Aleksander V. 2013. "Russian and European Mutual Perceptions: Foreign Policy Stereotypes in Mutual Perspective." In *Russia's Identity in International Relations: Images, Perceptions, Misperceptions*, edited by Ray Taras, 53–72. New York: Routledge.

Goss, Brian Michael. 2015. "The World Is Not Enough." *Journalism Studies* 16 (2): 243–258. https://doi.org/10.1080/1461670X.2014.882083.

Hesse-Biber, Sharlene Nagy. 2013. *Feminist Research Practice: A Primer*. Thousand Oaks, CA: SAGE Publications.

Italiano, Federico, and Michael Rössner, eds. 2012. *Translatio/n: Narration, Media, and the Staging of Differences*. Bielefeld, Germany: Transcript.

Krylova, Anna. 2000. "The Tenacious Liberal Subject in Soviet Studies." *Kritika: Explorations in Russian and Eurasian History* 1 (1): 119–146. https://doi.org/10.1353/kri.2008.0092.

Kwan, Uganda Sze-pui, and Lawrence Wang-chi Wong. 2014. *Translation and Global Asia: Relocating Networks of Cultural Production*. Hong Kong: Chinese University Press.

Lan, Shi-Chi Mike. 2016. "'Crime' of Interpreting: Taiwanese Interpreters as War Criminals of World War II." In *New Insights in the History of Interpreting*, edited by Kayoko Takeda and Jesús Baigorri-Jalón, 193–223. Amsterdam/Philadelphia: John Benjamins Publishing Company.

Lane, Julie B. 2010. "From Cab Rides to the Cold War: Richard Rovere, the New Yorker, and Postwar Washington." *Journalism History* 36 (1): 2–12.

Laqueur, Walter. 2018. *Russia and Germany: Century of Conflict*. New York: Routledge.

Le, Élisabeth. 2006. "Collective Memories and Representations of National Identity in Editorials." Journalism Studies 7 (5): 708–728. https://doi.org/10.1080/14616700600890372.

Macgilchrist, Felicitas. 2011. *Journalism and the Political Discursive Tensions in News Coverage of Russia*. Amsterdam; Philadelphia: John Benjamins Co. https://search.library.wisc.edu/catalog/9911070753702121.

Malia, Martin E. 2009. *Russia Under Western Eyes: From the Bronze Horseman to the Lenin Mausoleum*. Cambridge, MA: Harvard University Press.

Mitrofanov, Andrey, Nikolay Promyslov, and Evgenia Prusskaya. 2016. "Russian Threat in the French Press at the End of the XVIIIth — Beginning of the XIXth Centuries." *Istoriya* 7 (1 (45)): 10–20. https://doi.org/10.18254/S0001369-4-1.

Murrell, Colleen. 2015. *Foreign Correspondents and International Newsgathering: The Role of Fixers*. New York: Routledge.

Nygren, Gunnar, and Elena Degtereva. 2012. "Russian and Swedish Journalists." *Journalism Practice* 6 (5/6): 732–743. https://doi.org/10.1080/17512786.2012.667277.

Nygren, Gunnar, Michal Glowacki, Jöran Hök, Ilya Kiria, Dariya Orlova, and Daria Taradai. 2018. "Journalism in the Crossfire: Media Coverage of the War in Ukraine in 2014." *Journalism Studies* 19 (7): 1059–1078. https://doi.org/10.1080/1461670X.2016.1251332.

Nygren, Gunnar, and Karin Stigbrand. 2014. "The Formation of a Professional Identity." *Journalism Studies* 15 (6): 841–858. https://doi.org/10.1080/1461670X.2013.834163.

Ojala, Markus, and Mervi Pantti. 2017. "Naturalizing the New Cold War: The Geopolitics of Framing the Ukrainian Conflict in Four European Newspapers." *Global Media & Communication* 13 (1): 41–56. https://doi.org/10.1177/1742766517694472.

Palmer, Jerry. 2007. "Interpreting and Translation for Western Media in Iraq." *Translating and Interpreting Conflict* 28: 13–28.

Palmer, Lindsay. 2018a. *Becoming the Story: War Correspondents Since 9/11*. Champaign, IL: University of Illinois Press.

Palmer, Lindsay. 2018b. "Lost in Translation." *Journalism Studies* 19 (9): 1331–1348. doi:10.1080/1461670X.2016.1271284.

Palmer, Lindsay. 2019. *The Fixers: Local News Workers and the Underground Labor of International Reporting*. Oxford: Oxford UP.

Palmer, Jerry, and Victoria Fontan. 2007. "'Our Ears and Our Eyes': Journalists and Fixers in Iraq." *Journalism: Theory, Practice & Criticism* 8 (1): 5–24. https://doi.org/10.1177/1464884907072419.

Pasti, Svetlana, Beatriz Becker, Nagamallika Gudipaty, Yu Xu, and Musawekosi Ndlovu. 2018. "Profession and Practice: Re-Imagining the Future of Journalism." In *Contemporary BRICS Journalism: Non-Western Media in Transition*, edited by Svetlana Pasti and Jyotika Ramaprasad, 130–156. New York: Routledge.

Pennycook, Alastair. 2017. *The Cultural Politics of English as an International Language*. Oxfordshire, UK: Taylor & Francis.

Ramaprasad, Jyotika, Deqiang Ji, Zhou Ruiming, Paulino Fernando, Pasti Svetlana, Gavra Dmitry, Herman Wasserman, and Musawenkosi Ndlovu. 2018b. "Ethics: Ideals and Realities." In *Contemporary BRICS Journalism: Non-Western Media in Transition*, edited by Svetlana Pasti and Jyotika Ramaprasad, 72–103. New York: Routledge.

Ramaprasad, Jyotika, Svetlana Pasti, Fernando Oliveira Paulino, Ruiming Zhou, and Musawenkosi Ndlovu. 2018a. "Professionalism: Continuities and Change." In *Contemporary BRICS Journalism: Non-Western Media in Transition*, edited by Svetlana Pasti and Jyotika Ramaprasad, 23–48. New York: Routledge.

Roland, Ruth. 1999. *Interpreters as Diplomats: A Diplomatic History of the Role of Interpreters in World Politics*. Ottawa, ON: University of Ottawa Press.

Roudakova, Natalia. 2017. *Losing Pravda: Ethics and The Press in Post-Truth Russia*. Cambridge: Cambridge University Press.

Tessicini, Dario. 2014. "Introduction: Translators, Interpreters, and Cultural Negotiation." In *Translators, Interpreters, and Cultural Negotiators: Mediating and Communicating Power From the Middle Ages to the Modern Era*, edited by Federico M. Federici and Dario Tessicini, 1–9. New York: Palgrave Macmillan.

Tsygankov, Andrei P. 2019. *The Dark Double: Us Media, Russia, and the Politics of Values*. Oxford: Oxford University Press, Incorporated.

Tymoczko, Maria, ed. 2010. *Translation, Resistance, Activism*. Amherst, MA: University of Massachusetts Press.

Vartanova, Elena. 2014. "Constructing Ourselves Through Constructing Others." *Journal of Multicultural Discourses* 9 (2): 98–103. https://doi.org/10.1080/17447143.2014.923434.

Venuti, Lawrence. 1998. *The Scandals of Translation: Towards and Ethics of Difference*. New York: Routledge.

Weiss, Robert. 1995. *Learning From Strangers: The Art and Method of Qualitative Interview Studies*. New York: The Free Press.

Zelizer, Barbie. 2007. "On "Having Been There": "Eyewitnessing" as a Journalistic key Word." *Critical Studies in Media Communication* 24 (5): 408–428.

Reporting Global While Being Local—Commentary for Special Issue of Journalism Studies

Stephen Jukes

ABSTRACT
In the year 2000, Kurt Schork, a freelance journalist working for Reuters, was killed while on assignment in Sierra Leone. His death, along with that of Associated Press cameraman Miguel Gil Moreno de Mora, sent shockwaves through the news industry. But since the turn of the century, the death of journalists has become an all too familiar occurrence and while the targeting of high-profile international correspondents such as Marie Colvin has rightly caused international outrage, the overwhelming majority of those killed have been local journalists and fixers whose work often goes unheralded. Since the deaths in 2000, a number of trusts and foundations have been set up to support local journalists and fixers, while academic scholarship has started to focus on their work. But this commentary argues that much more needs to be done to recognise the invaluable role they play in today's newsgathering environment.

Commentary—It is Time to Recognise the Work of Fixers

The ambush came out of the blue at Rogberi Junction where the jungle road branches off to Sierra Leone's diamond mines. The Reuters correspondent Kurt Schork died instantly as rebels sprayed the convoy of journalists and government soldiers with automatic weapons fire. Two of Kurt Schork's Reuters colleagues scrambled out of the bullet-riddled blue Mercedes he had been driving and fled into the bush, hiding for hours and surviving the deadly attack. They later returned to the scene to find that Miguel Gil Moreno de Mora, the Associated Press cameraman who had accompanied them on their reporting trip to the frontline, had also been killed. This was Sierra Leone's bloody civil war, the year was 2000 and the deaths sent shockwaves through the tight-knit band of journalists who had formed their bond covering the Balkans conflict of the previous decade.

Almost 20 years on, the death of two journalists in a far away country is no longer a shock. The world has sadly become all too accustomed to learning of such killings. Of course, journalists have always been targeted, not least in Lebanon in the 1980s and during the long-running Chechnya conflict. But it is hard to escape the conclusion that there has been a step change in the twenty-first century, with increasing numbers intimidated, kidnapped and deliberately killed—often with seeming impunity—across the globe. While the murder of prominent foreign correspondents such as the *Sunday*

Times' Marie Colvin, targeted in Homs in 2012, is quite rightly greeted with international outrage, the vulnerability of local journalists and the fixers who work alongside foreign correspondents all too often goes unnoticed.

What can be done to draw attention to their role and, more importantly, support the vital work they do in today's newsgathering?

Many foreign correspondents working in the field who, like Kurt Schork and Miguel Gil Moreno de Mora, have specialised in covering conflict and tense international news stories, know all too well how difficult it can be to report in an unfamiliar location without the support of fixers with their diverse skills of translating, driving, local knowledge and "fixing." The fact that fixers are the subject of this special edition of *Journalism Studies* in itself demonstrates that their essential role in today's newsgathering is now being recognised in the area of academic scholarship. But in the world of journalism practice, far more needs to be done. Professional support for fixers is still patchy, and despite support from journalists in the field, this is not always replicated by editors back at head office; fixers often don't have access to the safety training, safety equipment and insurance that international correspondents can rely on; sources of financial support have grown partly through funds set up in memory of murdered journalists such as Kurt Schork and Miguel Gil Moreno de Mora but they are poorly co-ordinated; the level of public awareness about the vulnerability of local journalists remains low; and the British government has even refused visas for fixers who were due to attend awards ceremonies in London to be honoured for their courage.

According to the Committee to Protect Journalists (CPJ), 1454 journalists and media workers have been killed since 1992. Some of these deaths have been of high-profile correspondents—most recently Daphne Caruana Galizia killed in Malta in 2017 and the Saudi Arabian journalist Jamal Khashoggi murdered in Istanbul in 2018; others in the recent past have included Daniel Pearl, Anna Politkovskaya, James Foley, Steven Sotloff, and Marie Colvin. Some were well known international foreign correspondents, others freelancers whose name became known because of their abduction and murder. But for every name that makes it into the public consciousness, there are scores that do not. As long ago as 1997 UNESCO passed a resolution condemning violence against journalists, stating that attacks also curtailed freedom of expression and the rights of society as a whole. If that call fell on deaf ears then, the same is true more than two decades later. Shortly after the killing of Khashoggi, the *Guardian* newspaper highlighted in an editorial column the growing and widespread threat to journalists worldwide (2018). UNESCO itself, in its 2017/18 report on global trends in media expression and development, condemned what it called a "culture of impunity" which emboldens would-be perpetrators of violence against journalists and has meant nine out of 10 such crimes remain unresolved (2018, 17, 142). UNESCO points out that although the killings of foreign correspondents tend to garner publicity, 92% of the 530 journalists killed between 2012 and 2016 were in fact local reporters (2018, 16).

The vulnerability of fixers rarely comes into public view, and usually only when they become a casualty of war. The BBC's Middle East Editor Jeremy Bowen has spoken out about the death of his fixer and driver Abed Takkoush who was killed by Israeli mortar fire in 2000. His colleague John Simpson was caught up in a "friendly fire" attack by US jets which killed 18 people in Iraq in 2003, including his translator Kamaran Abdurazaq Muhamed. But these have tended to be exceptions to the rule, short-lived stories in the deluge of today's 24-hour news cycle.

The fact that fixers are now part of the academic debate and are slowly becoming a greater focus of professional practice owes as much to the changing nature of news gathering as it does to international pressure from organisations such as UNESCO. Since the turn of the century, the international news landscape has changed dramatically, offering new opportunities to local journalists and fixers and making their role arguably more essential than ever. International news organisations have been forced to rely more heavily on them as cost cutting driven by the erosion of traditional business models has seen the network of foreign correspondents and bureaux shrink. As Sambrook has pointed out (2010), the trend had begun as early as in the 1980s, pre-dating the Internet, but the contraction has gathered pace rapidly in the wake of social media disruption. International news organisations can now draw on a combination of local journalists and user-generated content to cover foreign news, far cheaper than maintaining a network of overseas bureaux. The breaking news story often initially relies on those caught up in natural and man-made disasters and their ability to capture and transmit in virtual real-time still images and video from their mobile phones. But Western news organisations still fly in high-profile correspondents to cover those breaking news stories, as the recent bomb attacks on churches and luxury hotels in Sri Lanka showed. It is in such circumstances that local journalists and fixers become invaluable. And it would have been virtually impossible for Western news organisations to cover the long-running civil conflicts in Iraq and Syria without them.

The increasing focus on fixers in the academic world reflects this shift in the news environment and the changing dynamic of news practice. Until recently, many academic studies had tended to look on the role of local journalists and fixers predominantly from the perspective of the Western foreign correspondent and international newsgathering (Hamilton 2009; Knightley 2004; Williams 2011). There had been some notable exceptions, with Mark Pedelty, for example, highlighting as far back as 1995 how the work of local journalists can sometimes be undervalued (1995). But only in the past few years has there been more consistent documentation of the invaluable role fixers play through their local knowledge (Bunce 2011; Murrell 2014; Palmer 2007), the fact that they can be still be undervalued (Palmer 2018) and how vulnerable they can be simply by dint of working for an international news organisation (Witchel 2004).

Sources of financial support in the West for local journalists and fixers have also increased markedly since the turn of the century although many of the trusts and funds set up represent a journalist's life lost. If any good came of the senseless killing of Kurt Schork and Miguel Gil Moreno de Mora in Sierra Leone, it is that their colleagues, friends and families set up foundations in their names to support local journalists and specifically the work of fixers. Numerous other foundations and prizes have been established to provide a far greater support network than was the case two decades ago. The Rory Peck Trust dates back to 1995 and supports freelance journalists in honour of the cameraman Rory Peck who was killed in Moscow in 1993. It has focused on welfare and safety and allowed countless freelancers to go on hostile environment training courses they would not otherwise have been able to afford. In 2015, the Martin Adler prize, in honour of the Swedish cameraman and freelance journalist killed in Somalia in 2006, was awarded to the Iraqi fixer Hassan Ashwor and the next year to Turkish fixer Angel Istek Alcu. The John Schofield Trust pays tribute to the BBC journalist killed in Croatia in 1995; the Simon Cumbers Media Fund pays tribute to a BBC cameraman shot dead in Saudi Arabia in 2004. And most recently, the Marie Colvin Memorial Fund and Marie Colvin Journalists' Network have been set up, the latter aimed at supporting women journalists working in the Arab world. Some of the winners of awards have also paid the ultimate price for their reporting. In 2007, the Kurt Schork award was made posthumously to the Iraqi journalist Sahar al Haideri, gunned down in Mosul after receiving death threats for a series of campaigning stories highlighting the influence of religious extremists, especially in curtailing the rights of women.

However, this diverse array of sources that local journalists and fixers can draw on for support sometimes appears bewildering from the outside and is crying out for better co-ordination. At a professional level, there have been attempts to bring some of the big players in news together. The International News Safety Institute (INSI), set up in 2003, has built a network of competing news organisations which agree to share confidential information that could help journalists stay safe in the field. The ACOS Alliance of journalism organisations came into being in 2015 following the deaths of James Foley and Steven Sotloff in Iraq, aiming to promote the safety of freelance and local journalists worldwide. It can draw on some powerful media organisations, including Reuters, the Associated Press, the Dart Center for Journalism & Trauma and the London-based Frontline Club's freelance register. A section of the Alliance's safety principles is clearly aimed at editors and head offices and states (2015): "Editors and news organizations should show the same concern for the welfare of local journalists and freelancers that they do for staffers." The ACOS Alliance is also working on plans to improve access to insurance for fixers, drivers and translators. But it is hard to escape the conclusion that there is a confusing array of organisations seeking similar goals. At times, there are positive signs that they can come together, as in March 2018 when 17 NGOs joined forces to condemn the killing of two journalists on European soil, Slovak journalist Ján Kuciak and Maltese journalist Daphne Caruana Galizia.

But while there has been progress on this front, the same cannot be said of the British government which prevented the first two winners of the Kurt Schork fixer award from visiting the United Kingdom to receive their prize. There is a deep irony here in that Britain, alongside Canada, is hosting an international conference to promote media freedom in London in July 2019. Indeed, the Canadian Minister of Foreign Affairs, Chrystia Freeland, is a former foreign correspondent and Reuters journalist and has been a vocal defender of a free press (2019). In 2017, the Kurt Schork award went to an Iraqi fixer, Makeen Mustafa, who worked with Western correspondents in Erbil. In 2018, the Syrian news fixer Wael Resol won the prize, having been nominated three times by international journalists who hired him during assignments in Iraq. The judges cited his courage, dedication and flexibility, saying he was a huge benefit to any journalist working with him. But despite such glowing endorsements and to the outrage of the community of international journalists, the British government did not offer either a visa to attend their respective awards ceremonies in London. It is deeply concerning that one of the governments driving a global campaign to promote media freedom could not support local journalists risking their lives to provide coverage of the Middle East conflict and to help keep Western correspondents safe. In its letter of rejection to Wael Resol, the British government cast doubt on his motives for visiting London (despite an official invitation from the awards committee and the Thomson Reuters Foundation) and whether he would return to Iraq where he is based. This is no isolated case. Winners of other international journalism prizes have also been barred from attending ceremonies in the United Kingdom. It is a problem the Kurt Schork awards and similar organisations have resolved to tackle this year and indicative of the work that still needs to be done to achieve recognition for fixers. When the British government co-hosts this summer's conference to promote media freedom, it would do well to remember their invaluable contribution to international newsgathering.

Disclosure Statement

At the time of Kurt Schork's death, I was the Head of News at Reuters. Since 2002 I have been a trustee of the Kurt Schork Memorial Fund set up in his memory and mentioned in this article.

ORCID

Stephen Jukes http://orcid.org/0000-0002-4364-4362

References

Acos Alliance. 2015. "Principles: For News Organizations Making Assignments in Dangerous Places." https://www.acosalliance.org/the-principles.

Bunce, M. 2011. "The New Foreign Correspondent at Work: Local-National 'Stringers' and the Global News Coverage of Darfur." *Reuters Institute for the Study of Journalism*.

Government of Canada. 2019. "Canada to Co-Host Media Freedom Conference." https://www.canada.ca/en/global-affairs/news/2019/02/canada-to-co-host-media-freedom-conference.html.

Hamilton, J. M. 2009. *Journalism's Roving Eye: A History of American Foreign Reporting*. Baton Rouge: LSU Press.

Knightley, P. 2004. *The First Casualty: The War Correspondent as Hero and Myth-Maker from the Crimea to Iraq*. Baltimore, MD: JHU Press.

Murrell, C. 2014. *Foreign Correspondents and International Newsgathering: The Role of Fixers*. Abingdon: Routledge.

Palmer, J. 2007. "Interpreting and Translation for Western Media in Iraq." In *Translating and Interpreting Conflict*, 11–28. Amsterdam/New York: Brill Rodopi.

Palmer, L. 2018. "Lost in Translation: Journalistic Discourse on News 'Fixers'." *Journalism Studies* 19 (9): 1331–1348.

Pedelty, M. 1995. *War Stories: The Culture of Foreign Correspondents*. New York: Routledge.

Sambrook, R. 2010. *Are Foreign Correspondents Redundant?* Reuters Institute for the Study of Journalism, Department of Politics and International Relations, University of Oxford.

The Guardian. 2018. "Opinion: The Guardian View on the Killing of Journalists: the Truth in Peril." *The Guardian*, October 9. https://www.theguardian.com/commentisfree/2018/oct/09/the-guardian-view-on-the-killing-of-journalists-the-truth-in-peril.

UNESCO. 2018. "World Trends in Freedom of Expression and Media Development." https://unesdoc.unesco.org/ark:/48223/pf0000261065.

Williams, K. 2011. *International Journalism*. London: Sage.

Witchel, E. 2004. "The Fixers." *Committee to Protect Journalists*, October 13. https://cpj.org/reports/2004/10/fixers.php.

Empowerment Journalism - Commentary for Special Issue of Journalism Studies

Maya Lefkowich, Britney Dennison and Peter Klein

ABSTRACT

Growing literature critiques the "parachute reporting" model of journalism. Briefly visiting communities as an outsider, overlooking local and cultural nuances, and prioritizing "audiences back home" can make this reporting practice problematic. Instead, we developed an approach called "empowerment journalism." Learning from foreign correspondence, citizen journalism, media activism, and community-based research, we challenge reporting inequities by centering on principles of accountability, reciprocity, collaboration, and local ownership. We develop community partnerships and work with story "subjects" to co-create content that matters to their communities. This commentary offers lessons learned from using this approach with varying levels of success across three projects. (1) In *Strangers at Home*, we launched a digital storytelling and social media project with members of marginalized communities about rising nativism in Europe. (2) In *Through Somali Eyes*, we collaborated with Somali journalists who documented their daily routines of reporting and navigating danger with wearable cameras. (3) In *Turning Points*, we are co-creating visual stories with Indigenous storytellers in Yellowknife that confront stereotypes about alcohol. By reimagining the "newsroom" within – rather than distinct from – communities, we illustrate tensions and opportunities for journalists to transition from gatekeeper to collaborator and empower story "subjects" to produce and own their content.

Introduction

In many ways, the "parachute journalism" model remains unchallenged in professional reporting practice. Yet, this model raises serious concerns about unintended harms, as journalists overlook local knowledge and capacity for storytelling, produce content for consumption and benefit elsewhere, and sidestep accountability to the communities in which they report (Klein 2016; McCue 2016).

Differing from parachute journalism, "citizen journalism" and media activism offer useful lessons in diversifying the newsroom and reporting practices, unearthing tensions for trained journalists who must confront their roles as gatekeepers in conversations about giving up control (Hermida 2010; Lewis, Holton, and Coddington 2013; Lewis, Kaufhold, and Lasorsa 2010). "Engagement reporting" is a nascent method that builds on citizen engagement to address community needs at the onset of a project and integrates professional journalists in the broader reporting. "Reciprocal" and "community" and "participatory journalism" promote sharing benefits and sustain engagement with audiences (Lewis, Holton, and Coddington 2013). Whereas these models primarily focus on audiences, Indigenous, community and arts-based research approaches (photo elicitation, narrative inquiry, storywork, and digital storytelling) illustrate the importance of reciprocal collaboration with "subjects" (Archibald 2008; Cox et al. 2014; Leavy 2015; Low et al. 2012). Without explicit ties to journalism, however, interpreting and applying these participatory research techniques to reporting is difficult.

The UBC Global Reporting Centre developed a new approach, which builds on these and other approaches to innovative journalism. Drawing on lessons learned from foreign correspondence, citizen journalism, media activism, and community-based research, "empowerment journalism" centers on principles of accountability, reciprocity, collaboration, and local ownership. Central to our approach is our partnerships with local storytellers or "subjects," who co-create the content that they deem useful and applicable in their communities and maintain editorial agency and ownership.

We adapted and used the empowerment journalism approach in three projects with varying levels of success: (1) *Strangers at Home*, a digital storytelling and social media project about the rise of nativism in Europe, (2) *Through Somali Eyes*, a documentary about Somali journalists' experiences of reporting on and navigating danger in Mogadishu, and (3) *Turning Points*, a collaborative digital storytelling project to co-create counter narratives about alcohol abuse with Indigenous storytellers in Yellowknife, NWT, Canada. In this article, we reflect on lessons learned about collaboration, communication, and ownership within interdisciplinary and intercultural projects.

Strangers at Home

In 2013, as nativist trends were strengthening in Europe, we wanted to design a journalism project to document varying forms of xenophobia emerging throughout the continent. Our working title for the project was "History Repeated," harkening to Nazi-era nativism. But, when we started researching the project, several experts warned us that our framing was flawed: Nazi-era Germany was a poor historical analogy, and the forms of xenophobia and racism are so diverse, no outsider could capture the complexity. Rather than finding stories to fit our frame, we put out a call for ideas throughout Europe, renamed the project "Strangers at Home," and handed the storytelling power over to those living the experiences of nativism and racism.

In a traditional journalistic context, this was a bold and controversial move. Most mainstream news organizations prohibit story subjects from reviewing final drafts or having editorial control over a story. The Canadian Association of Journalists' (2011) Code of Conduct notes:

> We do not show our completed reports to sources – especially official sources – before they are published or broadcast, unless the practice is intended to verify facts. Doing so might invite prior restraint and challenge our independence as reporters (page 3).

Veering from the standard norms of journalistic conduct, we decided to self-publish this project once complete.

We assembled a committee to review proposals and commissioned 10 short documentaries. We provided production funding and editorial support, but, ensured that the storytellers were the ultimate authors and directors of their pieces. Some storytellers – like Greek photographer Myrto Papadopoulos and famed Serbian graphic novelist Aleksandar Zograf – worked independently, producing compelling pieces with high production value. Other storytellers who had little or no storytelling experience required significant intervention by our production team, in some cases editing the stories together and presenting them back for approval.

With the pitch, funding, and editorial feedback, this project followed a more traditional practice of commissioning projects for a journalistic series. The Centre maintained ownership of the material and pulled the stories together into a curated multimedia project. The storytellers did not see the website until it was complete. Each individual story was released via social media, with a short "teaser" written by Centre staff. The project's research manager, Dr. Shayna Plaut, has presented *Strangers at Home* at 15 universities, as well as at the United Nations, and storytellers have all reported being satisfied with the end product.[1] The videos received more than 100,000 total views to date, and the project has been recognized with several journalism awards – a sign that, despite the irregular nature of this project's approach, *Strangers at Home* was being accepted in the mainstream media landscape.

Through Somali Eyes

As the European nativism project was starting, we turned our focus to another challenging story, the political and security situation in Somalia, and decided to take the empowerment journalism approach further by putting the storytelling power completely in the hands of local storytellers.

Somalia is one of the most dangerous countries in the world to be a journalist. Since 2015, the country has topped the Committee to Protect Journalists' Global Impunity Index, where journalists are specifically targeted for their work (Witchel 2018).[2] They are also at high risk for injury, kidnapping and death during assignments.[3]

To address these challenges in Somalia, we established a partnership with a group of Somali journalists, with the idea of having them document their day-to-day reporting activities with wearable cameras. These chest-mounted cameras would capture their daily routines, and footage could then be used to convey the effort it takes to keep media and journalism alive in their country. We worked with the University of British Columbia's general counsel to craft a Memorandum of Understanding, whereby Somali journalists owned the footage, with any profits from a potential commissioned project going directly to them.

The intent behind our approach was to create an empowerment journalism model where we provided resources and a distribution platform for local journalists, but for the most part allowed the local journalists to lead the project. Three wearable cameras and hard-drives were sent to our local partners in Somalia, and they initially met the idea with enthusiasm, making T-shirts to commemorate the launch of the project. But, the project faced several issues, and five years later it remains incomplete.

There were challenges in communication from the project's inception. Internet connections in Somalia were spotty, and phone calls were regularly dropped. The distance between our two teams meant we could not build authentic collaborative relationships. This, combined with the overall "hands-off" approach we took, led to too little guidance and support for the Somali collaborators.

We realized late in the process that we had not properly conveyed to our local partners the experimental nature of the project. Our partners' past experiences involved working with foreign media as freelancers/fixers, which meant they were understanding the project through a traditional foreign correspondent model – where foreign media leads the project and the local journalists fill a support role. We did not take this into consideration when deciding on factors like roles, responsibilities, and payment. Our team at the Centre understood the project as a partnership, but, upon reflection, we did not effectively communicate how that partnership would be different from the foreign correspondent model they were familiar with, which meant we placed too much responsibility on our local partners who received too little support – both editorial and financial.

Despite the challenges, *Through Somali Eyes* presented learning opportunities, helping us understand the need for truly collaborative partnerships, and for better cultural understanding of the communities with which we are partnering. We took these lessons to heart with a new project we were developing to address the complex topic of alcohol dependence in Indigenous communities in Canada.

Turning Points

Learning from our previous projects in Europe and Somalia, we shifted our attention to local inequities in Canadian journalism – adapting an empowerment journalism approach to reporting at home. *Turning Points* is a collaborative digital storytelling project in Yellowknife, Northwest Territories. By co-creating narratives with Indigenous storytellers, we confront both the media myth of the "drunk Indian" and a story-taking reporting approach.

While this work fits within a broader conversation about reconciliation in Canada, we were wary of using the language of reconciliation and decolonization or claiming to be different than our predecessors. As a predominantly non-Indigenous team, we continue to confront a history of prejudiced reporting techniques, and the colonial and racist roots of Canadian news media. From discriminatory training and hiring practices, to the production and reproduction of stereotypes in content about "the Aboriginal Problem," many challenges persist both in the newsroom and the field that prevent Indigenous peoples from being fairly represented (Anderson and Robertson 2011; Brady and Kelly 2017; Johnson 2016; McCue 2016; Morgan and Castleden 2014).

To address this, our first step was to build partnerships with local Indigenous community members in Yellowknife to whom we would be accountable. We created an advisory board to help us make informed decisions relative to local contexts and recruited storytellers to be directors and subjects of their own stories. Committing time to be present in the community and form face-to-face relationships with our partners was an important lesson we took from the previous projects. The first author, a PhD student reflecting on this project for her dissertation, committed to regular trips to Yellowknife, and all project team members were present in Yellowknife during filming.

Departing from a pitch model for stories, we conducted detailed pre-interviews with each storyteller to understand their goals and motivations for their unique stories and filmed their pieces accordingly. We have begun editing short documentaries with their guidance. With frequent editing meetings, we will incorporate their feedback into a final version that reflects their needs and desires. With storytellers' approval, we will share the finished short films first in a community screening event in Yellowknife, and then online through an interactive platform that encourages others to submit their own narratives. With a research component, we will also share reflections on the empowerment journalism approach to promote accountability and knowledge-sharing in the community.

The complexity of co-creating stories in collaborations between journalists, community advisors, storytellers, and academics is both the strength and challenge of our approach. For example, the project was initially called "Alcoholics Unanonymous," our nod to making stigmatized topics visible to promote conversation. Yet, the title later became a glaring illustration of our implicit colonial mentalities and cultural blind spots, since the play on "Alcoholics Anonymous" referenced a group founded by a Christian missionary and reinforced a pathology of alcoholism. The new title, *Turning Points,* was inspired by a conversation with one of the community advisors about creating counter-narratives about alcohol. They described the importance of capturing both honest struggles and resilience or willingness to change. The turning points in people's lives are key moments of strength that are lost in the one-dimensional stereotypes about "alcoholics." We made the change to better reflect the common goals of everyone involved in the project, and as a reminder of our commitment to confronting stereotypes.

Another key learning happened in our first trip to Yellowknife. Three initial advisory board members detailed a long history of researchers and journalists who come North, take stories and knowledge from communities, and never return to share their work. The advisors were clear: if we were going to do journalism differently, then the stories had to stay in and benefit the community, and storytellers had to own their own content.

We met frequently to strategize ideas and languaging around ownership and consent, and ran drafts of the protocol by community advisors. Our conversations were provocative as we confronted the reasons why journalists might not share their content with "subjects" to maintain impartiality and integrity, but why community-based researchers would prioritize trust-building by sharing findings. In developing a protocol based on trust, we decided to forgo fact-checking to acknowledge the value of storytellers' own "truths." Given how important it was for storytellers to help others in their community by sharing their knowledge, it would be inappropriate for us to invalidate their contributions. These conversations were uncomfortable, but eventually led to an ethics protocol that was approved by the advisory board, university and a research licensing board for the Northwest Territories. We do not require storytellers to give up control over or ownership of their content. All the raw footage was returned to each storyteller after filming, and drafts along with finished pieces will be returned upon completion. When the project is finished, we will relinquish our control over storytellers' content and promote their stories as they see fit.

Designing an ethics protocol around storyteller control was an important milestone that required a wealth of perspectives from Indigenous community members, journalists, and researchers to reach consensus. To act on – rather than pay lip service to – the principle of local ownership, we needed to solidify our role as a production team to support the storytellers' visions and priorities rather than our own. In moving through the editing phase now, we still confront our impulses to put a story together with our visions rather than the storytellers', and for an audience in Southern—rather than

Northern—Canada. It takes time and energy to genuinely address the remnants of parachute reporting that still surface in our work so that we can reflect, learn, and work in a better way.

Conclusion

All three projects challenged the norms and practices of the traditional "parachute reporting" model and brought us closer to an empowerment journalism approach. Yet, balancing control within partnerships is difficult, because there is no one-size-fits-all model. In *Strangers at Home*, our team co-created videos and relied entirely on local content, while retaining full control over the final output. In *Through Somali Eyes*, we completely relinquished control and only contributed resources to support our partners in Mogadishu. Yet, we failed to adequately articulate a shared vision or spend time in the community with our partners to complete the project. With *Turning Points*, we shared control in collaborations with community partners and storytellers in Yellowknife to co-create narratives for local audiences. Yet, collaboration is financially and emotionally costly. Working alongside community partners requires that they have the time and energy to review our materials, answer our questions, and highlight our blind spots. This is a substantial request, and the risk of burnout and emotional fatigue among community members and people of colour who work with/educate White settlers from institutions is well documented (Accapadi 2007; DiAngelo 2018; Irlbacher-Fox 2014; Watt 2007).

Our work to address inequitable reporting practices is far from over, and journalists who wish to use this approach must remember that strategies for communicating, collaborating, and navigating ownership are not transferable across projects and communities. In contexts where a commitment to social justice requires a methodological intervention, journalists should strive not to report *on*, but to report *with* communities. By reimagining the newsroom within rather than distinct from communities, we strive to be trustworthy collaborators and produce stories that matter to our partners.

Notes

1. One concern was raised by immigrant activists relating to the story "Fascist Logic," which gives voice to an Italian far-right organization, and how – out of context – our promotion of it could be construed as endorsement. We are addressing this concern by ensuring that the videos can only be viewed in aggregate on the website, and we are developing an introductory video to contextualize the project, noting that the nativist voices are being presented to give context to the marginalized voices that are being empowered by the project.
2. Since the CPJ began its data collection in 1992, 12 foreign journalists and 54 local journalists have been killed. The types of deaths recorded are: murder, crossfire and dangerous assignments.
3. Examples of foreign reporters targeted include Michael Scott Moore, who was kidnapped in 2012 and held for two and a half years, and Amanda Lindhout, a freelance journalist from Canada, and Nigel Brennan, a freelance photojournalist from Australia, who were kidnapped in 2008 and held for 15 months. Local journalists include Abdisatar Daher Sabriye from Radio Mogadishu who was killed when Al-Shabaab detonated a suicide bomb killing 14 people and leaving 20 injured and Abdiaziz Ali, a journalist for Radio Shabelle who reported on Al-Shabaab and corruption and was shot and killed.

Disclosure statement

No potential conflict of interest was reported by the authors.

ORCID

Maya Lefkowich http://orcid.org/0000-0003-3588-7150

References

Accapadi, M. M. 2007. "When White Women Cry: How White Women's Tears Oppress Women of Colour." *The College Student Affairs Journal* 26 (2): 208–215.

Anderson, M. C., and C. L. Robertson. 2011. *Seeing Red.* Winnipeg: University of Manitoba Press.

Archibald, J. A. 2008. *Indigenous Storywork: Educating the Heart, Mind, Body, and Spirit.* Vancouver: UBC Press.

Brady, M. J., and J. M. H. Kelly. 2017. *We Interrupt This Program: Indigenous Media Tactics in Canadian Culture.* Vancouver: UBC Press.

The Canadian Association of Journalists. 2011. "Ethical Guidelines." https://caj.starchapter.com/content.php?page=ethics-guidelines&bypassCookie=1.

Cox, S., S. Drew, M. Guillemin, C. Howell, D. Warr, and J. Waycott. 2014. *Guidelines for Ethical Visual Research Methods.* Melbourne: The University of Melbourne.

DiAngelo, R. 2018. *White Fragility: Why It's So Hard for White People to Talk About Racism.* Boston: Beacon Press.

Hermida, A. 2010. "Twittering the News: The Emergency of Ambient Journalism." *Journalism Practice* 4 (3): 297–308.

Irlbacher-Fox, S. 2014. "Traditional Knowledge, Co-existence and Co-resistance." *Decolonization: Indigeneity, Education & Society* 3 (3): 145–158.

Johnson, H. 2016. *Firewater: How Alcohol Is Killing My People.* Regina: University of Regina Press.

Klein, P. W. 2016. "Fostering a Grassroots Approach to International Reporting." *Nieman Reports,* October 27.http://niemanreports.org/articles/fostering-a-grassroots-approach-to-international-reporting/.

Leavy, P. 2015. *Method Meets Art, Second Edition: Arts-based Research Practice.* New York, London: The Guilford Press.

Lewis, S. C., A. E. Holton, and M. Coddington. 2013. "Reciprocal Journalism." *Journalism Practice* 8 (2): 229–241.

Lewis, S. C., K. Kaufhold, and D. L. Lasorsa. 2010. "Thinking About Citizen Journalism." *Journalism Practice* 4 (2): 163–179.

Low, B., C. Brushwood Rose, P. M. Salvio, and L. Palacios. 2012. "(Re)framing the Scholarship on Participatory Video: From Celebration to Critical Engagement." In *Handbook of Participatory Video*, edited by E. J. Milne, C. Mitchell, and N. De Lange, 49–64. Lanham: AltaMira Press.

McCue, D. 2016. "Storytakers." from http://riic.ca/the-guide/in-the-field/storytakers/.

Morgan, S. V., and H. Castleden. 2014. "Framing Indigenous Settler Relations within British Columbia's Modern Treaty Context: A Discourse Analysis of the Maa-nulth Treaty in Mainstream Media." *International Indigenous Policy Journal* 5 (3): 487–499.

Watt, S. K. 2007. "Difficult Dialogues, Privilege and Social Justice: Uses of the Privileged Identity Exploration (Pie) Model in Student Affairs Practice." *College Student Affairs Journal* 26 (2): 114–126.

Witchel, E. 2018. "Getting Away with Murder." *Committee to Protect Journalists.* https://cpj.org/reports/2018/10/impunity-index-getting-away-with-murder-killed-justice.php#infographic.

Index